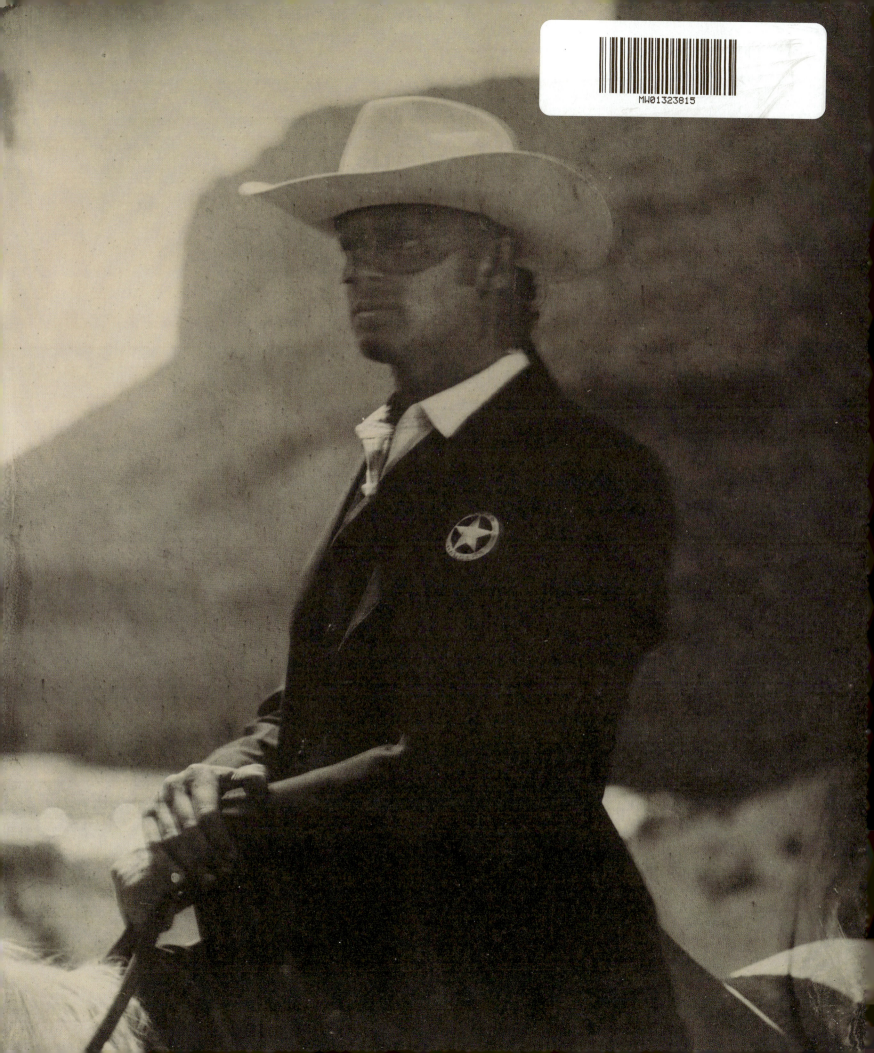

Disney THE LONE RANGER

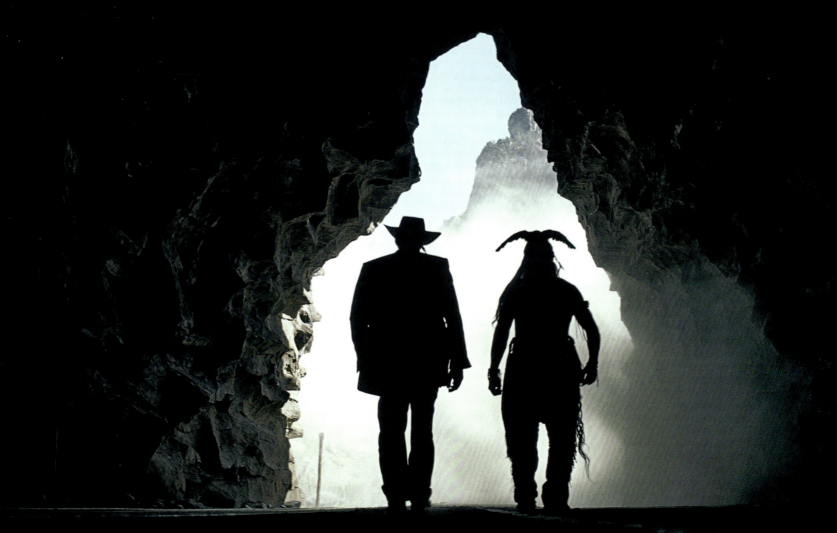

Disney THE LONE RANGER
BEHIND THE MASK

ON THE TRAIL OF AN OUTLAW EPIC

MICHAEL SINGER

FOREWORD BY
JERRY BRUCKHEIMER

INTRODUCTION BY
GORE VERBINSKI

AFTERWORDS BY
JOHNNY DEPP & ARMIE HAMMER

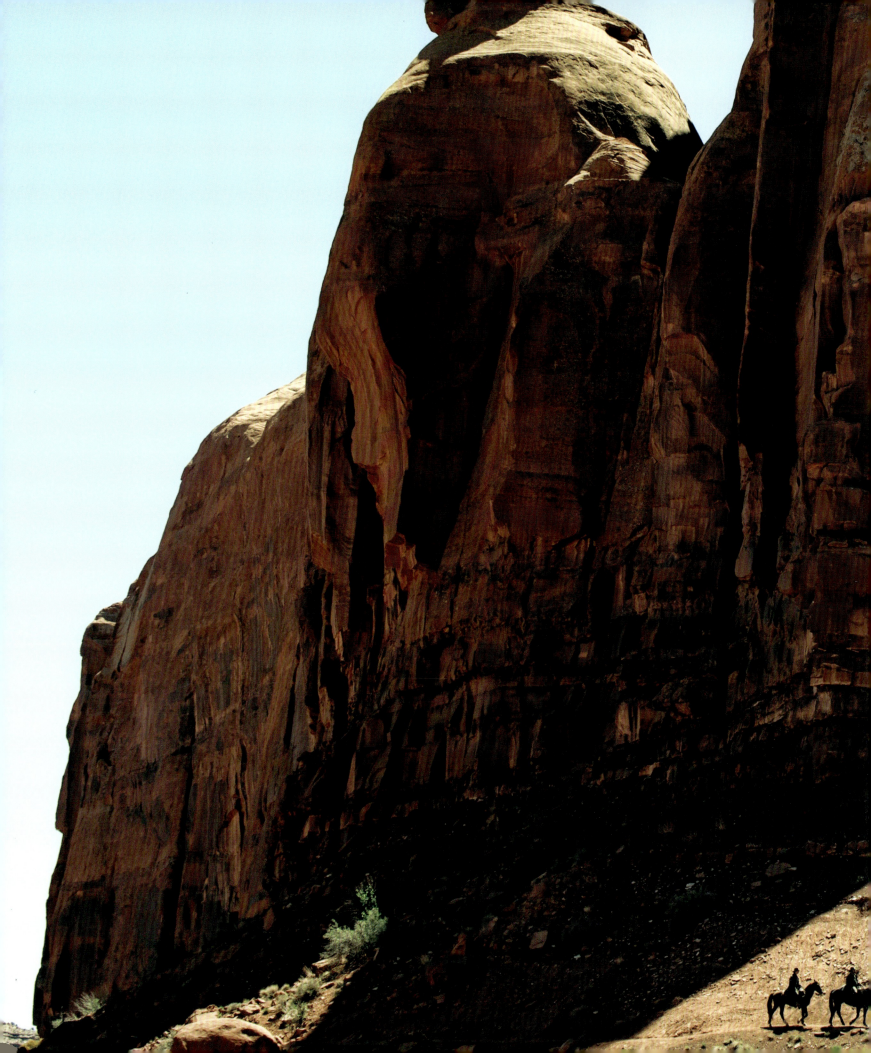

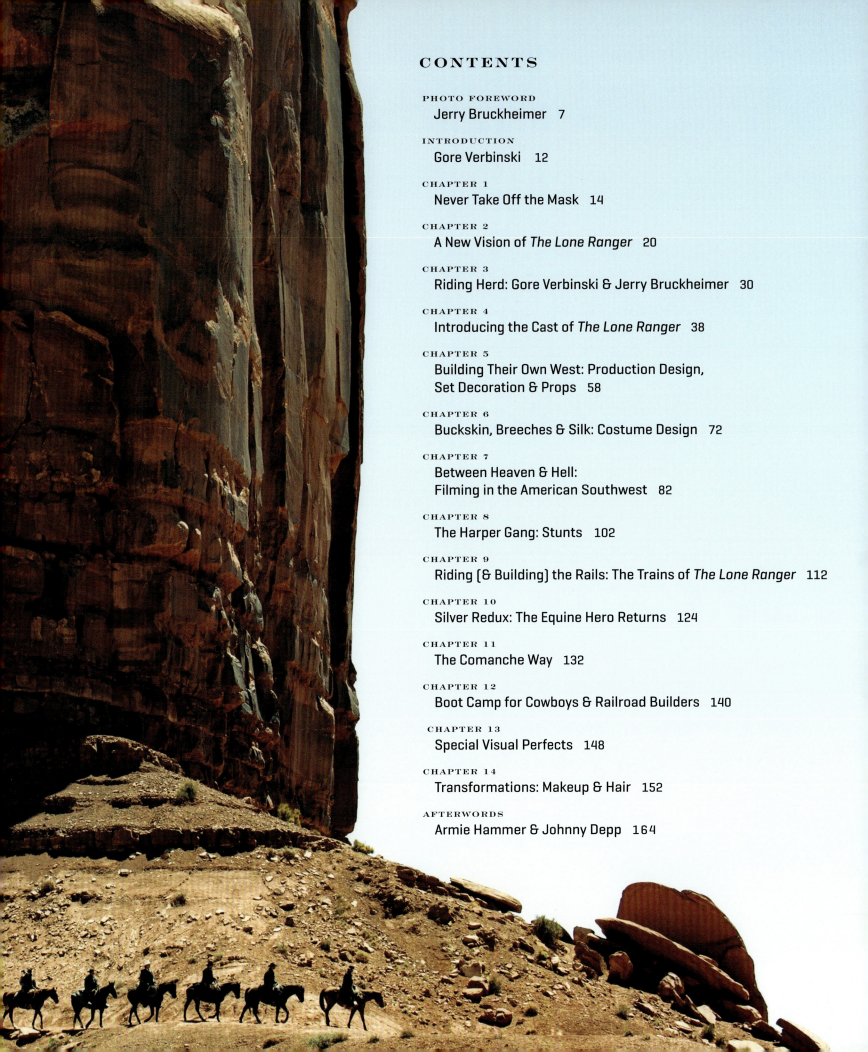

CONTENTS

PHOTO FOREWORD
Jerry Bruckheimer 7

INTRODUCTION
Gore Verbinski 12

CHAPTER 1
Never Take Off the Mask 14

CHAPTER 2
A New Vision of *The Lone Ranger* 20

CHAPTER 3
Riding Herd: Gore Verbinski & Jerry Bruckheimer 30

CHAPTER 4
Introducing the Cast of *The Lone Ranger* 38

CHAPTER 5
Building Their Own West: Production Design, Set Decoration & Props 58

CHAPTER 6
Buckskin, Breeches & Silk: Costume Design 72

CHAPTER 7
Between Heaven & Hell: Filming in the American Southwest 82

CHAPTER 8
The Harper Gang: Stunts 102

CHAPTER 9
Riding (& Building) the Rails: The Trains of *The Lone Ranger* 112

CHAPTER 10
Silver Redux: The Equine Hero Returns 124

CHAPTER 11
The Comanche Way 132

CHAPTER 12
Boot Camp for Cowboys & Railroad Builders 140

CHAPTER 13
Special Visual Perfects 148

CHAPTER 14
Transformations: Makeup & Hair 152

AFTERWORDS
Armie Hammer & Johnny Depp 164

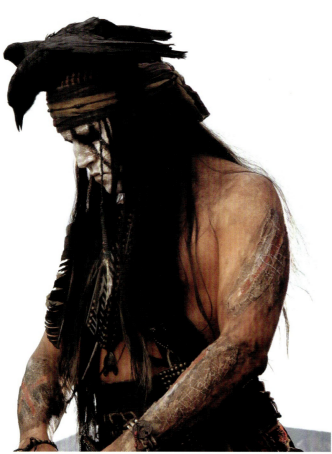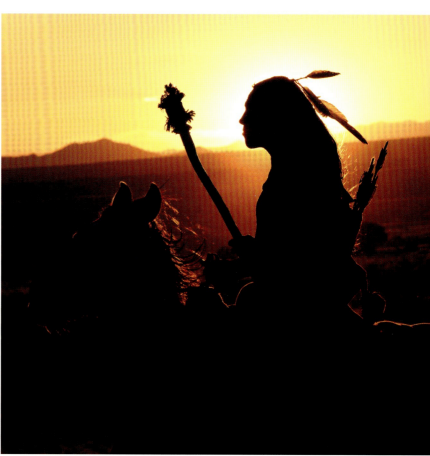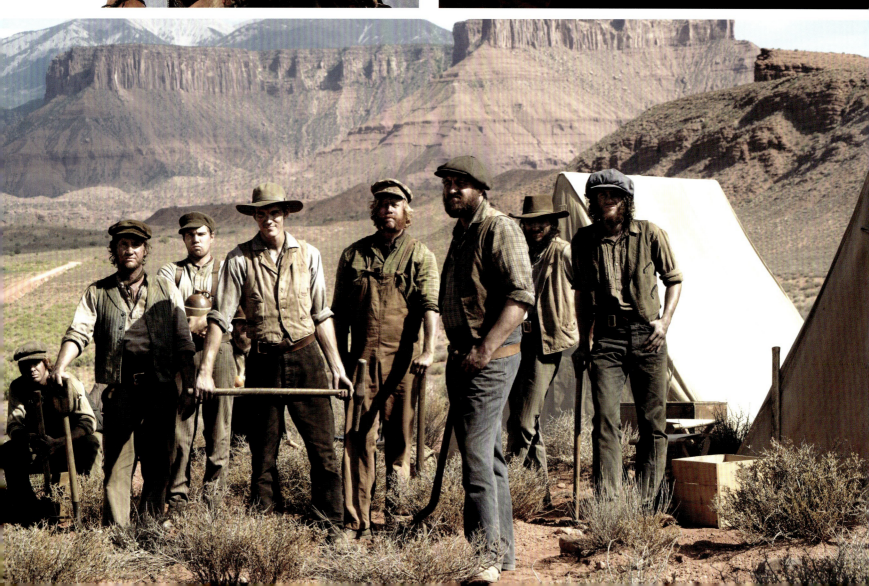

PHOTO FOREWORD
JERRY BRUCKHEIMER

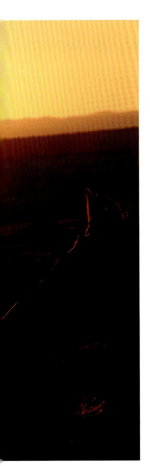

An exciting story based on two of the most famous characters in the history of American popular culture, a great cast, amazing director, the world's best crew, incredible sets and costumes, and some of the most astonishing and iconic landscapes in the United States. We pretty much had it all on *The Lone Ranger*, which also made it one of the most exciting of any of our films to be a part of. As we traveled with Johnny Depp, Armie Hammer, director Gore Verbinski, and the huge company from one astonishing location to another, throughout five states and filming for over seven months on a shoot that endured all four seasons and every conceivable kind of weather, the experience became more than a movie . . . It was an epic adventure. All of which gave me an opportunity to dust off my cameras and have a wonderful time trying to capture moments of this incredible journey, sometimes as amazed by what the lens was seeing as I hope you will be as you roam through the following photographs.

The ones who made this easy for me were director Gore Verbinski, who is an extraordinary visualist and incredible storyteller; our great director of photography, Bojan Bazelli, and visual consultant Mark "Crash" McCreery; an incredibly talented crew of artists and technicians working at the utmost of their considerable abilities; of course, fantastic actors like Johnny Depp, Armie Hammer, Tom Wilkinson, Helena Bonham Carter, Ruth Wilson, William Fichtner, and more; and, not least, Mother Nature herself. Talk about a winning team. Hope you enjoy this behind-the-scenes look at some of what we did from February through September 2012.

FAR LEFT: Johnny in a reflective moment between takes. Even the crow looks like he's catching a breather. **LEFT:** I took this picture of one of the fantastic Native American horsemen during a beautiful New Mexico sunset. **BELOW:** Armie's riding double, Lyn Clarke, in costume and mask astride Silver, assisted by horse trainer Jess Brackenbury (holding the reins) and assistant prop master Curtis Akin (holding a rope). **BOTTOM LEFT:** Penny Rose's authentic costume design extended to every background player, including this motley group in Moab, Utah, portraying Transcontinental Railroad workers.

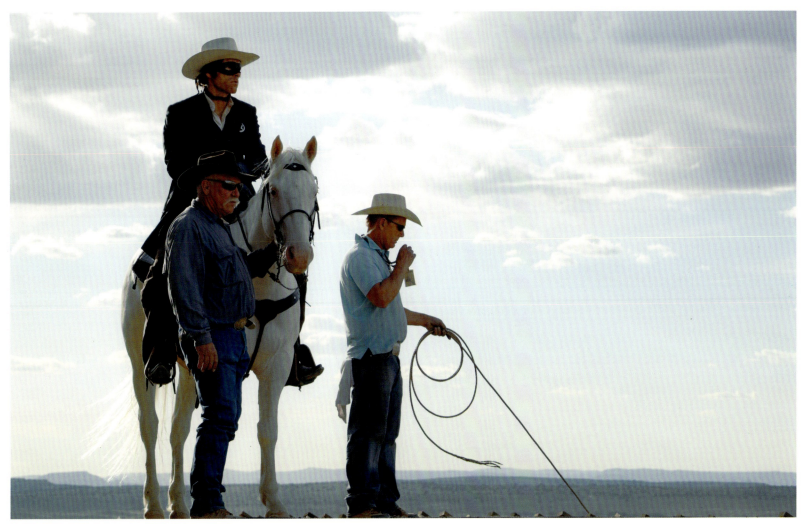

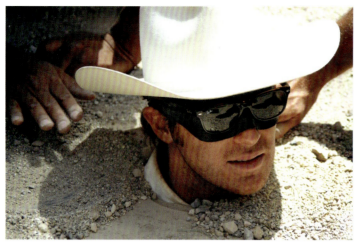

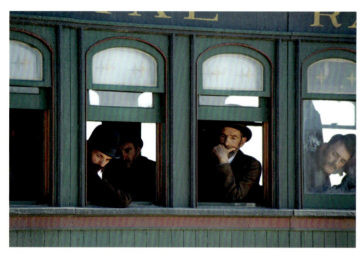

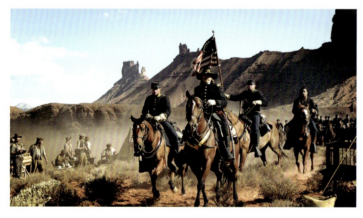

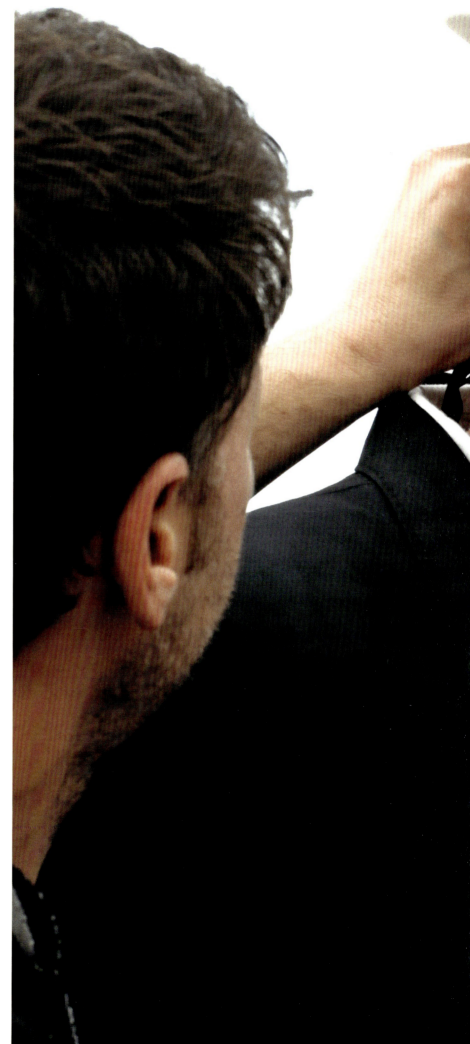

TOP: Up to his neck between shots in the Comanche village set at Valles Caldera, New Mexico, Armie wears shades to protect his eyes from the sun and sand.

MIDDLE: Background players in a railroad car were showing the effects of a long, hot day (note the gent on the right slumbering).

BOTTOM: A beautiful expanse of Moab was the perfect backdrop for a scene featuring Barry Pepper leading his cavalry as Captain Fuller.

RIGHT: Just before the camera rolls, Armie gets a helping hand with both his hat and his mask.

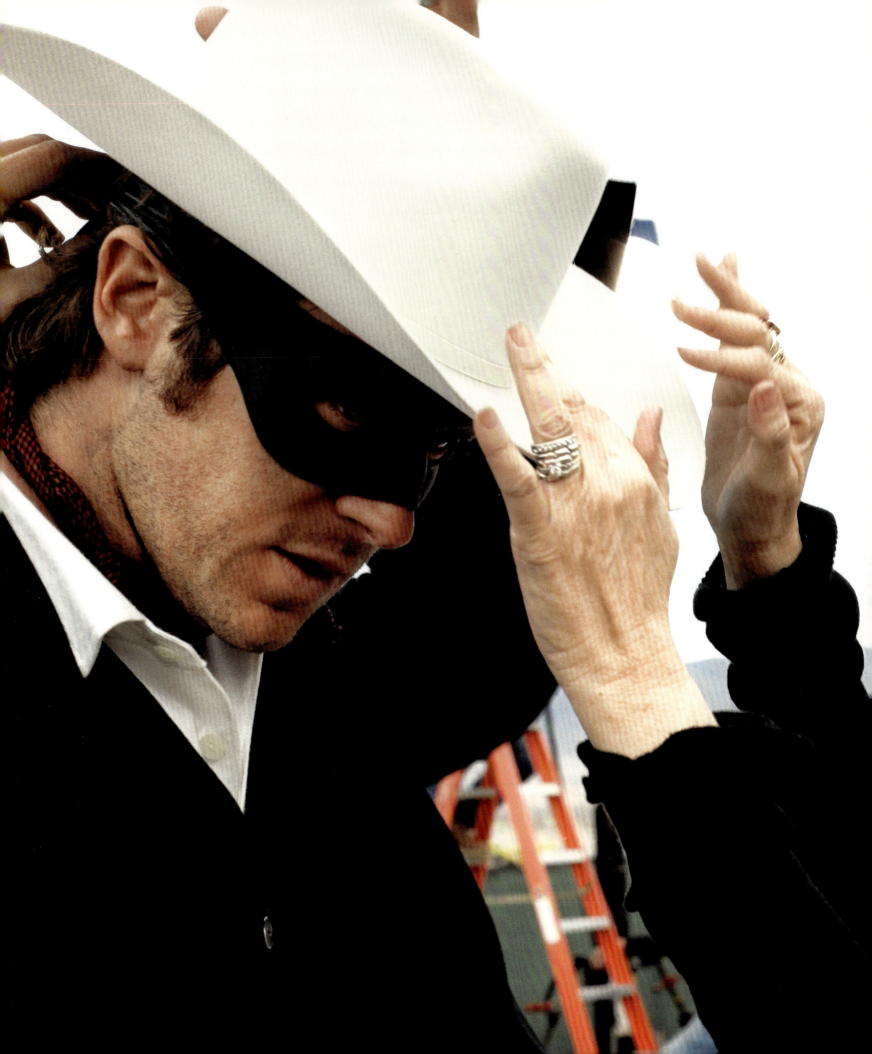

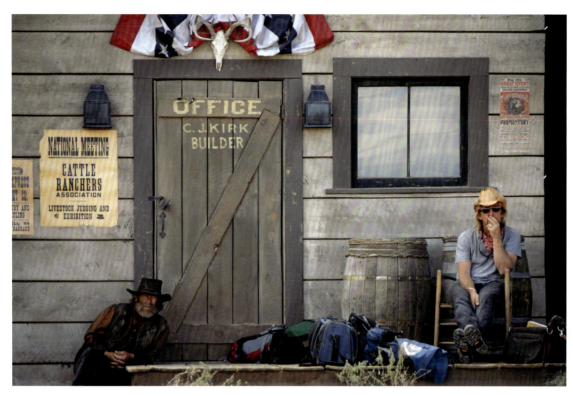

LEFT: Our visual consultant, Crash McCreery, takes a breather, along with an extra, on the Promontory Summit set he designed.

BELOW: How we got a full-size train to the top of Fossil Point in Moab is something that still amazes me. But we did, and here's the proof.

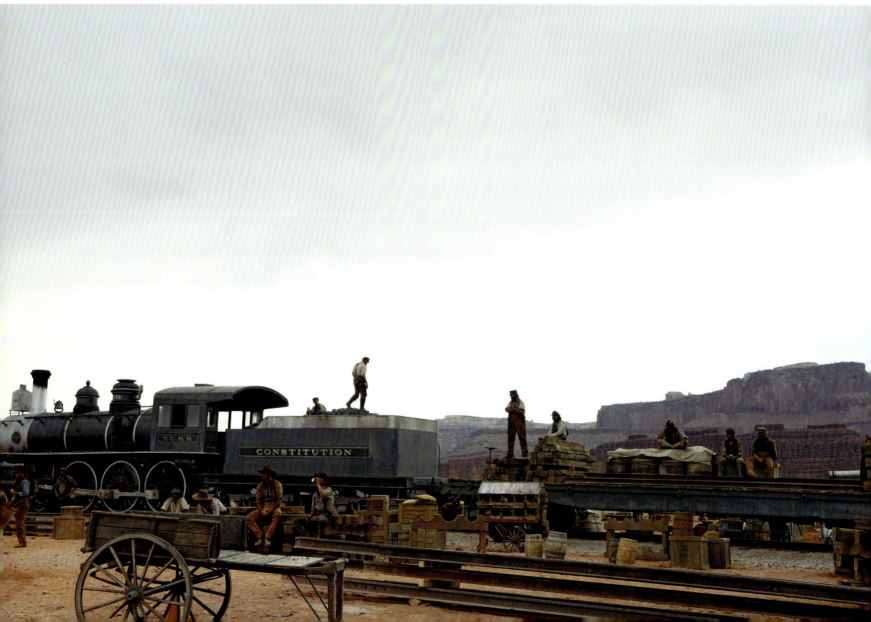

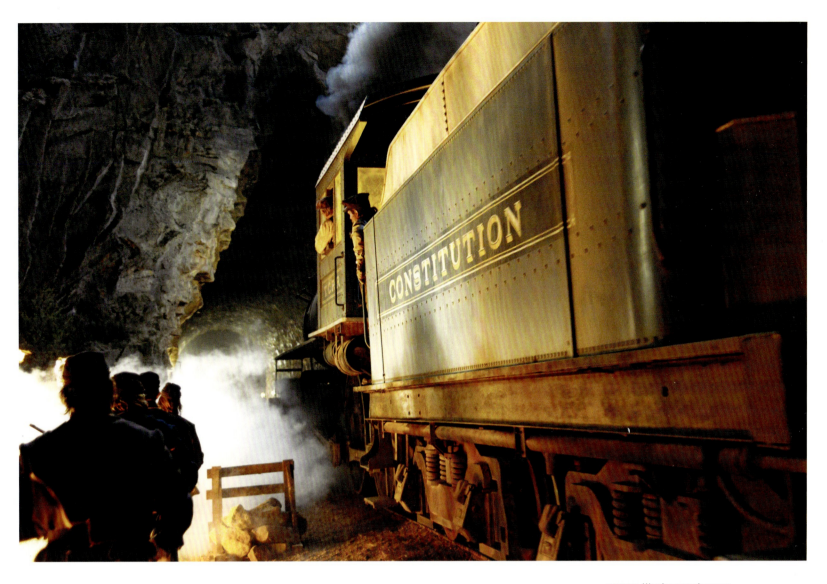

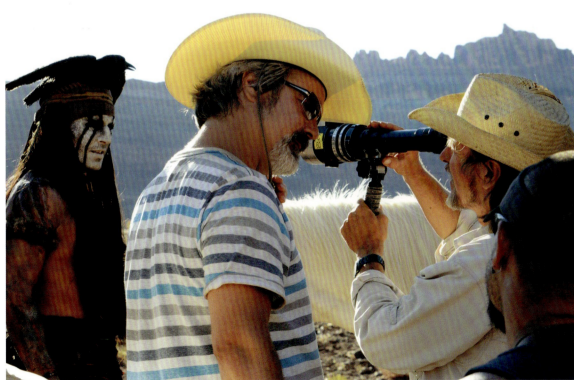

ABOVE: We also somehow got the Constitution train all the way to Creede, Colorado, and here it is entering a 200-foot-long rock tunnel built for the film at our Silver Man Mine set.

LEFT: Johnny and Gore prepare for action as camera operator Martin Schaer lines up the scene.

PHOTO FOREWORD: JERRY BRUCKHEIMER

INTRODUCTION
GORE VERBINSKI

THIS FILM IS ABOUT LOSS—a certain purity or innocence traded and enslaved to the algorithm of progress. Essential truths corrupted and deformed by the inevitable tick of a watch. Making a film often has a way of blurring the lines between story and storyteller. For those of us who lived it, we share a sense of that emptiness, knowing that there will never be another one quite like this.

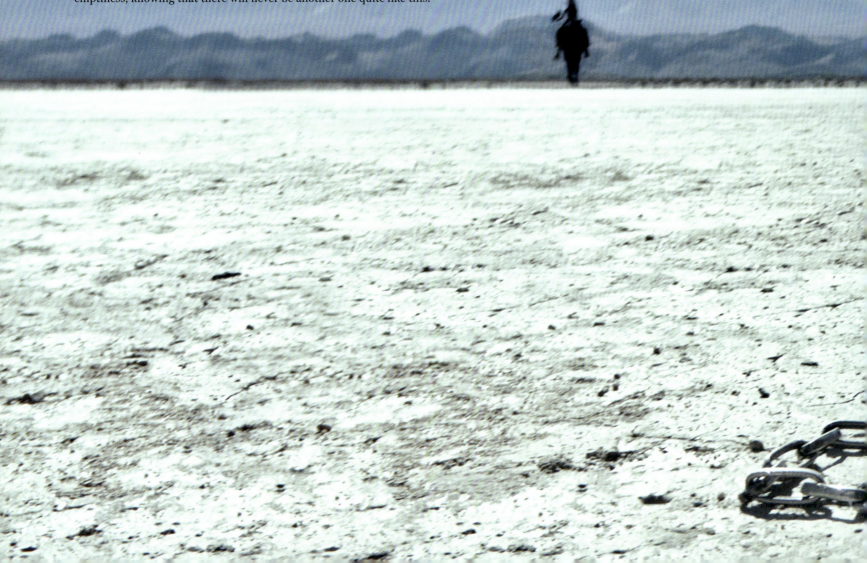

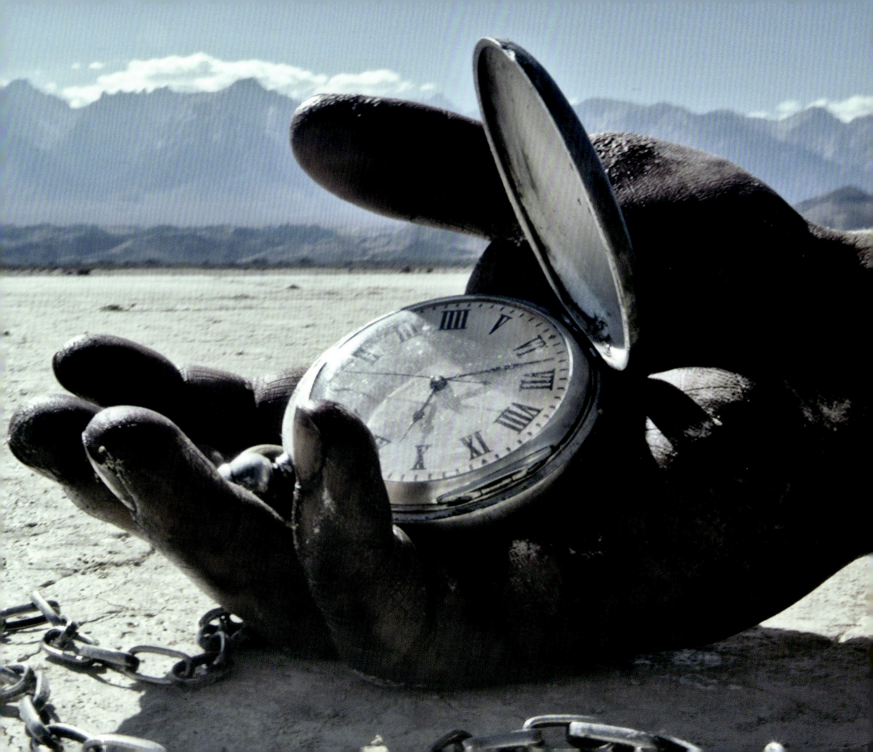

NEVER TAKE OFF THE MASK:
A BRIEF HISTORY OF *THE LONE RANGER*

ON MARCH 8, 2012, ALBUQUERQUE RESIDENT ANN SIMON AND HER TEN-YEAR-OLD DAUGHTER, BUDDING ACTRESS JENNA, FOUND THEMSELVES IN A PLACE THAT FULFILLED AN UNIMAGINABLE FAMILY DREAM. WALKING THROUGH AN ATMOSPHERIC WILD WEST EXHIBITION SET BUILT IN AN ALBUQUERQUE STUDIOS SOUNDSTAGE, THEY BOTH MUSED ON HOW WONDERFULLY STRANGE LIFE COULD BE. WEARING FASHIONABLE CIRCA-1933 PERIOD DRESS AND APPEARING AS BACKGROUND PLAYERS IN THE OPENING SEQUENCE OF JERRY BRUCKHEIMER AND GORE VERBINSKI'S BRAND-NEW MOVIE WAS PECULIAR ENOUGH, BUT THE FACT THAT THIS EPIC WAS *THE LONE RANGER* MADE THE SITUATION EVEN MORE UNUSUAL.

The reason can be found in Jenna's middle name, Jewell; for her great-grandfather, James Jewell, was instrumental in developing *The Lone Ranger* radio series in the early 1930s. "We were just excited to be part of the continuation of the history of *The Lone Ranger* story," enthuses Ann Simon. "*The Lone Ranger* was always our story in the family; it's always had a special meaning for us. And of course, they really belong to everybody who was a fan of *The Lone Ranger*, all the children who ran home after school to listen to the radio, and after that, when it was turned into a television series. And now, the characters will belong to yet a new generation. We're very proud!"

"There's something about these characters that have appealed to every generation since they were invented," notes producer Jerry Bruckheimer. "I grew up in Detroit, and *The Lone Ranger* TV show was part of my youth, and that of millions of others." On radio, television, theater screens, TV animation, comic strips, books, graphic novels, and video games, the perpetual popularity of these iconically American characters represents a continuum that confirms the fundamental genius of the men who created them.

BELOW: Storyboard artist Anthony Leonardi III created this evocative rendering of Tonto and John Reid chained one to the other in a wary dance of friendship.

OPPOSITE: The Lone Ranger in an iconic tableau, white hat held aloft, with Silver majestically rearing, perfectly recreated for the new film.

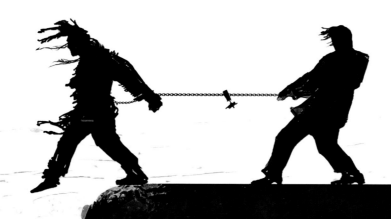

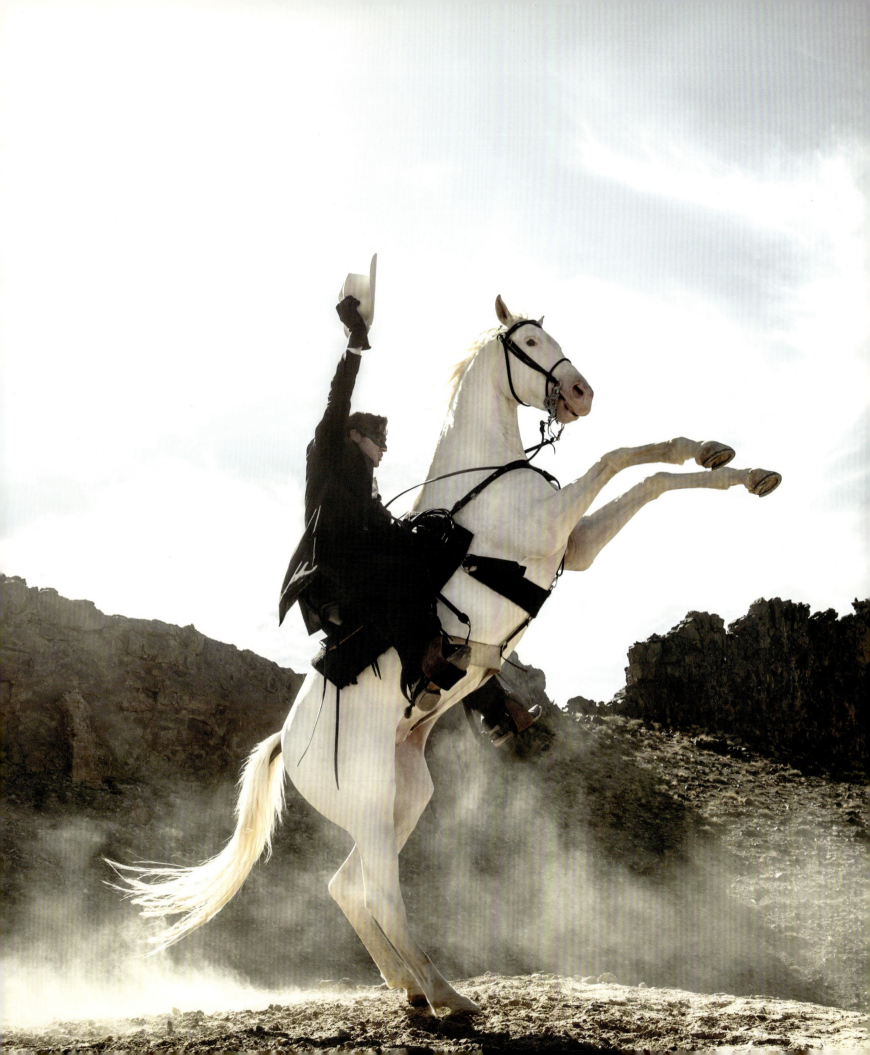

OPPOSITE: (clockwise from top left): The popularity of the character resulted in a huge number of tie-in products, including this "Lone Ranger Sport Shirt" aimed at youngsters; a vintage Lone Ranger kerchief highlights the character's famous "Hi-Yo Silver!" call; Clayton Moore and Jay Silverheels embodied the Lone Ranger and Tonto on TV and in theaters considerably beyond the eight years in which they played the roles; no youngster would want to be without this replica Lone Ranger mask.

BELOW: The Lone Ranger brings a rope-bound Butch Cavendish to justice.

THE BIRTH OF *THE LONE RANGER*

THE PROGRAM FIRST made its way onto the airwaves courtesy of WXYZ radio in Detroit, Michigan, on January 30, 1933. The station owner, George W. Trendle, wanted a Western that would appeal to a children's audience. The character he created was wholesome, honest and an authority figure kids could admire. The concept of the Lone Ranger was thus born and handed off to Fran Striker, a script writer from Buffalo, and the station's staff director, James Jewell.

Jewell went on to direct *The Lone Ranger* radio series through 1938, by which time it was a national phenomenon, and in the process was responsible for some of the most enduring keynotes of the legend. For example, Jewell's father-in-law owned a Kamp Kee-Mo-Sah-Bee in Mullet Lake, Michigan, the obvious linguistic inspiration behind Tonto's name for his friend, the Lone Ranger (Tonto was introduced eleven episodes into the series). It's believed that the camp was named after an Ojibwe word, "giimoozaabi," which has been varyingly translated as "trusty scout" or even "someone who does not follow the normal path." The name Tonto might also derive from an Ojibwe word, "N'da'aanh-too" (pronounced "Nduh-on-toe"), meaning "wild one" or "to change." It was also Jewell who suggested Gioachino Rossini's "William Tell Overture" as the program's theme music, which underscores the show's now-legendary opening lines, "A fiery horse with the speed of light, a cloud of dust, and a hearty 'Hi-Yo, Silver, Awa-a-ay!'" And, as Ann Simon notes, her Grandpa Jim's dog was named "Silver."

There were 2,956 radio episodes of *The Lone Ranger* (the last new one was broadcast on September 3, 1954) a twenty-one-year-long history that actually overlapped the hugely successful television series, starring stalwart Clayton Moore as the titular character and dignified Jay Silverheels

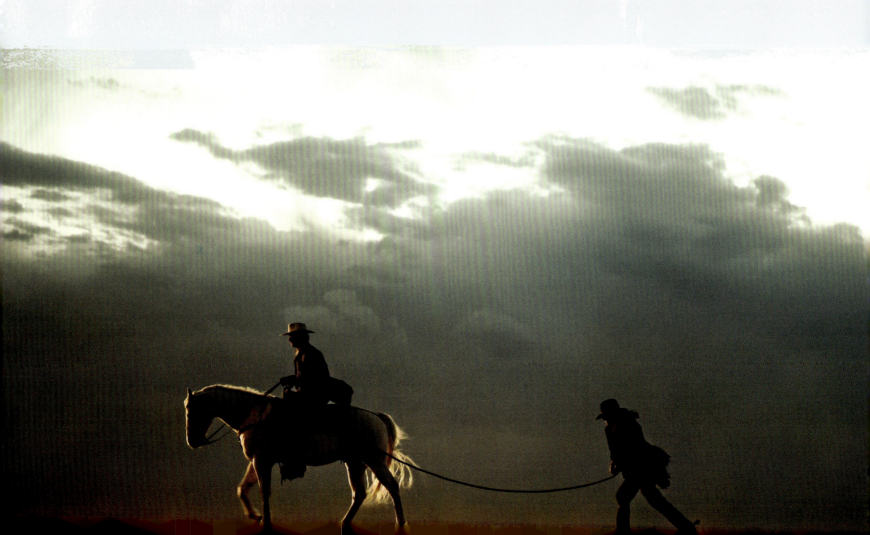

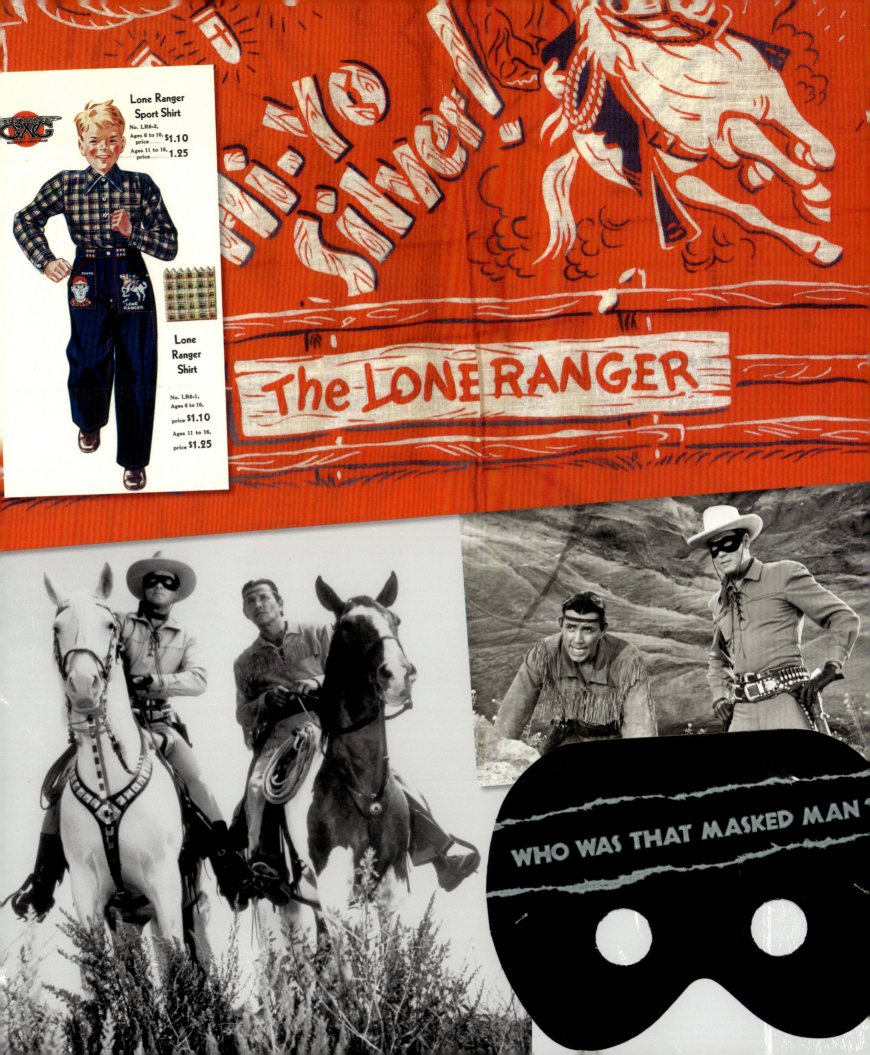

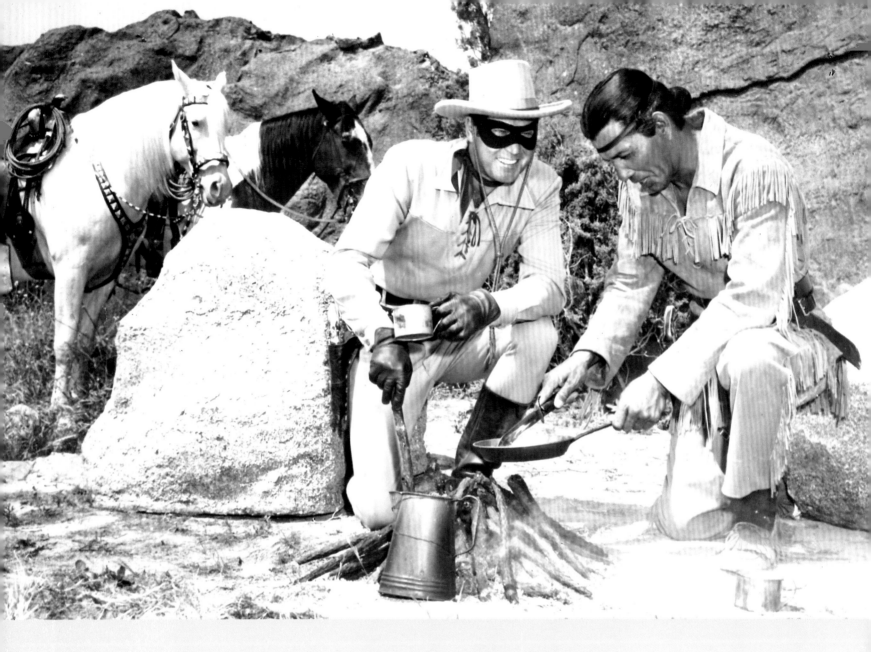

as Tonto. This program, which became an international phenomenon, began airing on ABC in 1949 and continued until 1957, bridging black-and-white to color TV and further enshrining the Lone Ranger and Tonto in the pop-cultural zeitgeist. *The Lone Ranger* radio and television programs revolutionized tie-in merchandising, and rare was the boy during those years who didn't have his very own Lone Ranger hat, mask, and toy six-shooters or eat breakfast from cereal boxes emblazoned with images of the masked hero and his Native American companion.

The huge popularity of the show also spun off into two theatrical feature films, *The Lone Ranger* (1956) and *The Lone Ranger and the Lost City of Gold* (1958). These arrived almost two decades after a pair of low-budget serials from Republic Pictures first appeared, *The Lone Ranger* in 1938 and then *The Lone Ranger Rides Again* the following year, neither of which pleased George W. Trendle with their thematic detours from his radio show.

Of course, until this point, the actors most closely associated with the roles of the Lone Ranger and Tonto are Moore and Silverheels from the television series. Numerous actors voiced the Lone Ranger on radio, including George Stenius, who later, under the name George Seaton, became one of Hollywood's most prominent film directors. Earle Graser and Brace Beemer also lent their voices to the stoic hero, and in the serials, he was played by Lee Powell in the first and Robert Livingston in the second. For the third season of the TV series, John Hart replaced Clayton Moore due to a contract dispute, and Tex Hill may

ABOVE: Clayton Moore and Jay Silverheels, as the Lone Ranger and Tonto, film a campfire scene for the popular television program.

RIGHT: Between takes Armie Hammer sits atop Silver on the rooftops of Promontory Summit as background players get into position below.

or may not have played the character in a 1961 pilot for a proposed television revival on CBS titled *Return of the Lone Ranger*. Mystery still surrounds Hill's involvement because there is no proof that it was ever actually filmed. For the ill-fated 1981 feature film *The Legend of the Lone Ranger*, the masked man was played by the unknown (then and since) Klinton Spilsbury but overdubbed in its entirety by the more experienced James Keach. Finally, Chad Michael Murray portrayed a very young masked man in a two-hour 2003 pilot (which also didn't go to series) simply titled *The Lone Ranger*. Fewer Tontos have been heard and seen: John Todd and Roland Parker on radio, Chief Thundercloud (aka Victor Daniels) in the two serials, Silverheels for the entire run of the TV series, Michael Horse in the 1981 film, and Nathaniel Arcand in the 2003 television pilot.

By this point in time, those three little words—*The Lone Ranger*—have entered the worldwide vernacular. As a result, any casual Internet search will bring up numerous daily references from the global media, often applied to sports or political figures from Albania to Zambia rather than to the enigmatic masked hero fighting for justice in the Old West. It's perfectly conceivable that several people now use the term without even knowing its origin!

But now it's time for Johnny Depp and Armie Hammer to put their own indelible stamps on Tonto and the Lone Ranger. As they respect some traditions established over the past eight decades, they also fearlessly interpret the characters for an entirely new generation, and for the parents and grandparents whose memories of the past will be matched by the thrilling reinvention of the present.

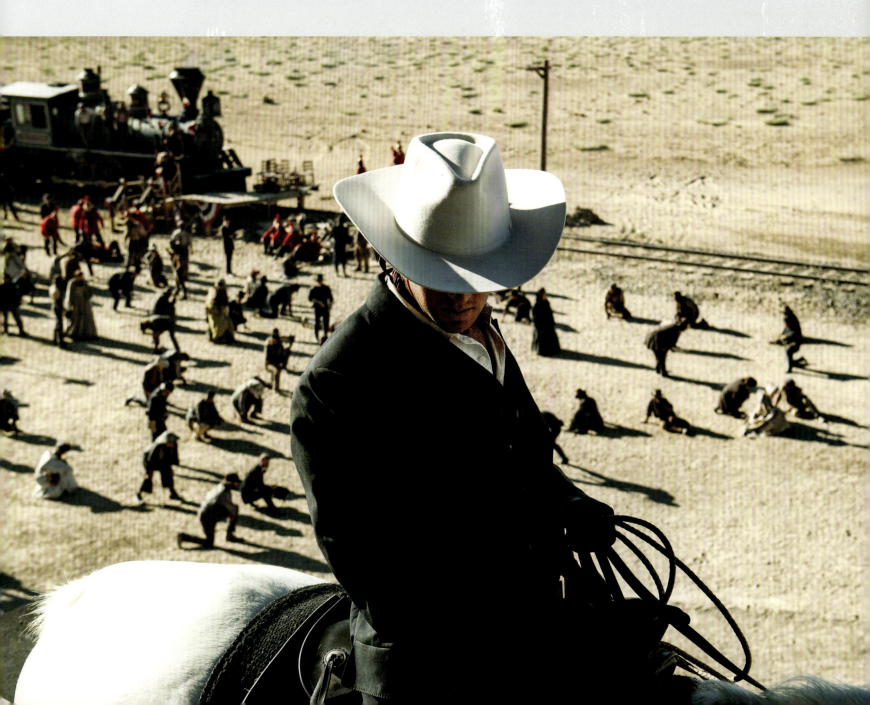

A NEW VISION OF THE LONE RANGER

THE JOURNEY OF A THOUSAND MILES BEGINS WITH ONE STEP," CHINESE PHILOSOPHER LAO-TZU IS BELIEVED TO HAVE SAID IN THE SEVENTH CENTURY. FOURTEEN CENTURIES LATER, IT'S NO LESS TRUE. JUST ASK JERRY BRUCKHEIMER AND GORE VERBINSKI. THE TALE OF THE DUO'S SEVEN-YEAR, AGAINST-THE-ODDS STRUGGLE TO BRING THEIR HUGELY AMBITIOUS VISION FOR *THE LONE RANGER* TO THE SCREEN BEGAN WITH ONE STEP IN THE DIRECTION OF A LEGENDARY EIGHTY-YEAR-OLD TALE. BY THE TIME THEIR JOURNEY WAS COMPLETED, CONSIDERABLY MORE THAN A THOUSAND MILES HAD PASSED BENEATH THEIR FEET. FROM THE ACQUISITION OF THE RIGHTS TO THE PROPERTY, TO THE HENRY KISSINGER-ESQUE DIPLOMACY THAT ENABLED ALL PRODUCTION ENTITIES TO AGREE ON THE FINE POINTS OF THE HUGE ENDEAVOR, TO GETTING OVER THE HURDLES OF A TEMPORARY TWO-MONTH HALT DURING PREPRODUCTION, AND THEN TRANSCENDING NEARLY EVERY METEOROLOGICAL AND GEOGRAPHICAL CHALLENGE POSSIBLE DURING THE SEVEN-MONTH SHOOT, THE DETERMINATION OF THE FILMMAKERS BREACHED EVERY OBSTACLE HURLED INTO THEIR PATH BY MAN OR NATURE.

Neither Bruckheimer nor Verbinski are men to be easily dissuaded once their hearts and minds are focused. "We knew that it was time for *The Lone Ranger* and Westerns to be reborn," says Bruckheimer, "just as Gore and I knew that it was time for pirate movies to be resurrected when we first developed *Pirates of the Caribbean* for the screen a decade ago. There's a reason why people have relished these characters and genres for decades, and we knew that if we reintroduced them in a fresh and exciting way, they would fall in love with them all over again."

As with many ambitious projects, there was a long and winding road to bring the new version of *The Lone Ranger* to fruition. During the overlapped filming of the second and third film in the *Pirates of the Caribbean* series, Bruckheimer and his two generals—Jerry Bruckheimer Films president Mike Stenson and president of production Chad Oman (later both executive

RIGHT: Fully transformed from a frontier lawyer into an enigmatic masked hero, the Lone Ranger rides away from Colby astride Silver.

BELOW: Another striking silhouetted rendering by Anthony Leonardi III.

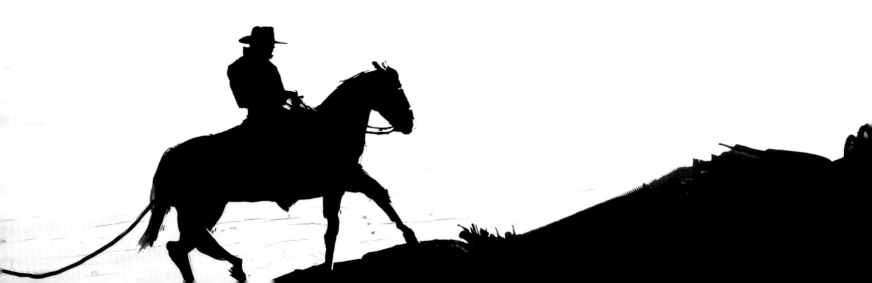

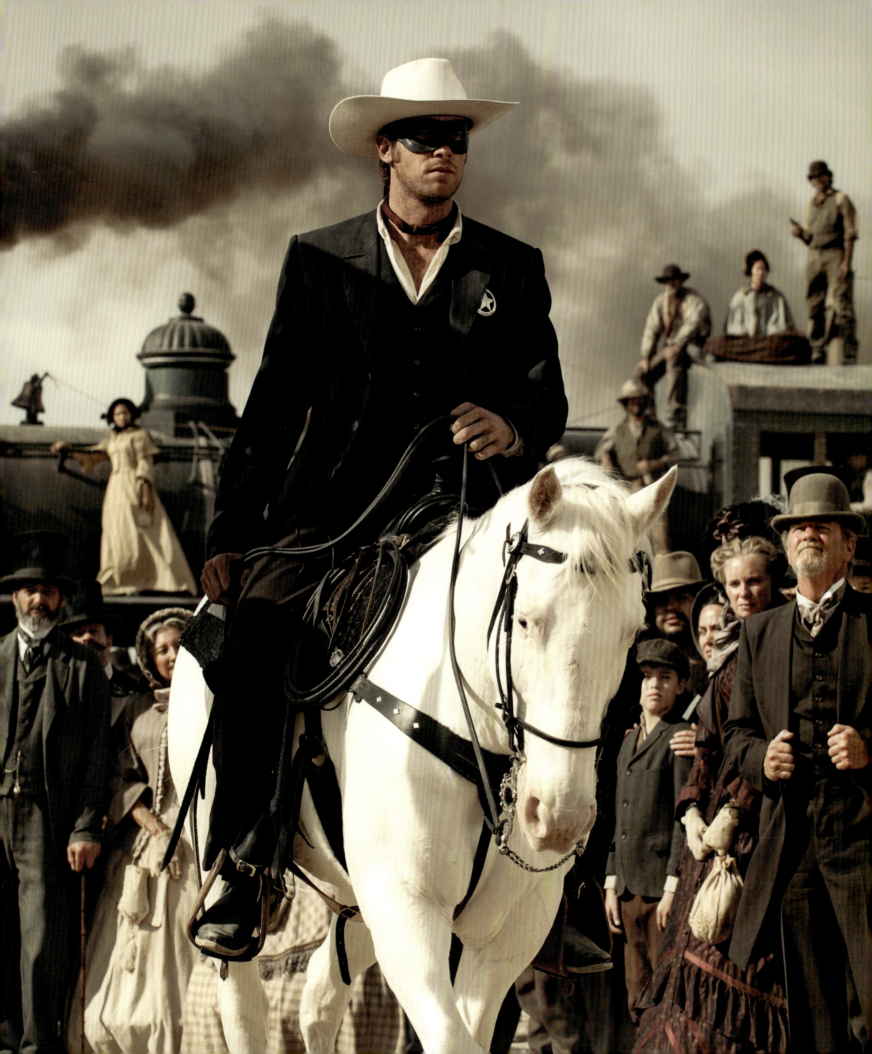

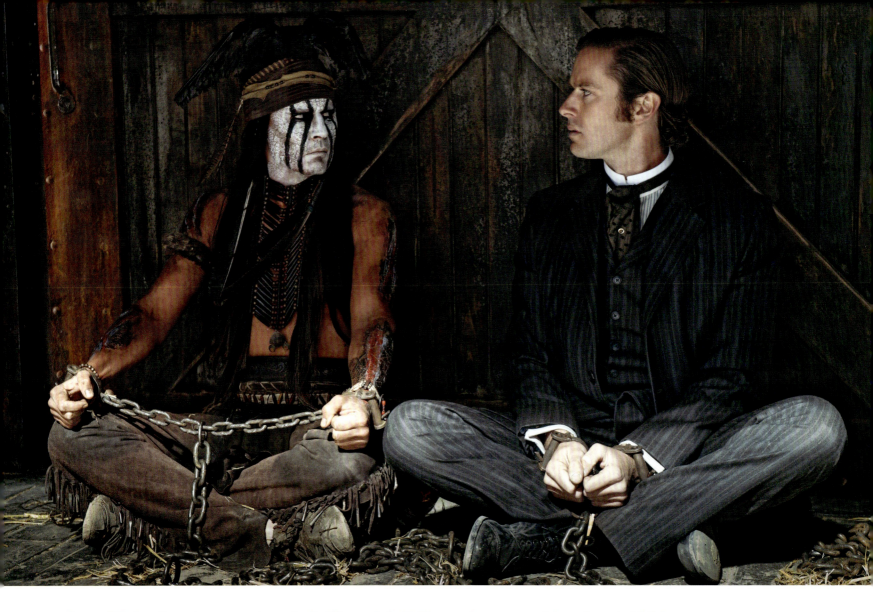

producers of *The Lone Ranger*)—saw a great opportunity. "We were in Dominica hanging out with *Pirates* screenwriters Ted Elliott and Terry Rossio and talking about what classic titles we would love to see as new movies," says Stenson. "They told us they had pitched a version of *The Lone Ranger* to Sony some years back. We discussed how great it would be for Gore to direct it, before talking about it with him, and then Johnny, who immediately came up with the unexpected idea of playing Tonto. Gore was really excited about the idea of making a great epic western." Recalls Oman: "Ted and Terry were in love with *The Lone Ranger*. Their passion for the material inspired us. Once we refamiliarized ourselves with the concept and basic tenets of the story and character, we became hooked."

"We had a personal relationship with the lawyer for *The Lone Ranger* rights owner, Classic Media," he continues. "Eric Ellenbogen, the founder of the company, loved how we handled *Pirates*, and was eager to support us in taking a shot at redeveloping the story and putting a movie together. When the option lapsed at Sony we were poised to quickly make a deal with Disney and pursue a new take on the material. Eric Ellenbogen has been a great partner since day one, supportive and very smart about the *Lone Ranger* brand and story."

Along with such films as *Aladdin* and *Shrek*, Elliott and Rossio had also scribed all four *Pirates of the Caribbean* movies, the first three of which were collaborations between Bruckheimer and Verbinski. The pair embarked on writing their version of *The Lone Ranger*, which Mike Stenson describes as, "For want of a better term, a *Pirates* approach with a number of supernatural elements, including coyotes, which embodied the spirit of avarice." Although deleted from later drafts and never filmed, this later gave rise to a long-lasting but misguided rumor that the story included werewolves!

In between the time when Verbinski first jumped aboard the project alongside Jerry Bruckheimer, Mike Stenson, Chad Oman, Ted Elliott, and Terry Rossio, and the time the film finally went before the cameras, the road to making *The Lone Ranger* became rather bumpy. There were several years of disagreements, multiple drafts of the script, a parting of

TOP: Tonto and John Reid's inauspicious first meeting, chained together in a railway car by the Cavendish Gang.

RIGHT: Tonto (Johnny Depp) and the Lone Ranger (Armie Hammer) gallop through the magnificent vistas of Monument Valley.

OPPOSITE TOP: Often confrontational, Tonto and the Lone Ranger ultimately find common ground when partnering for justice.

the ways between Verbinski and the project, and, ultimately, a welcome reunion. "Ted and Terry kind of had a different view of the film than I did," admits Verbinski. "It was a more traditional treatment of the story combined with supernatural ideas. No harm, no foul. I kind of went my way to finish the *Pirates* movies and then made *Rango*.

"Then, one night after finishing *Rango*, I was having dinner with Johnny and he pulled out a picture of himself in Tonto makeup with the bird on his head, and just slid it across the table. He had done his homework on the character, gotten underneath the guy, and that got me hooked. I wrote up an outline of how I saw the story, making Tonto the untrustworthy narrator and seeing the whole thing from his perspective, making the mythology be about how Tonto created the Lone Ranger. We've all heard the story from the Lone Ranger's point of view. We never heard it from (a) the guy who was there and (b) the Native American. The idea was that a very old Tonto is telling his story to a young kid who's sort of dressed up like the Lone Ranger, who knows the mass-produced, Happy Meal version but now hears it from the man himself, who has his own internal struggles and guilt."

"This is the story of how John Reid becomes the Lone Ranger," confirms Jerry Bruckheimer, "but in the framework of a 'dramedy' between two characters from totally different backgrounds who are really at odds at the beginning of the story and through the course of their relationship come to a kind of uneasy bonding. Our version has a lot of excitement, adventure, drama, comedy, spectacle, and emotion. And because of Gore's vision, it's also huge."

THE MASKED AVENGER REBORN

Gore Verbinski was interested in *The Lone Ranger* only if they could take the classic story and stand it on its ear. "I think if you're a fan of the original TV series," Verbinski says, "you're going to be surprised by the movie, because everybody knows that story, and that's not the story we're telling. We're telling the story from Tonto's perspective, kind of like Don Quixote told from Sancho Panza's point of view. I would say that at its core, our version is a buddy story and an action-adventure film with a lot of irony and humor and enough odd singularity to make it distinct."

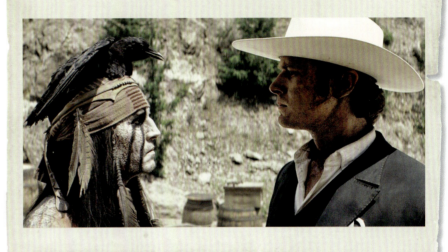

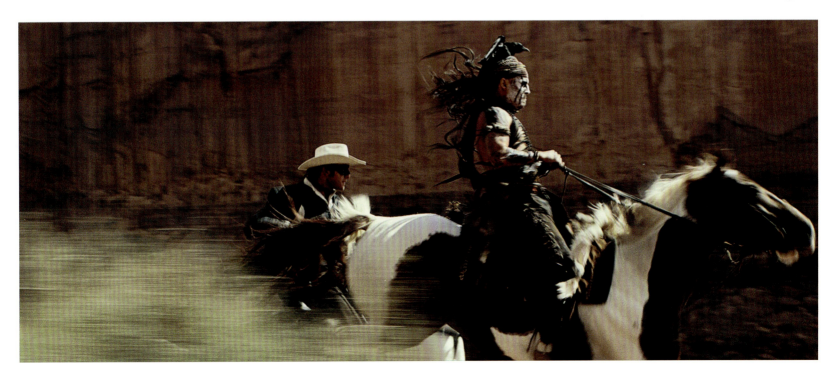

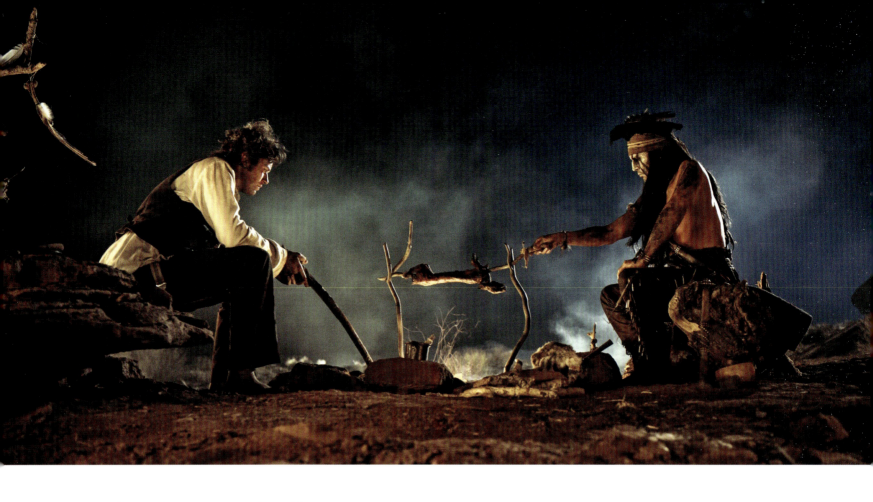

UPDATING A LEGEND

"Once we had the idea of casting Johnny as Tonto, you have to make his character relevant, or the whole thing's going to be tipped out of balance," notes Verbinski. "It's the Lone Ranger origin story, but told from Tonto's perspective and set against the backdrop of the Transcontinental Railroad's construction. During this time there was a tremendous amount of change going on in the West, and much would be lost in the forward thrust of progress. The Transcontinental Railroad was a tremendous achievement but also one that brought a sense of loss to many, particularly Native Americans. It's a story that is dramatic, comedic, and tragic at the same time. This *Lone Ranger* is a big action-adventure film, but at its core it's also the most unlikely two-hander because the Lone Ranger and Tonto are yin and yang. They're literally handcuffed together at the beginning of the story, both struggling to survive on their own, but becoming a whole through the very symbiotic relationship they develop.

"You've got the Lone Ranger, John Reid," Verbinski continues, "who believes in justice to the point where he's almost blind in a very unjust world. Imagine Jimmy Stewart stumbling into a Sam Peckinpah film—he's really out of time in this particular narrative. And then you've got this sort of crazy Native American who feeds this dead bird on his head, makes trades with dead people, reads messages in the blowing leaves, and has a kind of tragic core and his own unique outlook on things. He's an outcast from his own Comanche tribe, John Reid becomes an outcast from his own people, and together they're a band apart."

Verbinski was completely undaunted by the prospect of taking the classic story on different pathways, and in fact felt a responsibility to do so. "There are some great radio and TV episodes of *The Lone Ranger*," says Verbinski. "The stuff's still out there, and it's plenty good, so why retell it in the same way?" Verbinski, a passionate film buff, was interested in merging the traditional and postmodern western. "The traditional western is the solitary man, gun on his hip, silhouetted and juxtaposed against a vast emptiness," he says. "The postmodern western to me is the emptiness becoming cluttered. Objects, like trains, automobiles, hammers and nails flying, as progress starts to build. The silhouette is harder and harder to find, so the role of the hero in that modern world is harder to find. We've tried to contemporize what John Ford was doing in the heyday of westerns, and return the genre to an epic scale."

TOP: After being rescued by Tonto, John Reid watches him barbecue a rabbit for their wilderness dinner.
OPPOSITE: Visual consultant Crash McCreery created this remarkable illustration of Johnny Depp as Tonto.

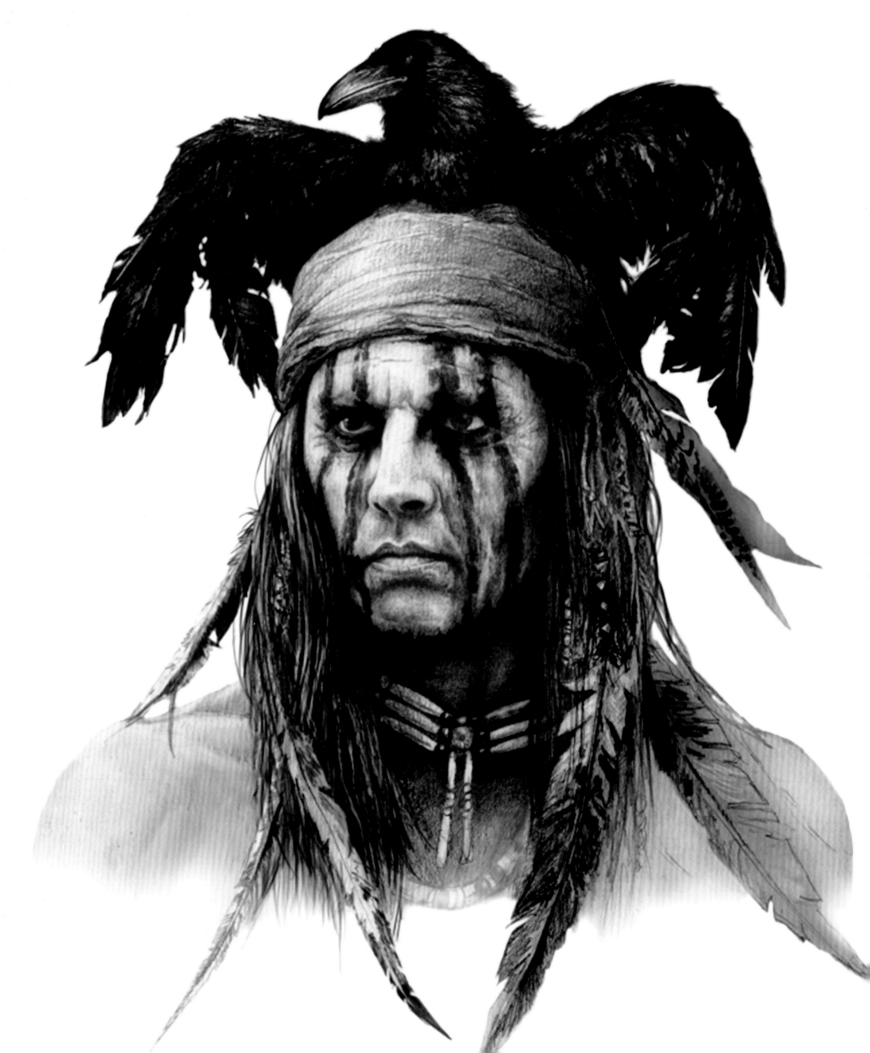

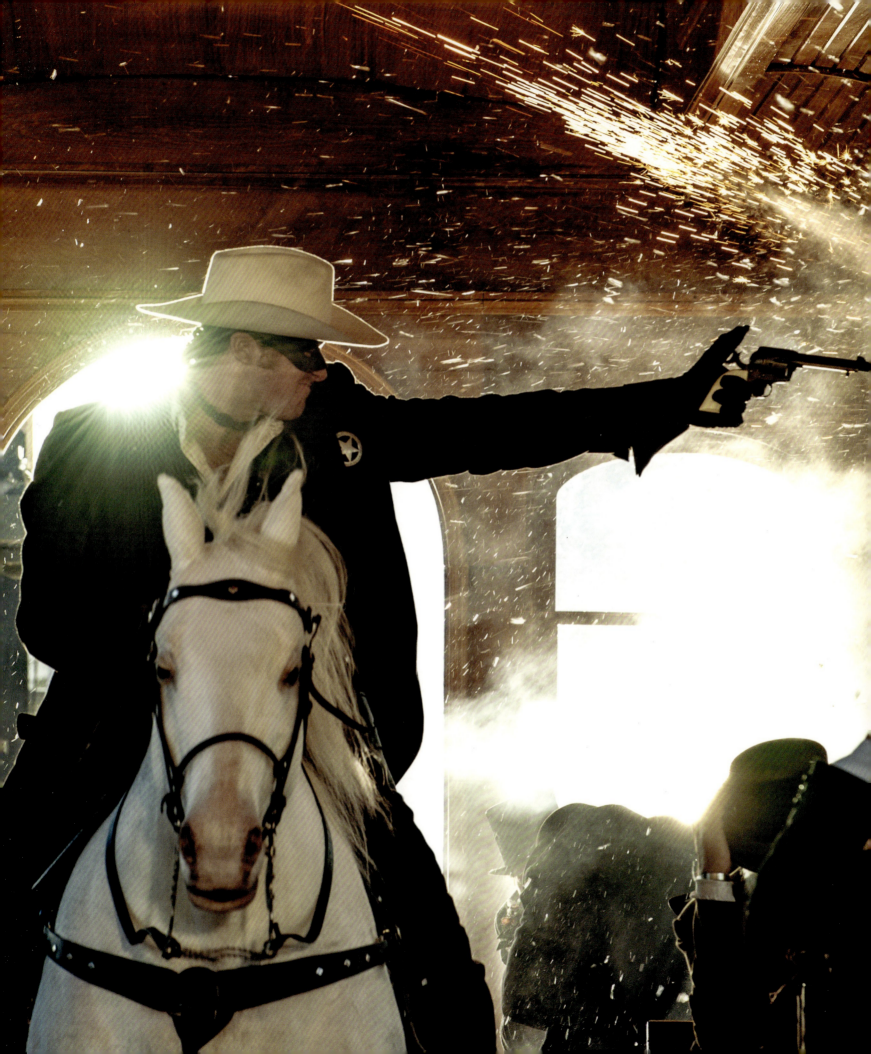

THE LONE WRITER

WITH ORIGINAL SCRIBES Elliott and Rossio having made their crucial contribution to the project, Bruckheimer and Verbinski then turned their attention to talented screenwriter and author Justin Haythe, who had adapted the novel *Revolutionary Road* for Sam Mendes's acclaimed film. Bruckheimer's production team of Stenson, Oman, and Melissa Reid had met with Haythe previously to discuss another project, and synchronistically, he was also on Verbinski's radar. A writer of uncommon intelligence and depth, British-born, Brooklyn-based Haythe was aligned with the producer and director on the new direction they all wanted *The Lone Ranger* to take. Despite the fact that previous incarnations of *The Lone Ranger* had been enjoyed by listeners and audiences of all ages, the property had always fallen within the realm of juvenilia, with stories and characters painted in black-and-white. "The TV show does feel dated to most people now," notes Haythe. "I grew up on it overseas and loved it, but watching it now, you realize that it was pretty much aimed at kids. The Lone Ranger was a mythic, but not fully developed, human character, and we wanted to paint him in four dimensions. Our version of *The Lone Ranger* wants to honor all the iconic aspects of the story—the mask, the silver bullet, the white horse, "kemosabe," the ambush at Bryant's Gap—but to do it in a way that they couldn't have fifty years ago when the television show was still being made.

"And our thinking about the story began at a simple question: Why does a good man have to wear a mask? And the answer is that a good man has to wear a mask because when doing the right thing, sometimes you have to go outside of society. Our version is essentially a conversion story. The movie begins with John Reid returning on a train to the West from the East, where he's studied law. He believes in modernity and pragmatism and is a devotee of liberal philosopher John Locke. But unknown to him, on the same train is Tonto, who's on a very different quest. Through a series of events, including the murder of John Reid's brother, Dan, his and Tonto's quest become one. So it's a conversion story in

LEFT: The Lone Ranger perilously gallops through a railroad car with guns blazing in the film's final chase sequence.

TOP RIGHT: Visual consultant Crash McCreery's detailed drawing of Armie Hammer as the Lone Ranger.

> "OUR THINKING ABOUT THE STORY BEGAN AT A SIMPLE QUESTION: WHY DOES A GOOD MAN HAVE TO WEAR A MASK?"

A NEW VISION OF *THE LONE RANGER* 27

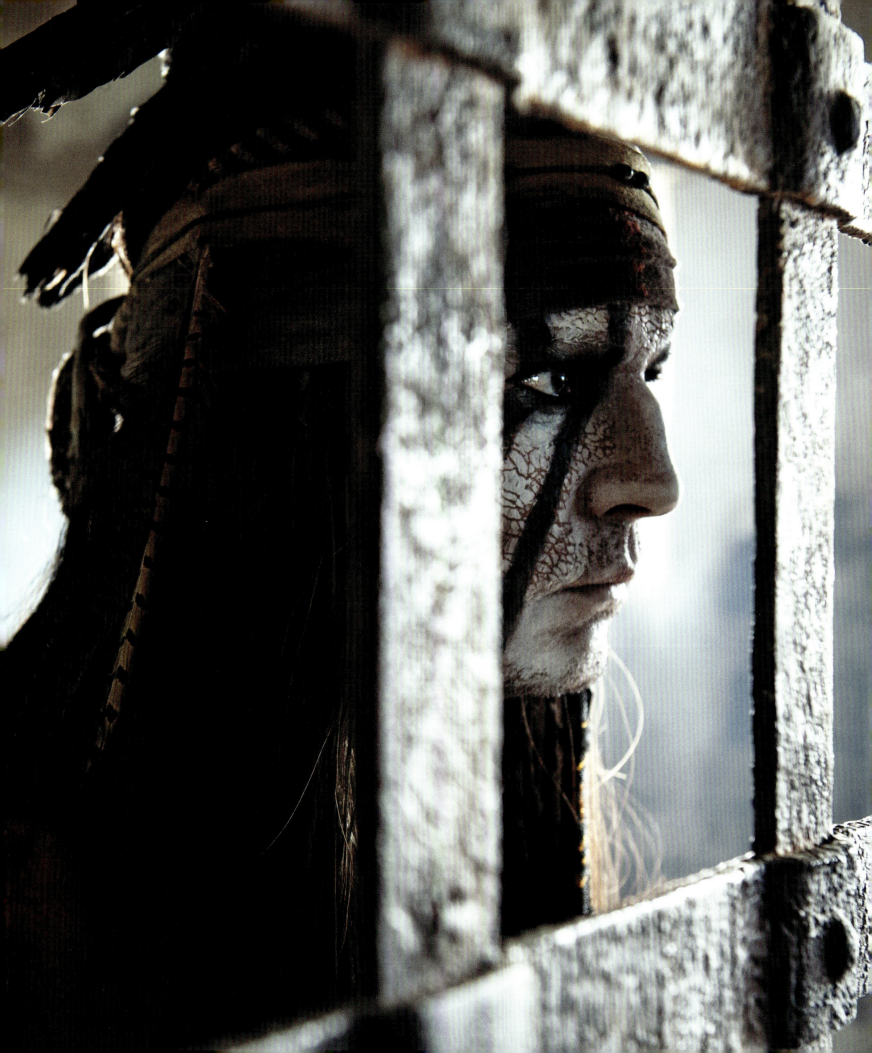

the sense that Tonto's the fulcrum by which this young man, John Reid, becomes the Lone Ranger, so everything we know about this iconic character all comes from Tonto.

"With Johnny Depp playing Tonto," adds Haythe, "we knew all bets were off. The relationship between the Lone Ranger and Tonto in the original series is an utter mystery. Tonto is the ultimate sidekick, but there's a genuine friendship there, which was something we really wanted to explore. The key of the movie was, how do you honor the creation myth of this icon, the Lone Ranger, but have a chance to explore that friendship? I thought that a cowboy in a mask, white hat, and white horse, in this day and age, had to be played with some humor. But it's not a send-up, or a lark, because there's real gravitas to the story. Early on, the white hat and mask are played for humor, but it becomes more serious as the story progresses."

LEFT: Tonto behind bars in the Colby sheriff's office.

BELOW: John Reid, made a Texas Ranger by his brother Dan, sets forth in pursuit of Butch Cavendish and his gang.

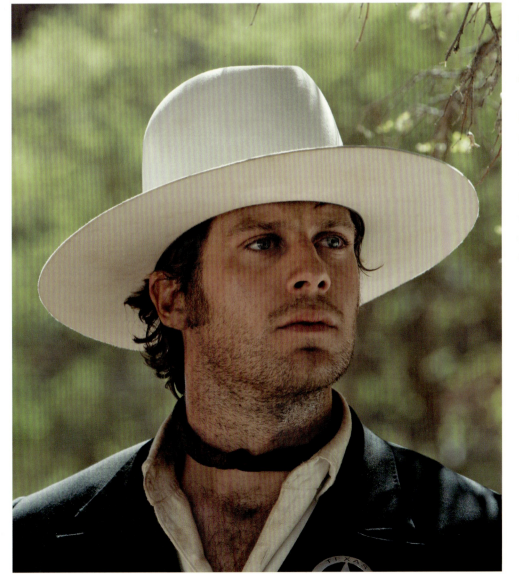

ACTING THE PART

WITH ARMIE HAMMER IN THE ROLE of John Reid/the Lone Ranger—an exciting new face whose acting chops equal his all-American good looks—and a truly brilliant group of supporting talent that includes the likes of Tom Wilkinson, William Fichtner, Barry Pepper, James Badge Dale, Ruth Wilson, and Helena Bonham Carter, the die was cast. The new *Lone Ranger*, as conceived by the filmmakers, deliberately echoes not only some of the most famous Western movies in cinema history, including works by the aforementioned Peckinpah, Italy's Sergio Leone (one of Verbinski's favorites), and John Ford, but also classic films from outside that genre as well. After all, it's no coincidence that Tonto and the Lone Ranger refer to themselves as "a band apart" in the film—two outcasts joining forces for a common cause. One of the films that heralded the innovations of French New Wave cinema during the early 1960s was Jean-Luc Godard's *Band of Outsiders*, or, in the original lingo, *Bande à part*. One can say the same about the hugely creative duo who brought *The Lone Ranger* to the screen—they too have one foot in the mainstream and the other very much outside of it.

Overcoming all hurdles on a journey that had already lasted several years, Bruckheimer and Verbinski finally started shooting *The Lone Ranger* on February 28, 2012. Brought to the screen by Disney and Jerry Bruckheimer Films, with Verbinski's Blind Wink and Depp's Infinitum Nihil also participating as production entities, this true team effort focused on a common goal: making a movie that would defy conventions and expectations, but satisfy audiences in ways they could never have expected.

"WITH JOHNNY DEPP PLAYING TONTO, WE KNEW ALL BETS WERE OFF...."

A NEW VISION OF *THE LONE RANGER*

RIDING HERD: GORE VERBINSKI & JERRY BRUCKHEIMER

GORE VERBINSKI IS A DIRECTOR WHO RARELY RAISES HIS VOICE ABOVE LOW-DECIBEL LEVEL, BUT ANYONE WHO MISTAKES THAT QUIETUDE FOR A SHY AND RETIRING NATURE IS IN FOR A MAJOR SURPRISE. WITH STEELY DETERMINATION AND AN UNWAVERING DEDICATION TO EMBLAZONING HIS EXTRAORDINARY CINEMATIC VISION ONTO THE SCREEN WITHOUT COMPROMISE, VERBINSKI DEFINITIVELY RIDES HIS OWN CINEMATIC TRAIL. IN THE PROCESS, HE HAS WON HUGE CRITICAL AND AUDIENCE ACCLAIM FOR FILMS RANGING FROM THE TERRIFYINGLY ATMOSPHERIC HORROR MOVIE THE RING TO HIS PIRATES OF THE CARIBBEAN EPICS (WHICH COLLECTIVELY GROSSED $2.8 BILLION WORLDWIDE), NOT TO MENTION HIS ICONOCLASTIC ANIMATED MASTERPIECE RANGO, WHICH REUNITED VERBINSKI WITH PIRATES OF THE CARIBBEAN STAR JOHNNY DEPP AND THEN WON THE DIRECTOR AN ACADEMY AWARD FOR BEST ANIMATED FILM. VERBINSKI IS PERHAPS THE MOST SUBVERSIVE DIRECTOR WORKING IN MAINSTREAM AMERICAN FILMMAKING TODAY, MELDING A TASTE FOR THE OFFBEAT, THE ECCENTRIC, AND THE SURREAL WITH A LOVE OF THE SPECTACLE THAT THIS EPIC FORM HAS TO OFFER.

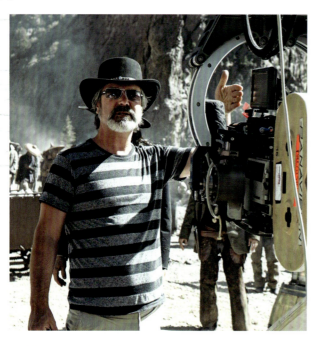

ABOVE: Director Gore Verbinski composes a shot on the Silver Man Mine set in Creede, Colorado.

OPPOSITE: Johnny Depp and Jerry Bruckheimer chat on the desert expanses of Rio Puerco, New Mexico.

"We could have made ninety different versions of a pirate film with the same script, the same story, and most of the same actors," comments executive producer Mike Stenson, "but we would not have had a multibillion dollar franchise without the vision of Gore Verbinski. The number of directors who can shoot great action, understand story, and have an encyclopedic knowledge of visual effects can be counted on one hand, but Gore is one of them."

Actors are eager to flock to Verbinski's team, which explains why *The Lone Ranger* marks his fifth collaboration with Johnny Depp and also elicited quick interest from rising star Armie Hammer. "He's had me since that Budweiser commercial," says Hammer, referring to the now-famous "Frog" spots, the first of which Verbinski directed. "Gore could not be more proficient at shouldering the entire burden. He's the smartest and hardest-working guy in the room. Gore will pose a question, and if someone is not right there with an answer in a second, he'll come

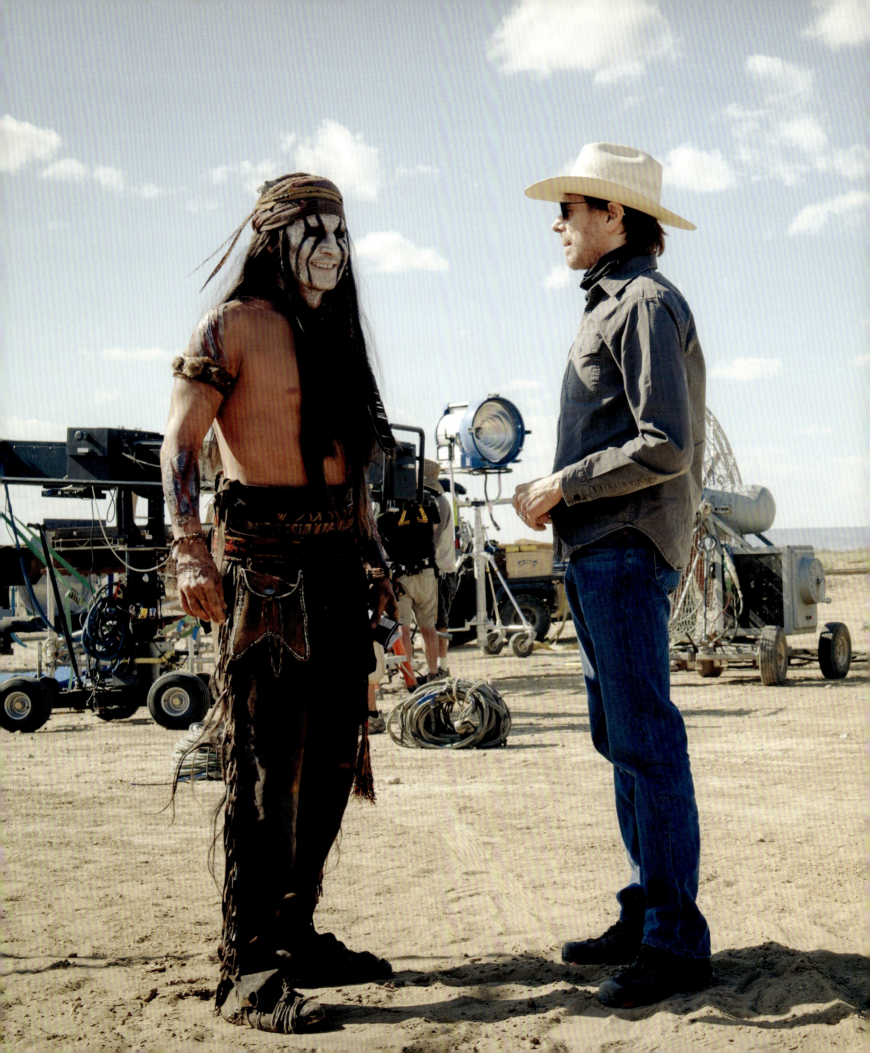

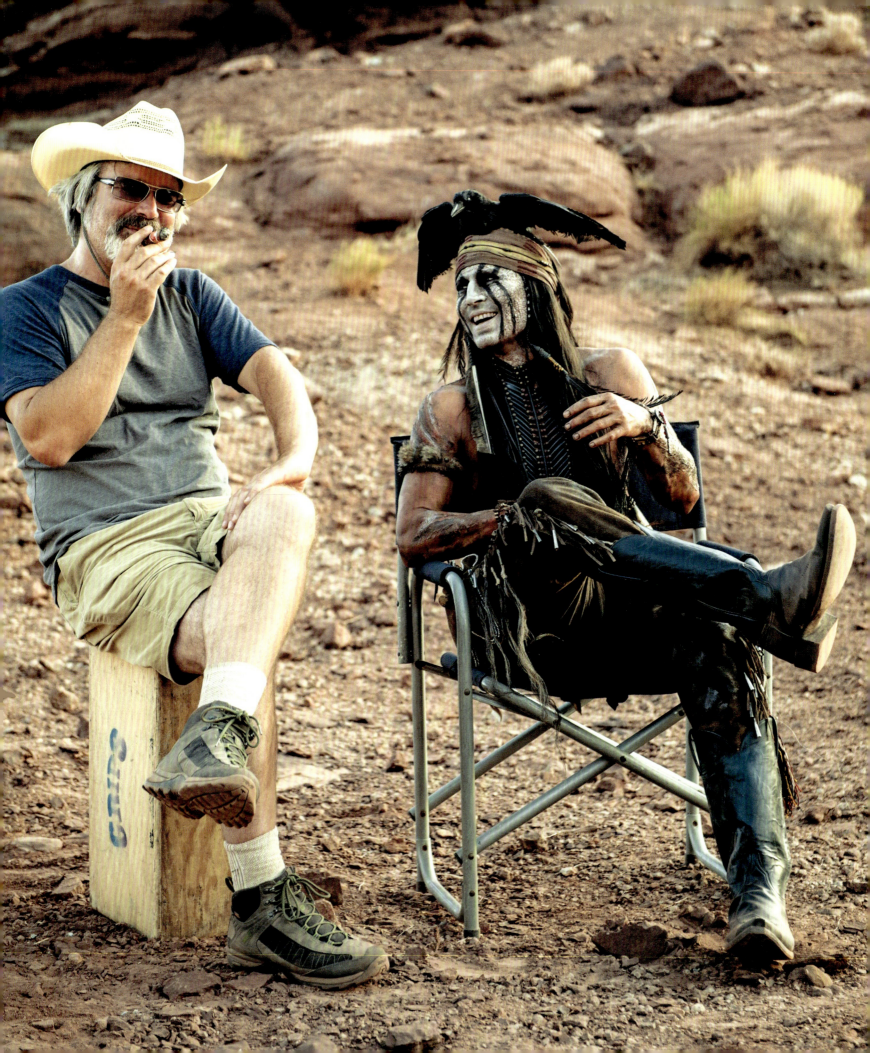

up with his own solution and it'll be better than anything that anyone else could have suggested."

Toward the latter part of The Lone Ranger shoot, Tom Wilkinson, the great British actor who portrays industrialist Latham Cole in the film, noted that "given that this is probably the biggest, most complicated movie that I've worked on . . . the fact that Gore can do it with such equanimity is amazing. At no point do you see him fly off the handle or go into a sulk. He just deals with it. And like all great directors, he won't compromise, something that can sometimes be uncomfortable, but that's what makes him who he is. He has a very, very clear image of what he wants to achieve with this film . . . and heaven help anybody who stands in his way."

"Gore creates a creative environment that is really infectious, and I think it makes you feel very safe to explore and experiment, which is a comforting feeling when you're on set," adds Ruth Wilson, who portrays Rebecca Reid. "The man at the center is protecting you, wanting the best out of you, and pushing you to be as wild and wonderful as he is."

"I do not like comfortable things," Verbinski has said more than once, borne out by the fact that as a filmmaker, he always takes the road less traveled. Or more to the point, not traveled at all. To access some of the utterly inaccessible locations he selected for Pirates of the Caribbean: Dead Man's Chest on the Caribbean island of Dominica, the company literally had to blaze new paths. Creating infrastructure where there was none, they constructed production offices and communications towers, even building entire roads into inaccessible sites and beaches. For The Lone Ranger, Verbinski continued his pioneering, not just geographically but also artistically. That's the way it's been for the filmmaker his entire life. Starting his creative career as a guitarist for such punk bands as the Daredevils and Little Kings, Verbinski has never lost his outlaw approach to life or art.

"Gore is an amazingly talented director, someone who encompasses it all," states Jerry Bruckheimer. "Sometimes you find a director who does comedy well but can't do action, or those who can only do action. Gore is one of the very few directors who can do everything—action, drama, comedy—with equal brilliance. He's highly visual and lets nothing stand in his way to create sequences that have never been seen before, and then he somehow finds a way to shoot them to maximum effect."

LEFT: Gore Verbinski and Johnny Depp share a laugh between takes.
BELOW: Gore Verbinski explains the upcoming action to a uniformed background player on the Promontory Summit set.

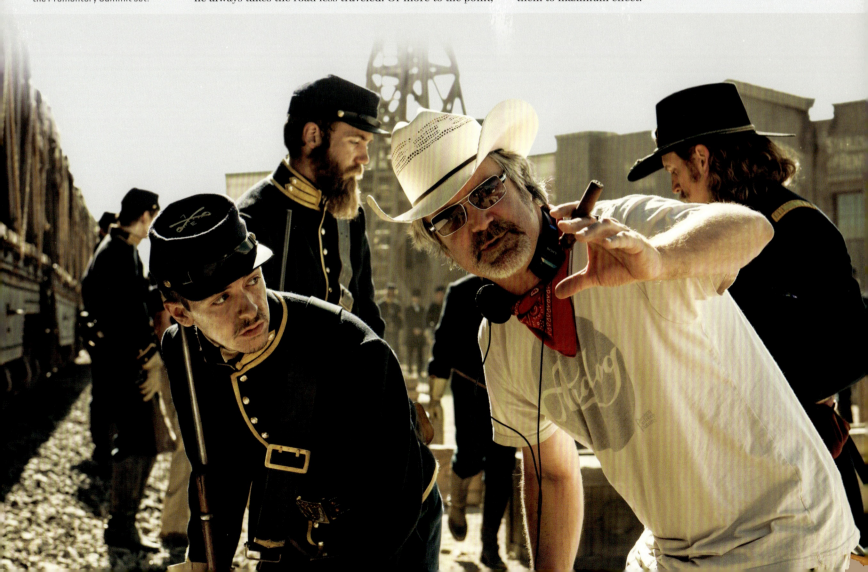

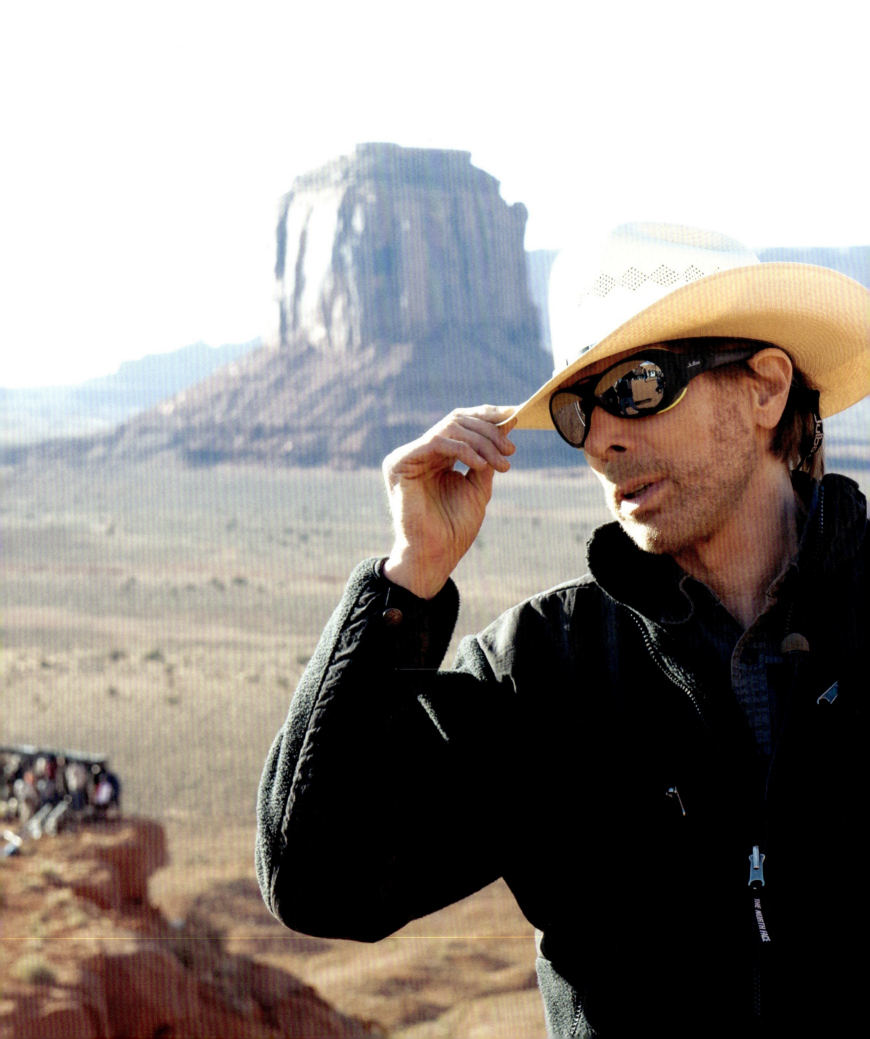

BELOW: Jerry Bruckheimer on location in Monument Valley.

PAGES 36–37: Johnny Depp, Armie Hammer, Gore Verbinski, and Jerry Bruckheimer enjoy a light moment during a long day of filming.

Somehow, there's poetic justice in the fact that forty monumentally successful years and forty-five feature films after his very first producing credit, Jerry Bruckheimer has finally made another Western. Bruckheimer was the associate producer of 1972's *The Culpepper Cattle Co.*, a modest venture that was nonetheless well received at the time. What's more, it's now seen as a model of genre revisionism for its gritty and realistic depiction of life on the frontier. While *The Lone Ranger* may also have revisionist elements, no one would describe the overwhelmingly ambitious film as modest, although that word has often been applied to Bruckheimer, despite his position as arguably the most successful producer in the history of the American motion picture industry.

The list of projects that Jerry Bruckheimer has produced since that first credit, either solo or in partnership with the late Don Simpson, reads like a checklist of the American pop culture zeitgeist: just a small sampling includes all four *Pirates of the Caribbean* movies, the two *National Treasure* and *Bad Boys* films, *Black Hawk Down*, *Enemy of the State*, *Armageddon*, *Con Air*, *The Rock*, *Crimson Tide*, the first two *Beverly Hills Cop* movies, *Top Gun*, and *Flashdance*, not to mention television's three *CSI* programs, *Without a Trace*, nine-time Emmy Award–winner *The Amazing Race*, and more.

Intriguingly, this giant of motion pictures and television is so unpretentious that, while indulging in his passion for taking photos on set, he's often mistaken for the company's unit photographer. Known for getting his points across with as few words as necessary, Bruckheimer utilizes his quiet strength to protect those he's chosen as collaborators. The Bruckheimer style is perhaps best described by an actor with whom he's collaborated five times, most recently on *The Lone Ranger*: "Jerry is sort of the Great Protector," explained Johnny Depp a few years ago. "He wards off any and all evil spirits. And if anyone had anything really grave at stake in the beginning of *Pirates*, it was Jerry. Talk about rolling the dice. I mean, for an actor, you come in, do your bit, and if it works, it works, and if it doesn't, it doesn't, and it's on to the next one. But Jerry really took a risk.

"We wouldn't have been able to get away with a third of what we got away with on the first *Pirates* without Jerry," Depp continues. "Without his support and his understanding of the material . . . the first film would have been much more generic, not much fun, and I would have been fired! Jerry knows these films well. I've been in umpteen script meetings with the guy, and whenever a false note comes up, he always comes up with something interesting. And if you're in a pinch, he's always the guy who says, 'Don't worry about it. We'll get it taken care of.' Jerry really produces; he's untamed all the time and allows us to be in an atmosphere that's conducive to making something interesting and different. There have never been pressures in that regard. It's always sort of, you know, Bruckheimer's got it. You know he's handling it. It's cool."

For Jerry Bruckheimer, his approach to film has always been the same: "We try to break the mold, always give the audience something unexpected and unique. That's why we work with actors like Johnny Depp and directors like Gore Verbinski, who are both total originals." Bruckheimer has spent his entire career championing new directors who went on to great success, including Michael Mann, Paul Schrader, Adrian Lyne, Tony Scott, Michael Bay, and, of course, Gore Verbinski. "There's nothing more exciting," says Bruckheimer, "than discovering fresh talent and giving them the room they need to be as creative as they can. I knew that Gore had what it takes, and he's amazed me, and audiences all over the world, with each successive film. He's the only one whose vision for *The Lone Ranger* was big enough, and the only one who could get it up on screen."

For Ruth Wilson, the young British actress who plays Rebecca Reid in *The Lone Ranger*, working on a Jerry Bruckheimer film meant that she had truly made it to Hollywood. "I was brought up on Jerry's movies; he's a huge part of my youth and my understanding of what film is. This film almost didn't get made, and it was Jerry fighting to keep it on track. He knows this project is very special, and it's a great comfort to know that your producer has that much faith."

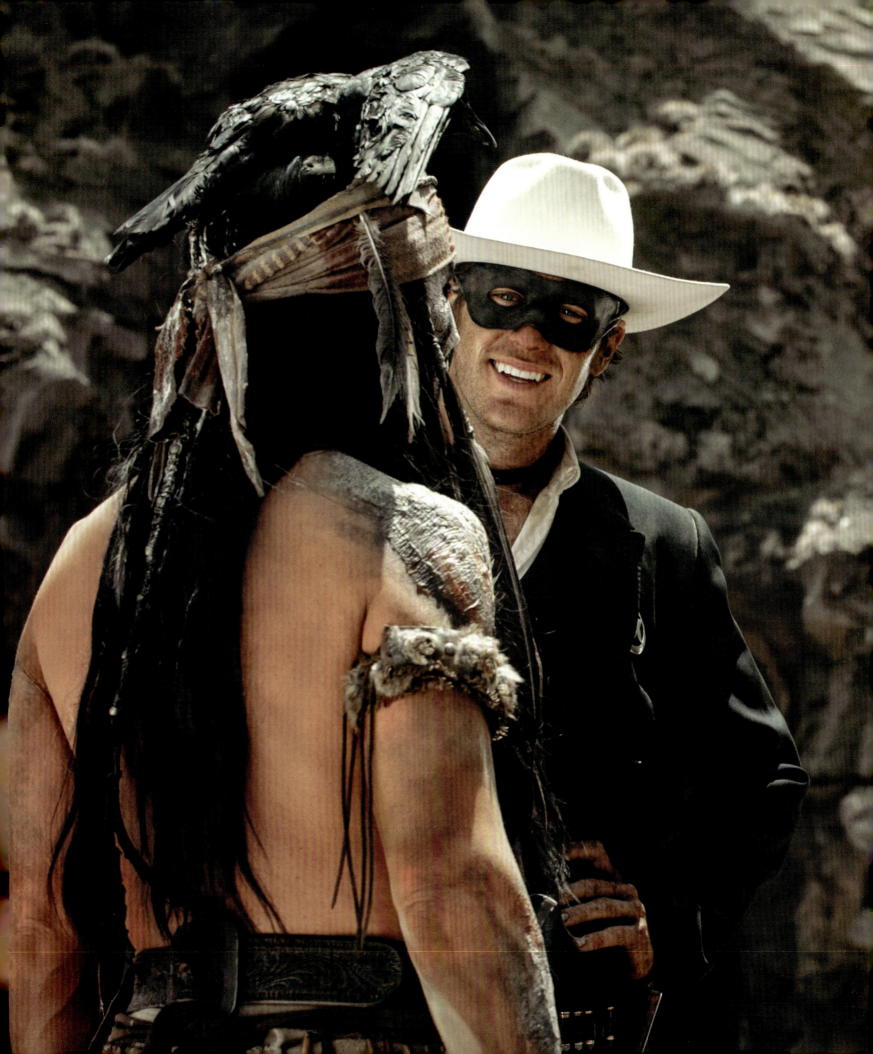

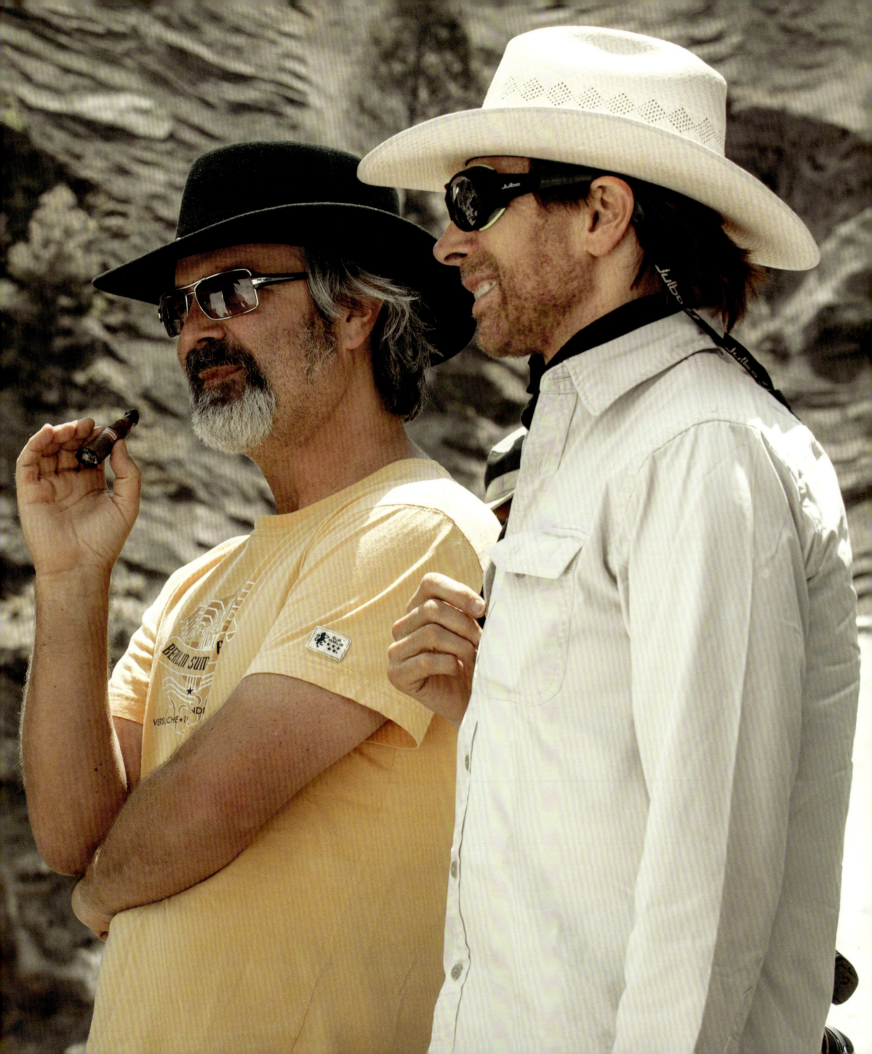

INTRODUCING THE CAST OF *THE LONE RANGER*

ARMIE HAMMER AS THE LONE RANGER/JOHN REID

As filming on *The Lone Ranger* entered its seventh exciting but unquestionably exhausting month, there was one man on set who embodied the spirit of the soldier who picks up the flag on the battlefield and leads his fatigued comrades in storming the hill that will secure a lasting victory. And he just so happened to be the guy playing the title character. Having already made a notable mark in Hollywood with his performance as the Winklevoss twins (yes, both of them) in David Fincher's *The Social Network* and starring opposite Leonard DiCaprio in Clint Eastwood's *J. Edgar*, Armie Hammer is a rising star, and Bruckheimer and Verbinski snagged him for *The Lone Ranger* at just the right moment.

"Armie Hammer is such a great find," says Bruckheimer. "Not only has he got classic movie star looks, talent, and charisma to spare, but he also has incredible spirit, drive, and a great sense of fun and adventure. When everyone else was dragging, Armie was always there with his bright smile and friendly conversation, lifting everyone's spirits. He's an action hero not just on screen but also in real life. Like Johnny, Armie also did many of his own stunts, and in his spare time on location in the Southwest, you couldn't keep him away from jumping into waterfalls, dirt biking, hiking in the mountains, rock climbing, you name it. And the more dangerous it got, the more he loved the challenge."

If Hammer's towering frame, all six feet five inches of it, and almost impossibly good looks recall movie stars of yesteryear, it's no accident that Gore Verbinski and Jerry Bruckheimer selected him for this much sought-after role. "A lot of names were thrown around," says the director, "but looking at Armie's picture, we just thought, 'If he has the chops, God willing, this is the right face.' Justin Haythe and I kept defining the Lone Ranger as Jimmy Stewart trapped in a Sam Peckinpah movie.

"Armie is a little out of time," Verbinski continues. "When you meet him, you soon realize that he doesn't have a cynical or jaded bone in his body. Armie has a kind of great, blind optimism in the way he looks at the world. We really needed someone you could believe could have old-fashioned ideas, and I think the world is starved for a good man. But, as we often say, the film deals with the question of why a good man has to wear a mask. And I think it's because to implement justice when it can be purchased by the highest bidder, you have to operate outside the law. The Lone Ranger and Tonto are outlaws for justice, and Armie was the perfect actor to embody that quest."

Hammer, who celebrated his twenty-sixth birthday during filming, was eager to tackle the complexities of the role. "John Reid's older brother, Dan, is a Texas Ranger," he says. "Their father was a Ranger. John could never throw the lasso or pick up a gun and twirl it quite as well as his brother. So my guess is that his father said, 'You know what, you're not meant for this, you've got soft hands. Go to the Northeast and become an educated man.' So John returns to his home in Colby, Texas, espousing these John Lockeian ideas and principles of how the world should work. But egalitarianism doesn't really have a place on the frontier, and so he gets an education of a very different kind in the course of the story, especially from his relationship with Tonto, which goes through many peaks and valleys. It's fun to watch the symbiosis develop between these two guys."

OPPOSITE: John Reid dons the mask of the Lone Ranger.

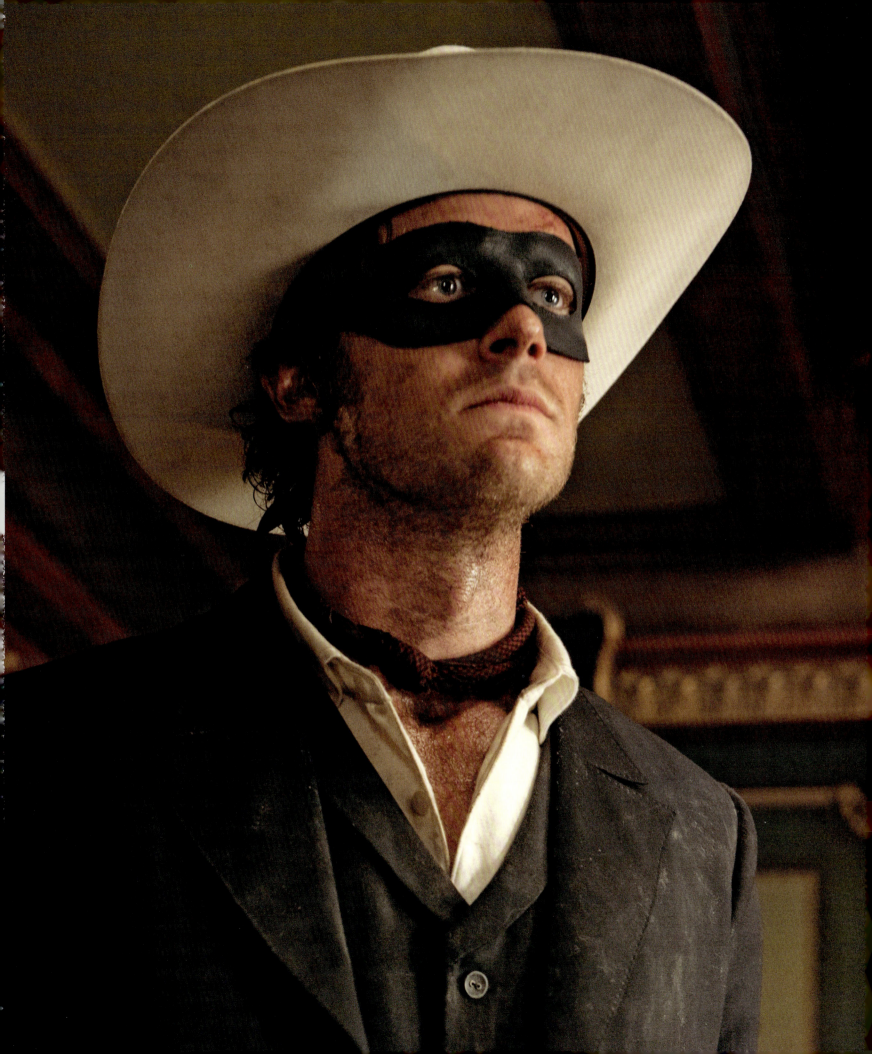

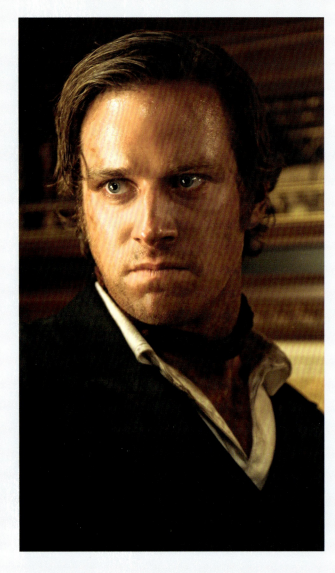

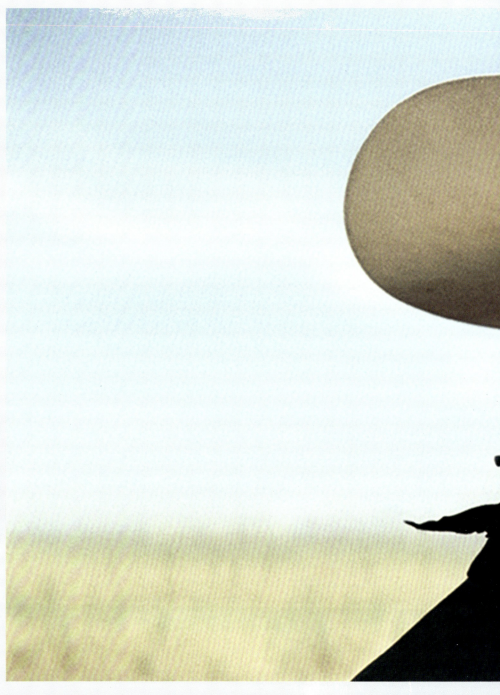

The actor, who was born in Los Angeles but grew up in the Cayman Islands (which might explain his passion for nature and adventure), divides his time between Los Angeles and San Antonio, Texas, hometown of his beautiful and talented wife, TV personality Elizabeth Chambers and the site of her heralded Bird Bakery (which opened during the shoot of *The Lone Ranger* and instantly became *the* destination for gourmet cupcakes). Often buried in a book, tying complex rope knots, or amiably chatting with fellow cast and crew, and when not zooming through buttes, valleys, and mesas on his dirt bike between shots or playing with Archie, his beloved Welsh terrier, the articulate Hammer brought an irrepressible ebullience to the nearly year-long shoot. "What did I love about this project?" Hammer said on one of his last days of filming. "There weren't many things that you couldn't love. We traveled all over the American Southwest; we spent months on the road in a different city almost every two or three weeks. I rode my dirt bike around Indian reservations and national parks. I got to work with Johnny Depp. I got to work with Gore Verbinski. I got to work with Jerry Bruckheimer. The list of things that I loved is too long. It's been a great project."

And there was one other way in which Armie Hammer would remember his experiences starring as the Lone Ranger—he got to keep one of the masks!

TOP LEFT: A determined John Reid learns some of the hard lessons of the West.

ABOVE: Hiding his identity, John Reid re-emerges as the masked warrior for justice known as the Lone Ranger.

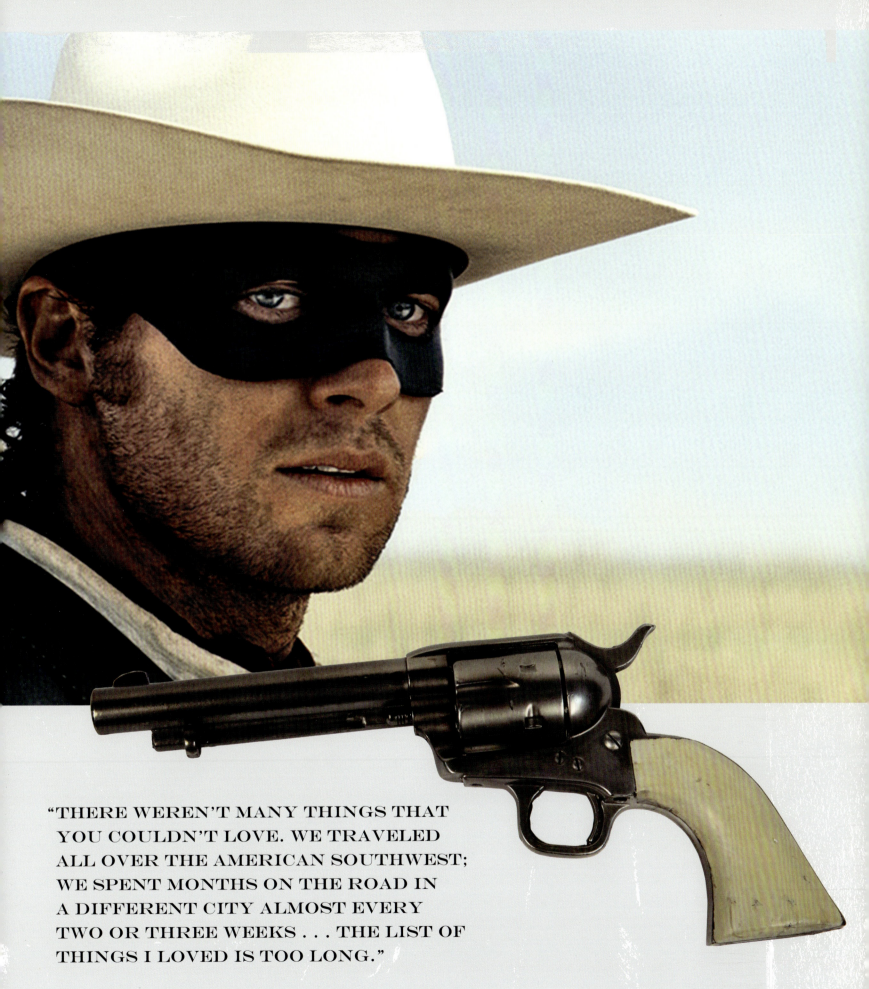

"THERE WEREN'T MANY THINGS THAT YOU COULDN'T LOVE. WE TRAVELED ALL OVER THE AMERICAN SOUTHWEST; WE SPENT MONTHS ON THE ROAD IN A DIFFERENT CITY ALMOST EVERY TWO OR THREE WEEKS . . . THE LIST OF THINGS I LOVED IS TOO LONG."

INTRODUCING THE CAST OF *THE LONE RANGER*

JOHNNY DEPP AS TONTO

In May 2012, in a leafy Albuquerque backyard at the home of LaDonna Harris, the now-legendary human rights activist who has spent the better part of her eight decades campaigning to improve the lives of Indigenous peoples around the world, Johnny Depp was "taken" into Harris's own Tabbytite family in the presence of Harris's extended family, staff members of her activist organization Americans for Indian Opportunity, and a few friends. Depp, himself of partial Cherokee heritage, was now a part of her own nation, the Numunu, Lords of the Plains, and better known to most of the world as the Comanche. In the tradition of such adoptions, a new name for Depp was announced by Wahathuweeka-William Voelker—more commonly known to the company as just "Bill"—of Sia, the Comanche Nation Ethno-Ornithological Initiative who officiated the ceremony with his associate, Troy "The Last Captive" (so named because he was "taken" into the Ohnononuh band of the Comanche "in the old way," according to an official proclamation of the Nation). The distinguished assemblage also included the tribal chairman of the Comanche Nation, Johnny Wauqua, who, sadly, has since passed on. The name chosen for Depp was Mah-woo-meh, which, in an approximate translation, means "He Can Change" or, perhaps more in the vernacular, "shapeshifter."

A more appropriate appellation could not be found for this world-renowned actor, musician, and visual artist who was born in Owensboro, Kentucky. Following no path other than his own and liberated from the dictates of any known authority, he has transformed himself into a brilliant and varied rogues' gallery of on-screen characters for more than thirty years. This remarkable canon has included playing the title characters of *Edward Scissorhands*, *What's Eating Gilbert Grape*, *Ed Wood*, *Don Juan DeMarco*, *Donnie Brasco*, and *Sweeney Todd: The Demon Barber of Fleet Street*, and providing the voice, soul, and spirit of Gore Verbinski's *Rango*. He also utterly embodied the alter ego of writer and close friend Hunter S. Thompson in both *Fear and Loathing in Las Vegas* and *The Rum Diary*. Other memorable performances include Ichabod Crane in *Sleepy Hollow*, James Barrie in *Finding Neverland*, Willy Wonka in *Charlie and the Chocolate Factory*, John Dillinger in *Public Enemies*, and the Mad Hatter in *Alice in Wonderland*. However, Depp's most celebrated role is perhaps that irascible, delightfully irredeemable, and downright loveable scoundrel Captain Jack Sparrow in the four *Pirates of the Caribbean* movies, all of which were produced by Jerry Bruckheimer, with the first three being directed by Gore Verbinski. It should come as no surprise that Depp is a great admirer of silent movie actor Lon Chaney, who was dubbed the "Man of a Thousand Faces." More than any other actor since Chaney, Depp has made every effort to shapeshift with the same frequency, a quality that makes each of his roles unique, surprising, and effortlessly enthralling.

Tonto promises to be another unforgettable addition to Depp's oeuvre. Painted, tattooed, bare-chested, adorned with an impressive bone choker, and with an inanimate crow perched on top of his head (along with a beaded bag of bird seed used to "feed" his feathered friend), Tonto possesses a somewhat foreboding visage. Even the actor admits, as he did to *USA Today* during filming, "This is not the look you want to wake up to in the middle of the night and see

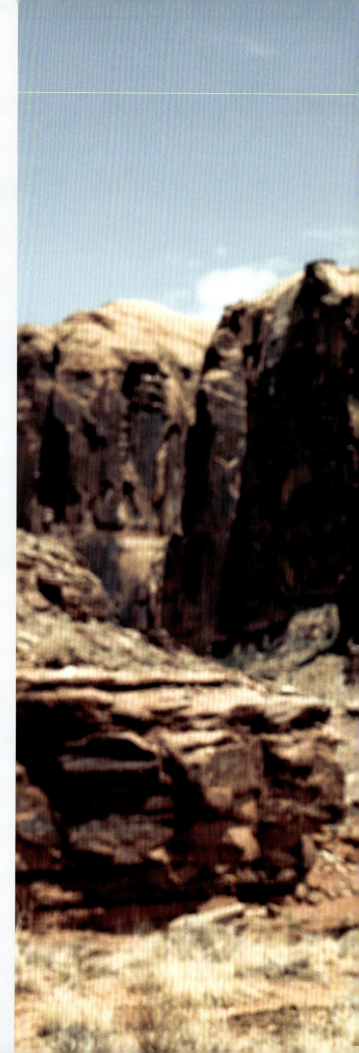

RIGHT: Tonto rides through the harsh and jagged Western landscape that has helped form him.

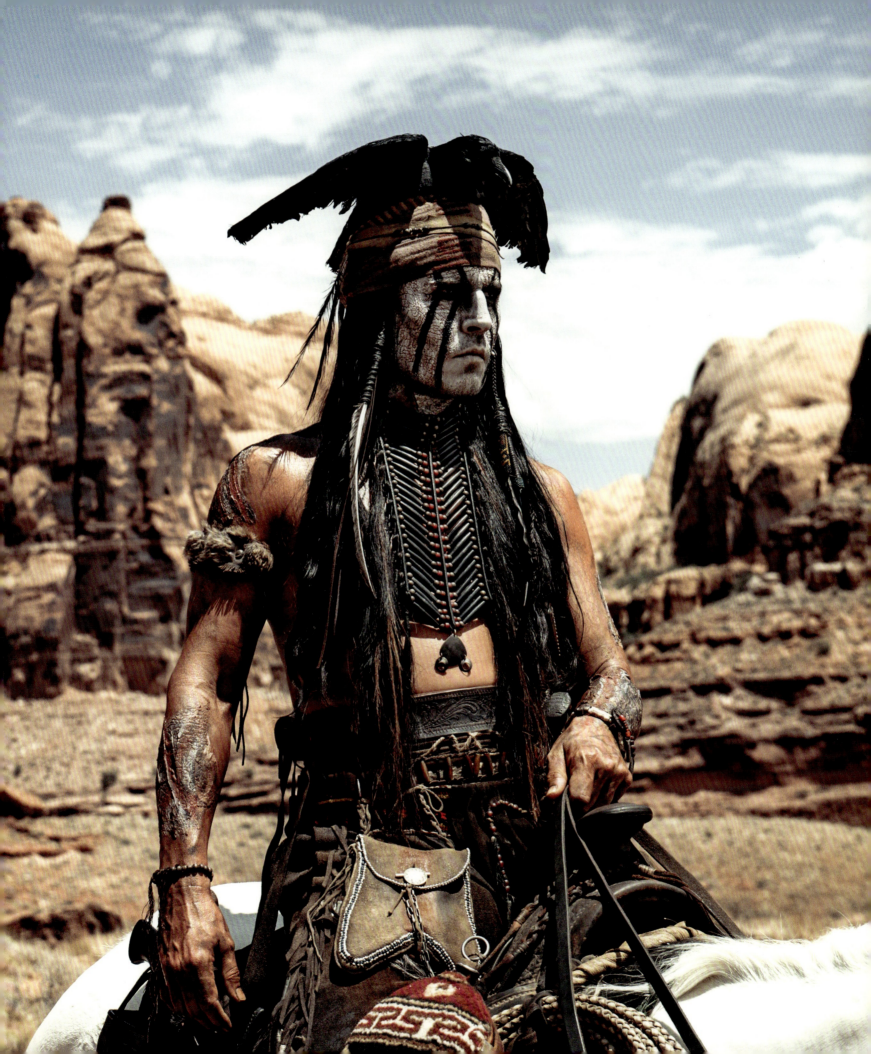

hovering above you." But as the story progresses, we learn about Tonto's background and why he, like the Lone Ranger, must wear a mask—in his case the paint that perpetually adorns his face. With pathos, humor, physical dexterity, and the fearlessness of the great silent-screen comedians, Tonto becomes an utterly singular character in this version of *The Lone Ranger*; a solitary warrior who lives in a mystical world with a reality all its own—an outlook diametrically opposed to John Reid's scientific reason and pragmatism.

Depp's alchemical technique is known only to him. But he seems to find the center of gravity to each character he plays before purposefully tilting it. The results are always just skewed enough to keep the audience unsettled, anticipatory, and in a place to expect the unexpected, knowing that as far as Depp's work is concerned, the conventional is unwelcome.

Depp's fervent desire to portray Tonto in *The Lone Ranger* was born out of his firm belief that he could honor the role by taking the character to places unimagined in previous incarnations while at the same time respecting Jay Silverheels's classic take on the character. Just as important, Depp also felt a duty to help set right Hollywood's negative treatment of Native Americans during a century or more of film history. It's well chronicled that the proud, dignified Silverheels attempted to imbue his Tonto with greater depth but was thwarted by the tenor of the times. Depp, who closely developed his take on the character with Verbinski and Bruckheimer, was excited by the possibilities afforded by their mutually adventurous spirit. "I think I have interesting plans for the character, and I think the film could be entertaining and very funny," Depp told *The Hollywood Reporter* before the cameras started to turn. "But I also like the idea of having the opportunity to make fun of the idea of the Indian as a sidekick . . . I don't see Tonto that way." Depp added to *Entertainment Weekly* magazine, "I always felt Native Americans were badly portrayed in Hollywood films over the decades. It's a real opportunity for me to give a salute to them." With Depp's acceptance into the Comanche Nation, and his warm embrace during filming from the people of the Navajo Nation and other tribes, including several Pueblos in New Mexico, clearly the salute has already been returned in kind to Mah-woo-meh.

On set and throughout every location, the endlessly gracious Depp, a brother-in-arms to the cast and crew and so devoted to his fans that he would often spend hours signing autographs for them after a twelve- or fourteen-hour day of filming, proved multiple times why he's achieved such a rarified position in his field. "There's really no one like Johnny," notes Bruckheimer. "He's one of the most original, adventurous, and exciting actors of all time, always surprising us with one fantastic creation after another. Johnny is creating a Tonto unlike any we've seen before, a character with multiple levels, with great humor but a really moving core of pathos and emotion. What's more, Johnny is just a wonderful human being, and we're so lucky to work with him again."

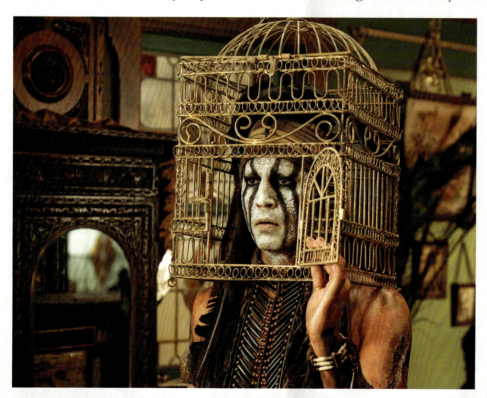

LEFT: In Red Harrington's chambers, Tonto attempts to protect the crow on his head from a cat.

RIGHT: Tonto adorns his face with war paint until his quest for vengeance is fulfilled.

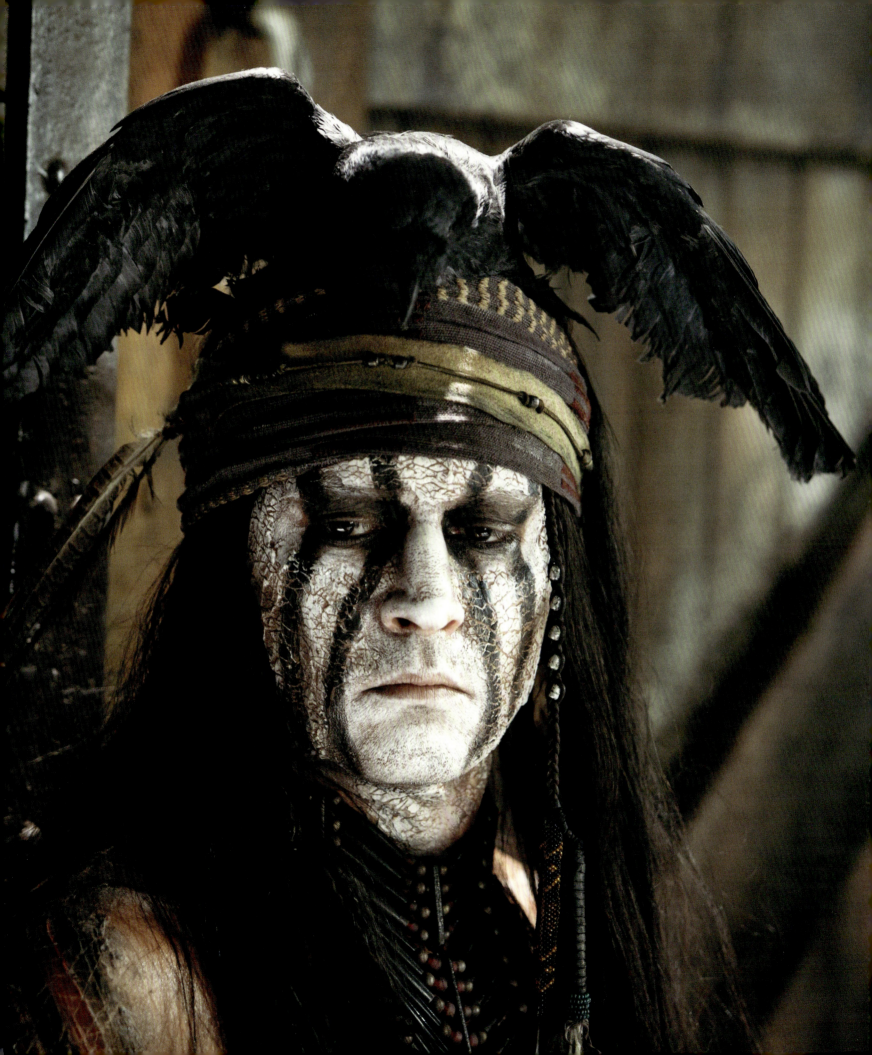

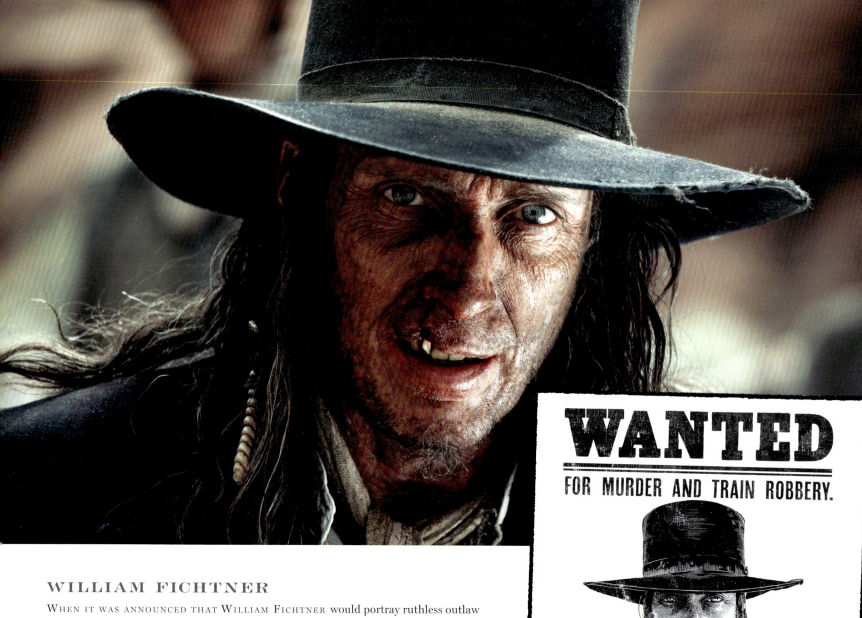

WILLIAM FICHTNER

When it was announced that William Fichtner would portray ruthless outlaw Butch Cavendish, the Lone Ranger's archenemy and a character known to all fans of the legend, movie websites lit up like Christmas trees. As the online outlet Indiewire posted, "William f****** Fichtner . . . who has worked with a pretty wide berth of Hollywood . . . has never crossed paths with Depp, but he couldn't ask for a better project to do it with," adding that the actor would be "bringing his brand of badass to *The Lone Ranger*." And badass is just the word to describe Cavendish, his terribly scarred and torn face a reflection of the bottomless pit of darkness in his soul. By now, it's agreed that there's little that Fichtner can't do on screen or television, as evidenced by his work in more than sixty roles, including three previous smash-hit films produced by Jerry Bruckheimer: *Armageddon*, *Pearl Harbor*, and *Black Hawk Down*. Unrecognizable in his makeup as Cavendish, Fichtner nonetheless found a core to the character that makes him more than just a monster. "Sometimes I play people rougher in nature, but I always try to find something to make them real," he says. "Cavendish is pretty simple in his thought process about what he wants, but he's smart and focused. I think it's safe to say that out of all the amazing characters that you'll see in this film, the last person you would want to find in a dark alley is Cavendish. I don't even think Cavendish would want to run into himself, let's put it that way."

TOP: The combination of William Fichtner's great talent and the transformational skills of makeup department head Joel Harlow created an unforgettably villainous Butch Cavendish.

ABOVE: Graphic designer Dianne Chadwick created this period-authentic wanted poster of Butch Cavendish for Kris Peck's prop department.

OPPOSITE: Barry Pepper brings both versatility and originality to his role as rigid martinet Captain J. Fuller.

BARRY PEPPER

The wonderfully unpredictable Barry Pepper made his mark portraying real-life figures (Robert F. Kennedy in *The Kennedys*, for which he won an Emmy; baseball great Roger Maris in *61**) and creating unforgettable characters in a wide range of genres (the sharpshooting Private Jackson in Steven Spielberg's *Saving Private Ryan*, Dean Stanton in *The Green Mile*, his namesake Lucky Ned Pepper in the Coen brothers' *True Grit*). He set his targets on the role of *The Lone Ranger*'s Captain Fuller based on the track record of the filmmakers. "I think Gore, Jerry, and Johnny set the gold standard for the pirate movie, and I think they are now going to reshape the Western because they bring such spectacle, intrigue, and singular characters to the film," says the Canadian actor. "I was sent a few pages of the script, which had this really bizarre, eccentric character by the name of Captain Fuller. He had this one line of dialogue in which he expressed his feelings about hygiene that was the germination of the character for me, and I thought we could have a lot of fun with this. I'm a huge fan of spaghetti Westerns, and I love the more villainous characters from those films. There's a playfulness and singularity to those characters that is similar to what Gore has achieved with this film. He's constantly searching for the awkward truth, and this was totally in my wheelhouse." In researching the role, Pepper read about such famous "Indian fighters" of the late nineteenth century as George Armstrong Custer and Ranald Mackenzie. "They were all very egotistical and had grander plans for themselves in mind," he says. "You can almost hear the campaign speeches and slogans stirring in Fuller's mind. I saw him as this sort of preening peacock involved in the grotesque task of ridding the Indians from the plains."

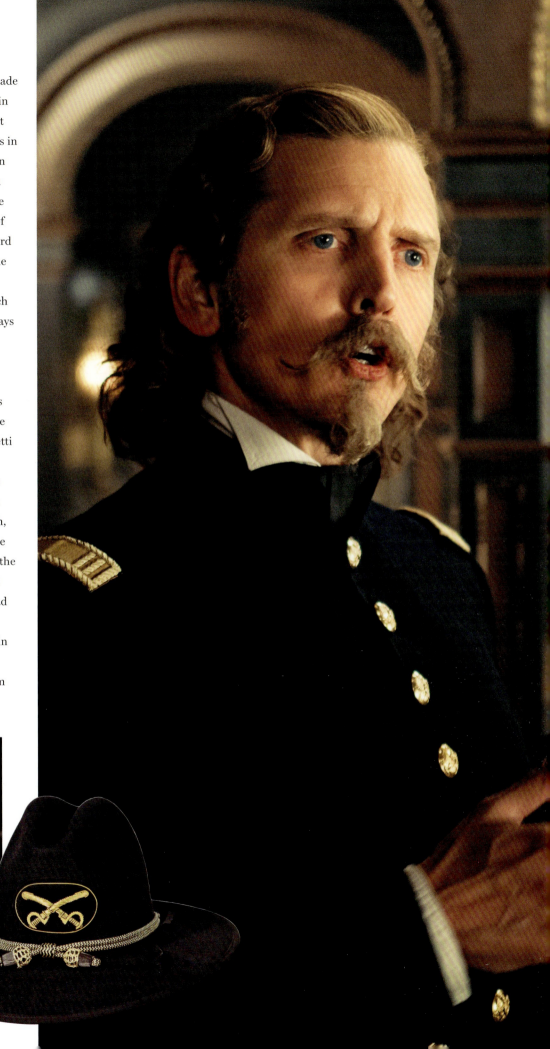

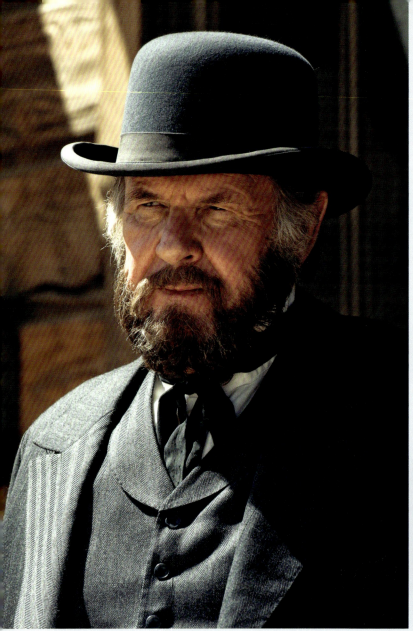
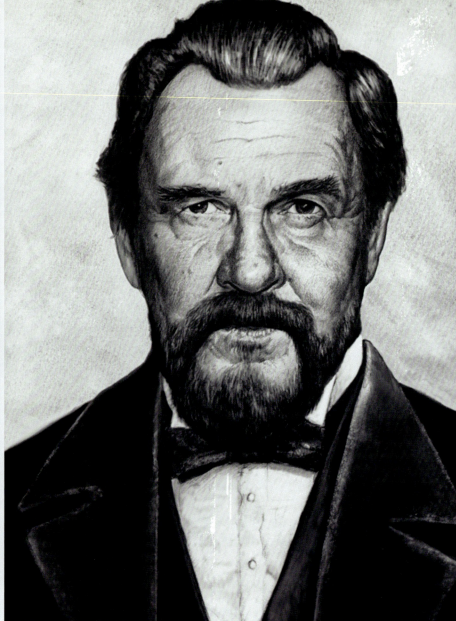

TOM WILKINSON

Tom Wilkinson, who portrays railroad and nation builder Latham Cole, is acknowledged as one of Britain's finest and most versatile actors, and is a two-time Academy Award nominee (for *In the Bedroom* and *Michael Clayton*) and four-time Golden Globe nominee, winning for his performance as Benjamin Franklin in the HBO miniseries *John Adams*. "Latham Cole is, in a certain sense, one of the fathers of America as it is today," explains Wilkinson. "Today he would be called a venture capitalist. For Cole, building the Transcontinental Railroad isn't just an opportunity to make money, but also his vision for unified greatness. But Cole is not always overfastidious in how he achieves what he needs to achieve, but I guess that's always been the case. The people who have the big vision are not reluctant to tread on the legal rights of other people."

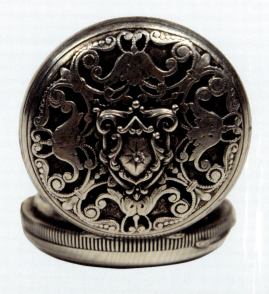

TOP LEFT: Tom Wilkinson, one of Britain's greatest character actors, as American railroad tycoon Latham Cole.

TOP RIGHT: Another finely rendered Crash McCreery drawing, this one of Tom Wilkinson as Latham Cole.

LEFT: Latham Cole's beautifully tooled pocket watch was provided by property master Kris Peck.

OPPOSITE: The brilliant Ruth Wilson brings strength, fortitude, and beauty to her role as Rebecca Reid.

RUTH WILSON

GORE VERBINSKI AND JERRY BRUCKHEIMER really grabbed the brass ring when they decided to cast British actress Ruth Wilson as Rebecca Reid, a spirited frontierswoman married to Texas Ranger Dan Reid. Unfortunately, younger brother John has carried a torch for Rebecca since they were teenagers, which results in what Gore Verbinski calls "a very classic love triangle." Wilson, who makes her American film debut in *The Lone Ranger*, was the perfect choice following two Olivier Award–winning performances, one for her luminous work playing Stella in *A Streetcar Named Desire* at London's famed Donmar Warehouse and another for her title role in *Anna Christie*. She has also won acclaim for her beautifully complex performance as the alluring and dangerous Alice Morgan opposite Idris Elba in the BBC series *Luther*, along with her portrayal of Jane Eyre in the celebrated BBC miniseries adaptation of the literary classic. "When Ruth came in and read for the part, she just blew us away," says Verbinski. "She can act circles around most people, and she's really got it going in those eyes. She's going to be a huge movie star." Wilson herself was keen to tackle the role of Rebecca, by no means a damsel in distress but a tough, independent woman who can handle herself. "What Gore and Justin Haythe have done with the characters Helena Bonham Carter and I played is to make them much stronger, more independent, and more characterful than you might normally expect in these sorts of films. *The Lone Ranger* is a dream come true," she says. "It's full of action. It's got great amounts of humor. It's also about an amazing part of American history. I've never been in anything of this scale, so it was a complete shock to me, and every day on set was amazing. You've got to pinch yourself every now and then."

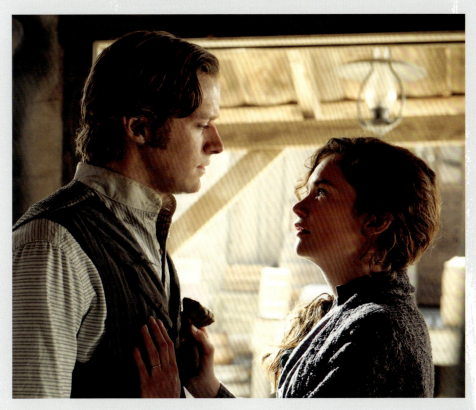

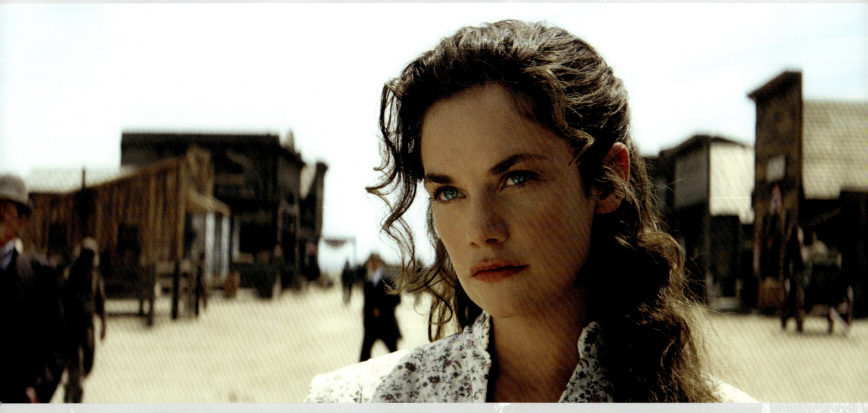

HELENA BONHAM CARTER

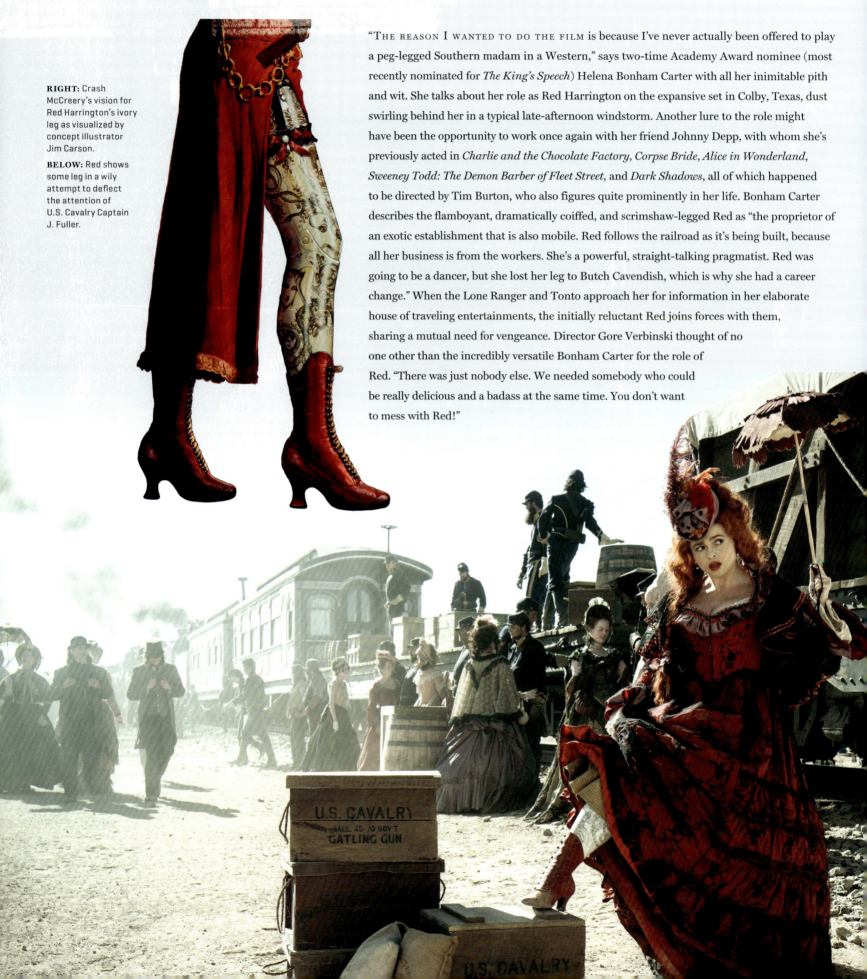

RIGHT: Crash McCreery's vision for Red Harrington's ivory leg as visualized by concept illustrator Jim Carson.

BELOW: Red shows some leg in a wily attempt to deflect the attention of U.S. Cavalry Captain J. Fuller.

"THE REASON I WANTED TO DO THE FILM is because I've never actually been offered to play a peg-legged Southern madam in a Western," says two-time Academy Award nominee (most recently nominated for *The King's Speech*) Helena Bonham Carter with all her inimitable pith and wit. She talks about her role as Red Harrington on the expansive set in Colby, Texas, dust swirling behind her in a typical late-afternoon windstorm. Another lure to the role might have been the opportunity to work once again with her friend Johnny Depp, with whom she's previously acted in *Charlie and the Chocolate Factory*, *Corpse Bride*, *Alice in Wonderland*, *Sweeney Todd: The Demon Barber of Fleet Street*, and *Dark Shadows*, all of which happened to be directed by Tim Burton, who also figures quite prominently in her life. Bonham Carter describes the flamboyant, dramatically coiffed, and scrimshaw-legged Red as "the proprietor of an exotic establishment that is also mobile. Red follows the railroad as it's being built, because all her business is from the workers. She's a powerful, straight-talking pragmatist. Red was going to be a dancer, but she lost her leg to Butch Cavendish, which is why she had a career change." When the Lone Ranger and Tonto approach her for information in her elaborate house of traveling entertainments, the initially reluctant Red joins forces with them, sharing a mutual need for vengeance. Director Gore Verbinski thought of no one other than the incredibly versatile Bonham Carter for the role of Red. "There was just nobody else. We needed somebody who could be really delicious and a badass at the same time. You don't want to mess with Red!"

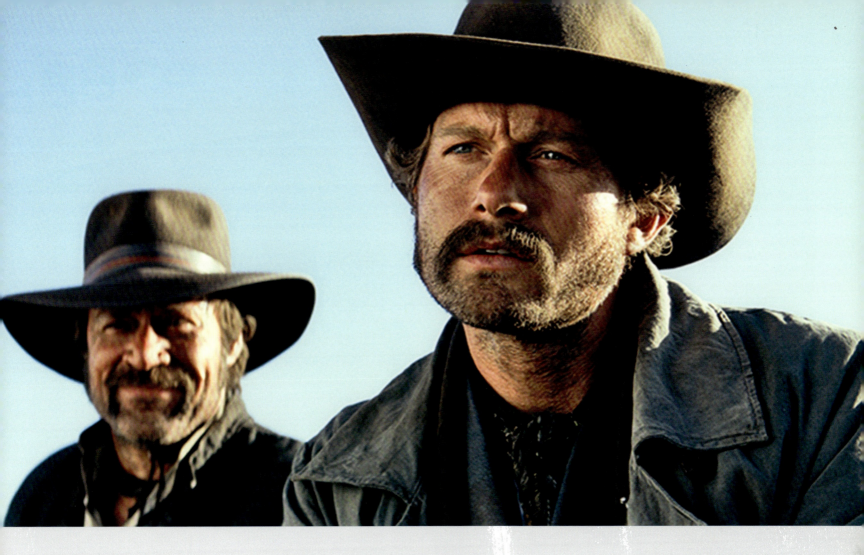

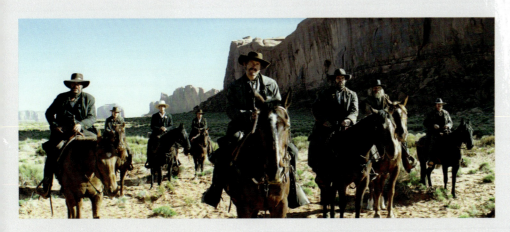

TOP: James Badge Dale, a city slicker from New York City, transformed himself into tough and courageous Texas Ranger Dan Reid.

ABOVE: Dan Reid rides with a posse of fellow Texas Rangers in pursuit of Butch Cavendish and his gang.

JAMES BADGE DALE

THE FILMMAKERS' DETERMINATION to marry the best possible talent to their specific roles paid off again with the selection of New York City–born James Badge Dale to play Dan Reid, a Texas Ranger whose rough frontier nature is a striking contrast to that of his refined and highly educated brother, John. Dale, known as "Badge" to colleagues and friends, has excelled in such roles as Chase Edmunds in *24*; Will Travers, the leading role in *Rubicon*; Robert Leckie in the Steven Spielberg–produced miniseries *The Pacific*; and serial killer Henry Darius, a character who crossed over from *CSI: NY* to *CSI: Miami*. Having made his film debut at the age of twelve in *Lord of the Flies*, Dale has also continued to work in films, including *The Departed*, *Shame*, *The Grey*, and *Iron Man 3*. "Dan Reid is John's dirtier, more world-weary older brother," notes Dale of his character in *The Lone Ranger*. "There are lots of shades of gray in Dan's worldview, and perhaps in another world and another time, he might have ended up on the outlaw side of things. Right and wrong don't seem to be that clear to him anymore."

INTRODUCING THE CAST OF *THE LONE RANGER* 51

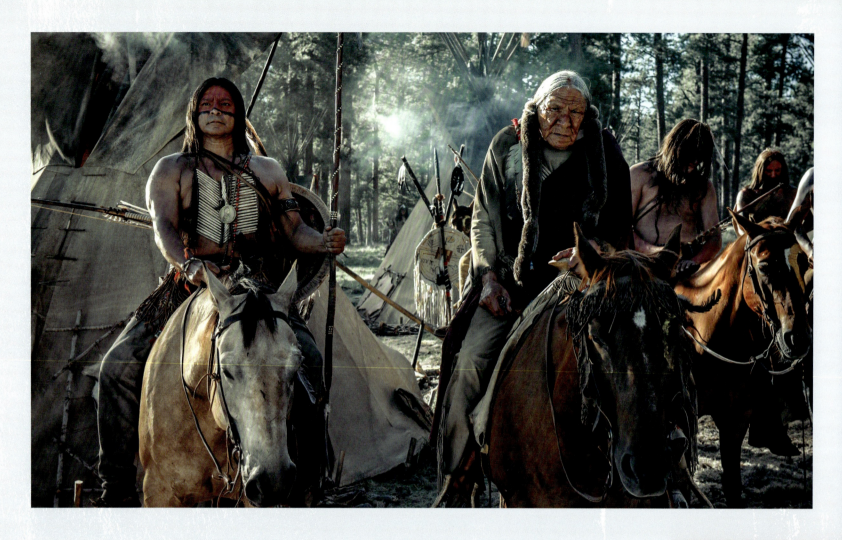

SAGINAW GRANT & GIL BIRMINGHAM

TWO DISTINGUISHED ACTORS WERE SELECTED to portray Comanche warriors facing an uncertain future with all the dignity and bravery they can muster. Saginaw Grant, a greatly respected actor/educator/activist from the Sac and Fox, Iowa, Nation and Otoe-Missouria Nation, portrays Chief Big Bear, still a great leader despite the advance of both his older years and the railroad into Comanche territory. Gil Birmingham, himself a Comanche, plays Chief Big Bear's trusted advisor Red Knee. He is perhaps best known for his role as Billy Black in the *Twilight* saga, and he previously worked with Johnny Depp and Gore Verbinski in *Rango*, providing the voice of Wounded Bird. "The way I was taught in my clan," explains Grant, whose expressive face is like a road map, "I know how Chief Big Bear would act and the things he would say. He wouldn't be hollering around barking orders. He would take care of his people like any great chief would. He would make everyone feel proud of their tribe, and of themselves." Looking at the authentic teepees constructed for a Comanche camp built in Valles Caldera (sacred Native American land in New Mexico) complete with background players from the area adorned in their period costumes, Grant added, "I know that every one of these extras will be proud to have been in *The Lone Ranger* when it opens." On the same set, Gil Birmingham commented on why the classic tale has endured through the decades: "I think the integral component is the friendship between the Lone Ranger and Tonto, but the dynamics between the characters in this one are very different. The older version was more of a sidekick thing; it didn't integrate the Native American aspect nearly as much. And there have been great efforts made by the production, working with Comanche advisers, to make it as authentic as possible in many respects. My costume features sacred eagle feathers, the Comanche horses were painted in an authentic, sacred way, and for the first time audiences will see the cut of the teepees in the original Comanche way, facing east, as the sun rises. We've got many years of stereotypical portrayals that we've been trying to change, and this is one way to do it."

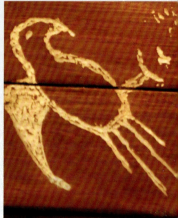

TOP: Saginaw Grant (right) and Gil Birmingham (left) as Comanche warriors Chief Big Bear and Red Knee.

ABOVE: A Native American petroglyph hand carved by visual consultant Crash McCreery.

OPPOSITE: Butch Cavendish's colorful if unsavory cohorts: (left to right) Skinny Kyle (Matt O'Leary), Frank (Harry Treadaway), Collins (Leon Rippy), Barret (James Frain), Ray (Damon Herriman) and Jesus (Joaquin Cosio).

A ROGUES GALLERY

The actors selected to portray the nefarious and very distinct members of Butch Cavendish's gang all knew that they wouldn't be playing your run-of-the-mill Western outlaws. All of them have outstanding traits that mark them as interesting individuals, however repugnant their actions may be. This gnarly lot includes Frank (Harry Treadaway), a young gunslinger with an unusual affection for ladies' garments; Barret (James Frain), a gunman who is perhaps Cavendish's most ruthless enforcer; Jesus (Joaquin Cosio), whose penchant for stealing rings occasionally includes removing the fingers wearing them; Ray (Damon Herriman), who once barely escaped a hanging and now wears the scar around his neck as a reminder; Skinny Kyle (Matt O'Leary), a disheveled, bearded whipping boy for Cavendish's outbursts of rage; and Collins (Leon Rippy), a veteran scout and old friend of the Reid family whose betrayal of the Texas Rangers sets not only the plot in motion but also his own fate. The actors formed a small League of Nations, as Treadaway and Frain hail from the United Kingdom, Herriman is Australian, and Cosio is a major star in his native Mexico. "The Cavendish Gang is a hodgepodge of various individuals," notes Treadaway, "and I think in that time period the West was a kind of cocktail of people from different regions and parts of the world." Adds Frain, who gained popularity with his roles in television's *The Tudors* and *True Blood*, "We're a desperate bunch of reprobates, and if we didn't work for Butch, we'd probably function as a fairly competent gang of robbers and thieves. There are no bonds of affection between Butch and his gang; they kind of pull together out of necessity, really." "There are no simple

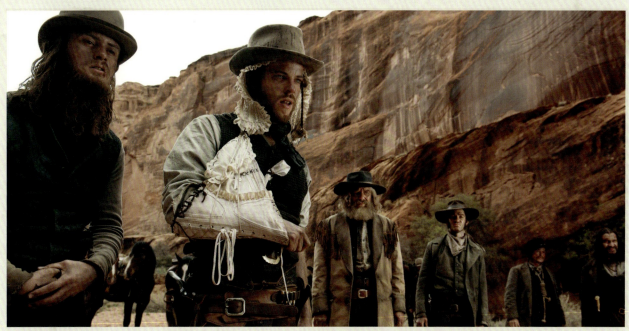

characters," notes Cosio, who has been nominated for two Ariel Awards, Mexico's version of the Oscar. "We're all bad guys, but everyone has a personal character. Barret is something of a gentleman. Skinny is very freaky. Frank is really crazy. And all of us are very fast with the gun. We are all killers." Damon Herriman, whose physical appearance was completely altered by makeup department head Joel Harlow so that he could portray the scarred Ray, notes that "it's a real testament to all the elements of the film's design that the Cavendish Gang have been made so specific and not just a cookie cutter of five bad guys. They've really taken the time to make these guys all very unique."

BRYANT PRINCE & MASON COOK

BRYANT PRINCE AND MASON COOK BOTH FELT like kids working and playing amid the massive sets and hardware created for *The Lone Ranger* for a very good reason—they are kids! For ten-year-old Prince—a North Carolinian who had only done one TV movie before Verbinski and Bruckheimer summoned him—portraying Danny Reid, the son of Texas Ranger Dan Reid and his wife, Rebecca, allowed him an opportunity to pretend to be someone he really admired. "I thought Danny Reid was a very cool boy and I would love to be like him," he says. "He sticks up for his mother a lot. He knows how to handle weapons, and he knows how to ride a horse. Danny isn't afraid of anything." From "Cowboy Boot Camp" to the third-from-final day of the shoot, Bryant experienced the full range of the marathon *The Lone Ranger* shoot, much of it in the company of Ruth Wilson, who plays his mother. "People on set say I'm Ruth's shadow because I'm with her so much," he says. "She's helped me a lot through this movie. In the beginning, I was too shy to ask for a glass of water, but Ruth was like, 'Dude, you can just say, "Can I please have water?" This is a movie set, and you're an actor on this!'" Eleven-year-old Mason Cook plays Will, a young boy of the early 1930s dressed in a Lone Ranger costume, replete with mask, hat, and toy six-shooter, who finds himself the sole audience of a story being told in a Wild West Exhibition tent. Mason was lucky enough to act all his scenes with only one other performer: Johnny Depp. "I thought I was dreaming when I got the role," he recalls, "because Johnny Depp was someone I had always wanted to work with ever since I started acting. He was really nice to me and really, really funny too. He's a great role model."

ABOVE: Danny Reid (Bryant Prince) has definitely inherited both grit and courage from his Texas Ranger father Dan and stalwart mother Rebecca.

BELOW: Dressed as his favorite legendary hero, Will (Mason Cook) finds himself hearing the "true" story of Lone Ranger and Tonto in a Wild West exhibition tent.

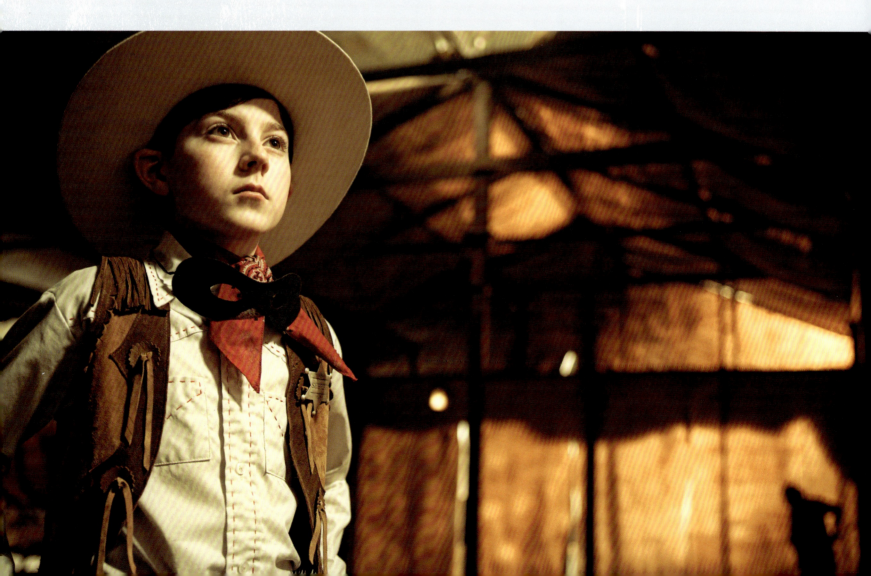

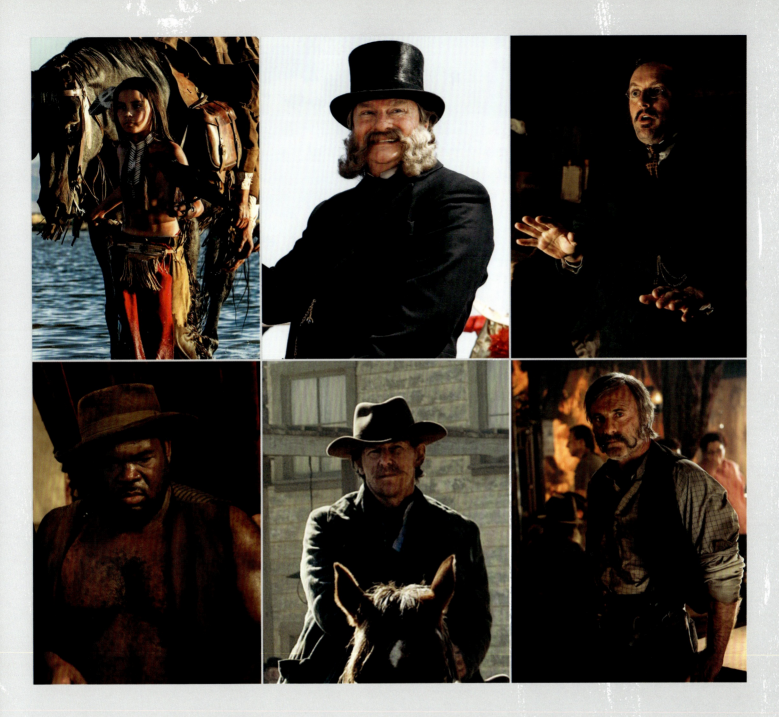

ESSENTIAL SUPPORT

The nearly one hundred speaking roles of *The Lone Ranger* are populated with many fine performers, including JD Cullum as Latham Cole's functionary Wendell; W. Earl Brown as a mustached Texas Ranger who meets his fate at the hands of Butch Cavendish; Timothy V. Murphy (from Jerry Bruckheimer's *National Treasure: Book of Secrets*) as hardened Transcontinental Railroad foreman Fritz; Stephen Root (who also provided one of the voices in Verbinski's *Rango*) as railroad executive Habberman; Leonard Earl Howze as Red Harrington's imposing aide and bodyguard Homer; Joseph Foy, a young boy from the Mescalero Apache Reservation who had never before been in front of a film camera, plays Tonto as a lad; and, as the Texas Rangers who ride into Bryant's Gap with John Reid and his brother Dan, Damon Carney as Blaine, Kevin Wiggins as Clayton, Chad Brummett as Martin, Robert Baker as Navarro, and Lew Temple as Hollis. Even legendary eighty-four-year-old character actor Rance Howard, father of Ron Howard, grandfather of Bryce Dallas Howard, and a man who has acted in some 250 film and television roles, appears as the engineer of the steam engine Constitution. All were a testament to director Verbinski's desire to paint the film's huge cast of characters in fine detail rather than broad strokes.

ABOVE: (clockwise from top left): Joseph Foy as Young Tonto; Stephen Root as Transcontinental Railroad executive Habberman; JD Cullum as Latham Cole's subordinate Wendell; Timothy V. Murphy as Transcontinental Railroad foreman Fritz; Lew Temple as Texas Ranger Hollis; Leonard Earl Howze as Red Harrington's enforcer, Homer.

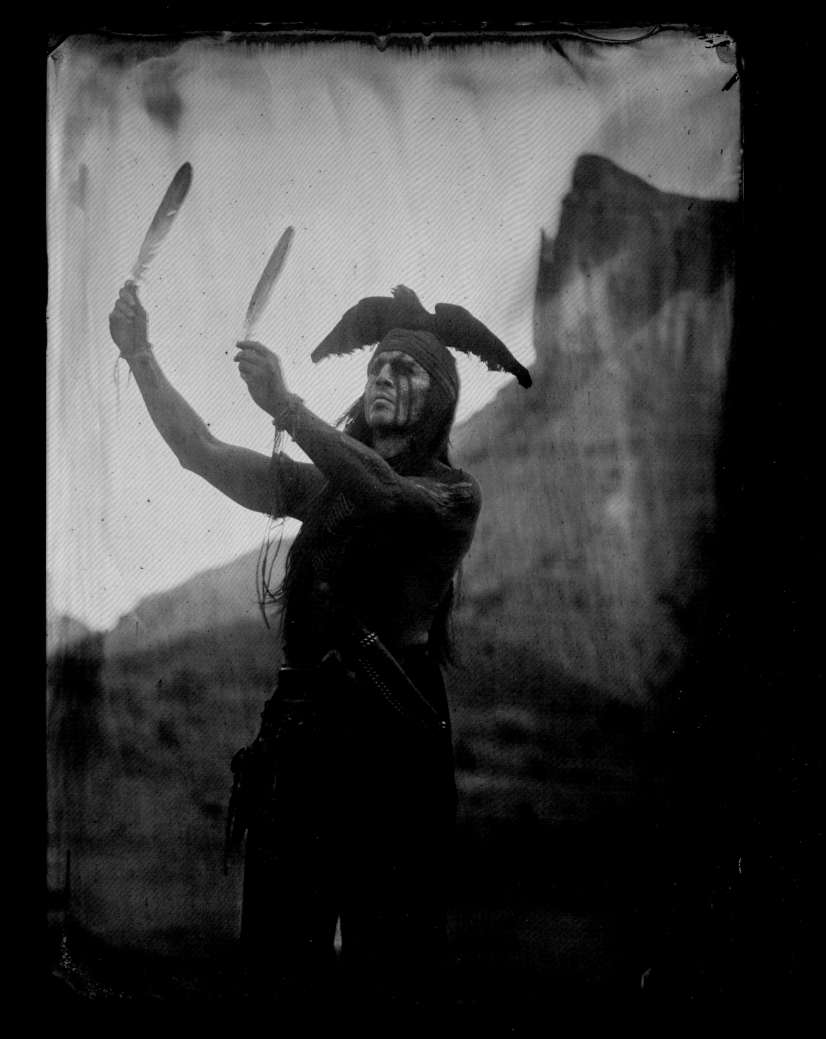

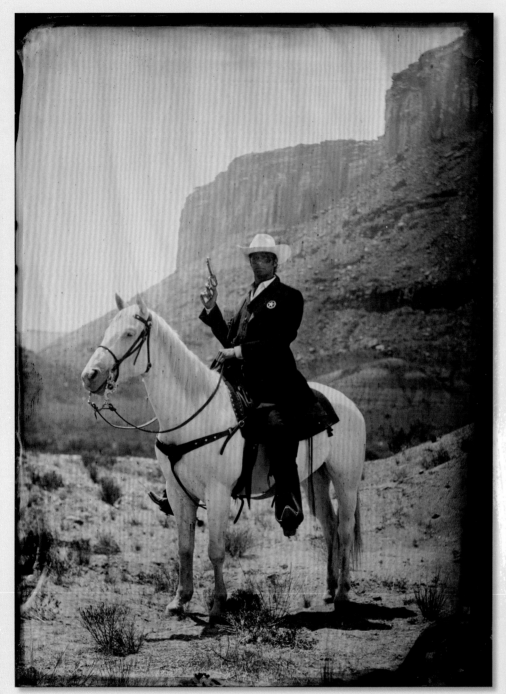
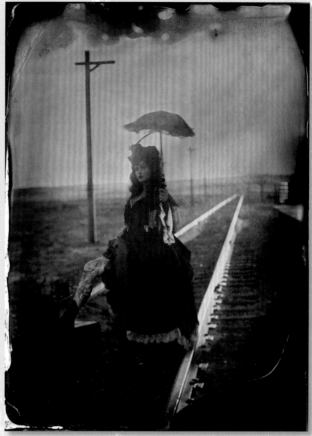
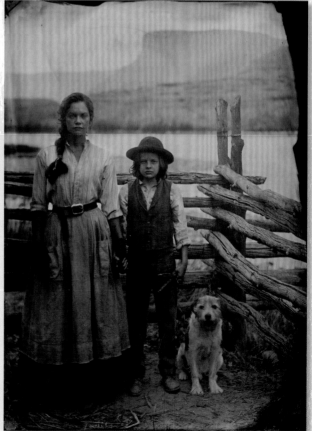

PORTRAITS FROM THE PAST

STEPHEN BERKMAN, a specialist in the art of 19th century photography, took these evocative tintypes of the leading players of *The Lone Ranger* with a view camera and Dallmeyer lens, utilizing the Wet-Collodian Process. Berkman also appeared in the film behind this vintage camera in scenes set in both Colby and Promontory Summit.

5

BUILDING THEIR OWN WEST: PRODUCTION DESIGN, SET DECORATION & PROPS

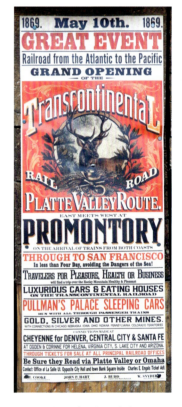

Although *The Lone Ranger*'s talented visual consultant Crash McCreery enjoyed a large staff—composed of six art directors, eleven set designers, two illustrators, a scenic artist, several storyboard artists, two graphic designers, two model makers, a research coordinator, an art department production assistant, and 274 members of the construction team—sometimes he just liked to do things on his own. He hand-carved the Native American petroglyphs that adorn the wooden frame around Old Tonto's diorama in the Wild West Exhibition tent, for example, and personally painted symbols on the walls of a two-hundred-foot-long train tunnel he designed and built in Creede, Colorado.

But McCreery's predilection for the personal touch makes perfect sense. The endlessly affable designer, whose beard and shaggy long hair make him look exactly like what he is—an artist—has spent much of his career being totally hands-on, his considerable practical experience having led to his reputation in the industry as a legendary character and creature designer. First working with the late, great creature effects guru Stan Winston, then collaborating with Tim Burton on *Batman Returns* and *Edward Scissorhands* and Steven Spielberg on his two *Jurassic Park* movies, *A.I. Artificial Intelligence*, and many more, McCreery was eventually enlisted by Gore Verbinski to create conceptual and creature designs for his three *Pirates of the Caribbean* films. There he designed one of the trilogy's most memorable elements, the extraordinary look of Davy Jones, which would later be brought to life by actor Bill Nighy and the visual effects wizards of Industrial Light & Magic. It was Verbinski who then raised McCreery to the rank of production designer on the Academy Award–winning *Rango*, before giving him the mighty opportunity of creating the visual universe of *The Lone Ranger*. "I work great with Gore," says McCreery. "We seem to have the same kind of aesthetic, and a good shorthand has developed between us. But never having designed a live-action film before, I didn't realize what it really meant until now. This has been a huge, but fantastic, learning experience for me."

"Crash is a total maverick," says Jerry Bruckheimer, "with a limitless imagination and tons of energy. We've been lucky enough to work with Crash as a creature designer on several films, and it really was time for him to take a step up and show the full range of his abilities."

Gore Verbinski knew that he was putting a weight of expectations on his longtime friend and colleague—a burden that could break a lesser spirit. "I just sort of woke up one morning thinking that maybe Crash could do this," Verbinski recalls. "I believed in him. The truth is that it's somewhat unconscionable, because you can't go from being an illustrator to a production designer on a movie this big. What we did to him was cruel, there's no doubt about it. I mean, you could see Crash's physical

ABOVE: An authentic period poster advertising the grand opening of the famed Transcontinental Railway at Promontory Summit.

RIGHT: The ornate yet rustic spectacle of Red's Traveling Entertainments.

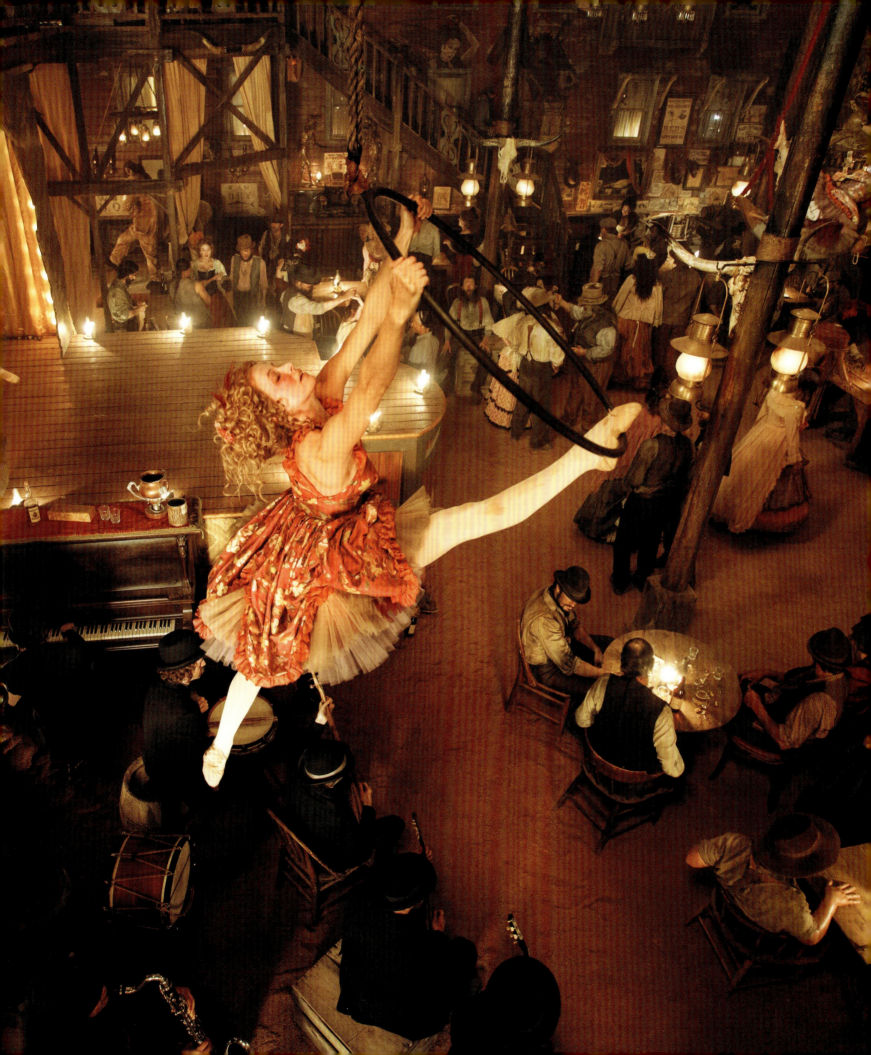

exhaustion; the rubber bands in his brain were twisted and fraying just from the workload. But it's wonderful how much he learned. And you know, he doesn't have to tell illustrators what to do. If something doesn't look right, he can draw it in five minutes, and everybody goes, 'Ah, okay, yeah, I see what you mean.' And Crash is so loved by his crew. His spirit is what got him through. Nobody else could have done it."

Among those applying their artistry alongside McCreery were five-time Academy Award–nominated set decorator Cheryl Carasik, and prop master Kris Peck, both *Pirates of the Caribbean* veterans. For the demands of the film, Carasik maintained a thirty-thousand-square-foot warehouse in Albuquerque that was worthy of the finale in *Raiders of the Lost Ark* and packed to the rafters with a cornucopia of items that included furniture, wagons, drapery, bottles, paintings, posters, and even pulled teeth.

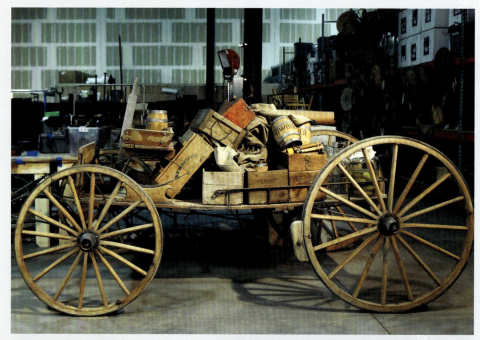

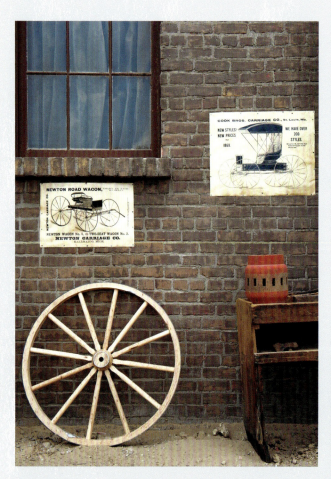

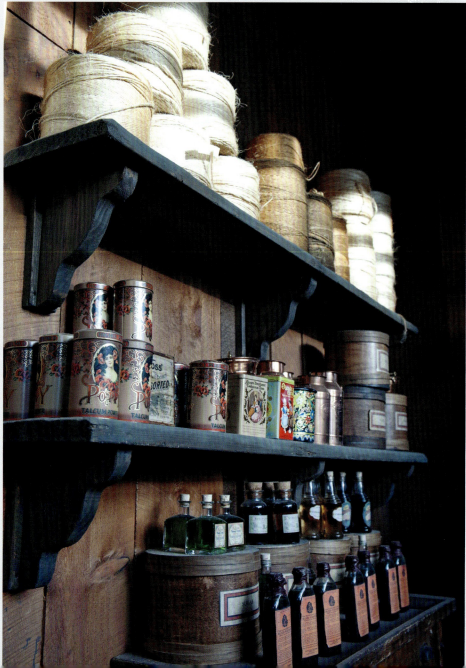

THIS PAGE: Whether they were creating wagons, posted bills, or general store goods, meticulous attention to detail was paramount for the film's art department.

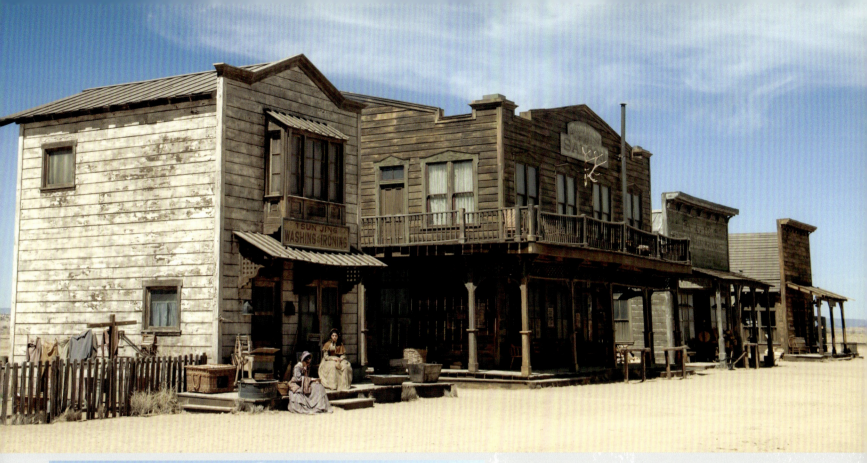

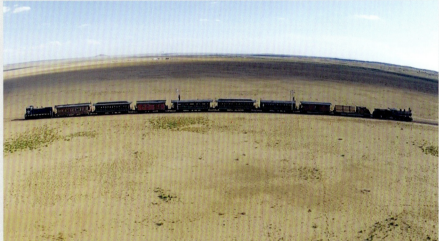

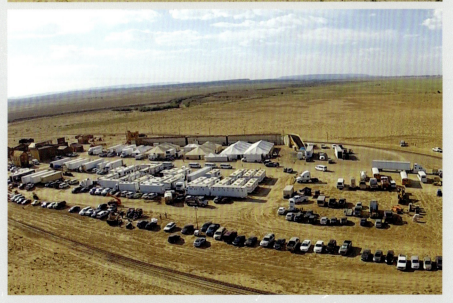

COLBY

McCreery's challenges included designing several massive sets on which the drama, comedy, and adventure of the film could play out. Built by construction supervisor Jonas Kirk's vast department, the sets were created on exteriors spread across five different states as well as a few soundstages at Albuquerque Studios. Fictional Colby, Texas, a hardscrabble, dusty frontier town that is home to John Reid and his brother, Dan, seems almost a cousin to the delightfully forlorn desert hamlet of Dirt, which McCreery designed for Verbinski's *Rango*. As the modest McCreery is quick to note, some of the designs for Colby had been started in preproduction by Jess Gonchor, who was the film's production designer before he moved on to another project following a temporary production hiatus.

"Colby is realism mixed with absurdity," notes McCreery. "Anything with a straight line doesn't feel right. Gore likes things that feel lived in, which is why you have a balcony smashed on one end or a missing railing, or paint splatter on the side of a building. It adds to the character of the town; you start to

TOP: This section of Colby's main street demonstrates the extraordinary detail that went into its design and construction.

MIDDLE: One of the trains built for *The Lone Ranger* on the tracks built at Rio Puerco, with a modern diesel locomotive giving the train a power boost.

LEFT: An aerial shot of the vast production setup in Rio Puerco, New Mexico, including the towns of both Colby and Promontory Summit, the armada of trailers, equipment trucks, and personal vehicles, and a section of the five miles of railroad track built for the film.

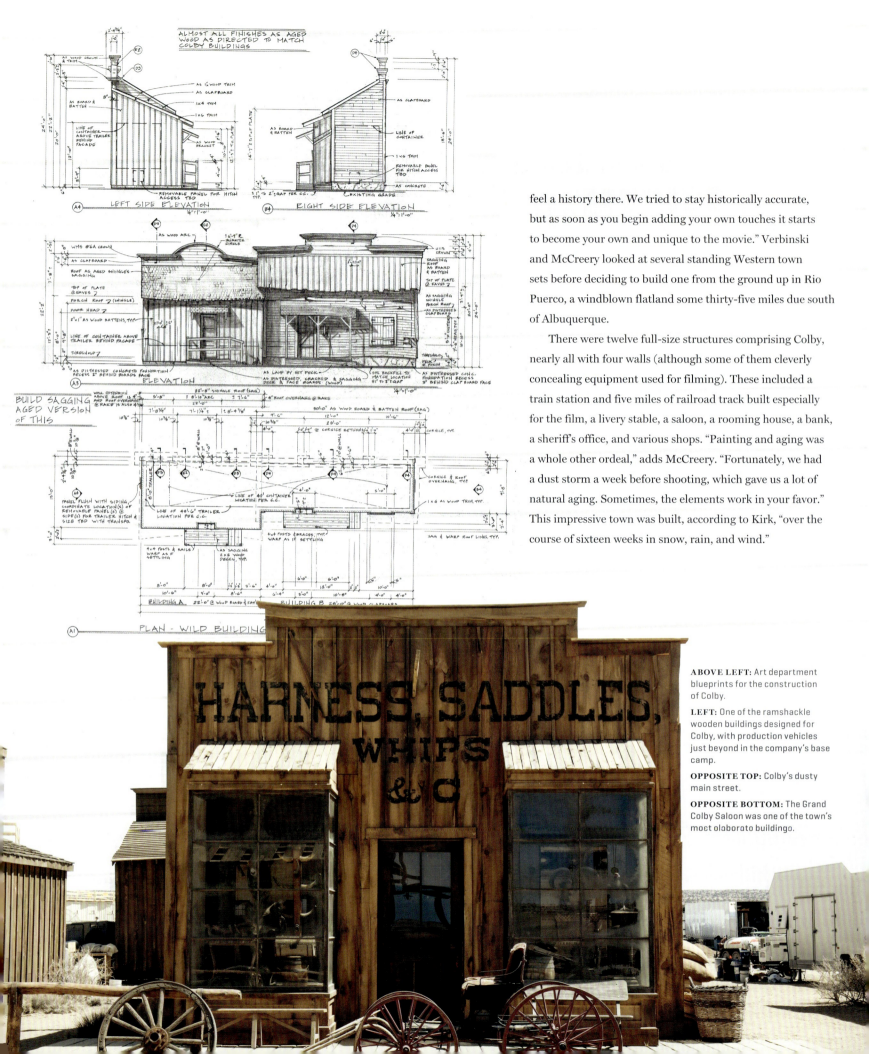

feel a history there. We tried to stay historically accurate, but as soon as you begin adding your own touches it starts to become your own and unique to the movie." Verbinski and McCreery looked at several standing Western town sets before deciding to build one from the ground up in Rio Puerco, a windblown flatland some thirty-five miles due south of Albuquerque.

There were twelve full-size structures comprising Colby, nearly all with four walls (although some of them cleverly concealing equipment used for filming). These included a train station and five miles of railroad track built especially for the film, a livery stable, a saloon, a rooming house, a bank, a sheriff's office, and various shops. "Painting and aging was a whole other ordeal," adds McCreery. "Fortunately, we had a dust storm a week before shooting, which gave us a lot of natural aging. Sometimes, the elements work in your favor." This impressive town was built, according to Kirk, "over the course of sixteen weeks in snow, rain, and wind."

ABOVE LEFT: Art department blueprints for the construction of Colby.

LEFT: One of the ramshackle wooden buildings designed for Colby, with production vehicles just beyond in the company's base camp.

OPPOSITE TOP: Colby's dusty main street.

OPPOSITE BOTTOM: The Grand Colby Saloon was one of the town's most elaborate buildings.

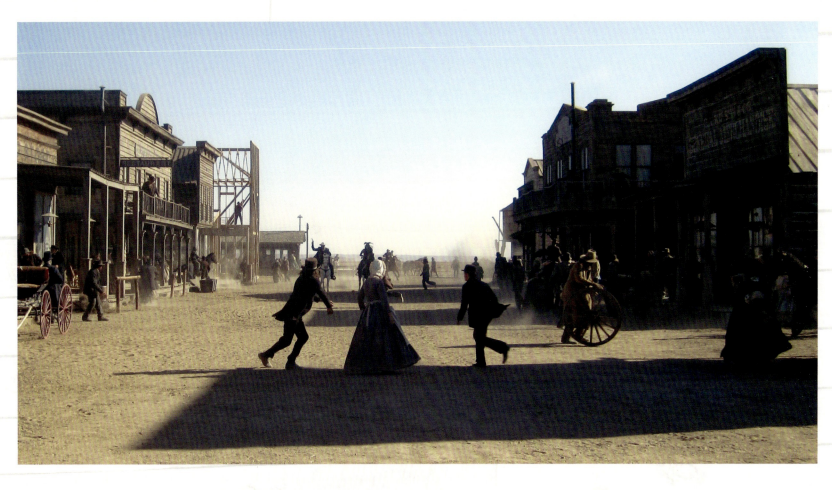

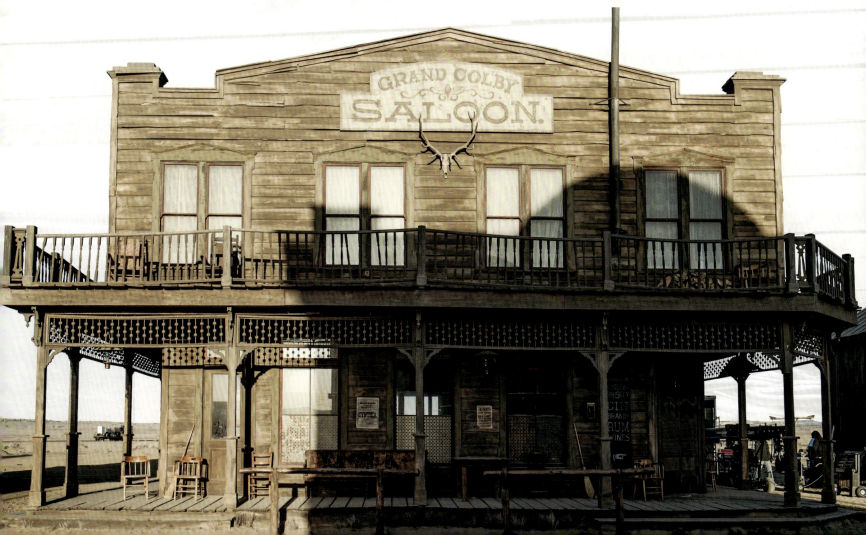

PROMONTORY SUMMIT

BUILT ADJACENT TO COLBY IN RIO PUERCO was the set for another town, Promontory Summit, the historic site where the Union Pacific and Central Pacific trains met head-to-head after completion of the Transcontinental Railroad. The famed Golden Spike ceremony that took place on May 10, 1869, to commemorate the event is elaborately and fancifully re-created in *The Lone Ranger*. Promontory Summit as built for the film has a very different feeling from the decidedly ramshackle Colby, more solidly built with brick and wood, indicating greater prosperity and a longer history. Also prominently featured in Promontory Summit is an impressive courthouse building, the largest on the set, with a screened-in porch area, which also functions as an important location in the film's Golden Spike ceremony sequence.

"Promontory was built more as facades than the three-dimensional buildings of Colby," admits McCreery, but there was a specific reason for such construction. The storefronts (which included one door humorously marked J. C. KIRK, BUILDER) were constructed with their backs against two levels of shipping containers for one of the film's greatest stunts involving the Lone Ranger and Silver, the masked avenger's trusty steed. "We had to get the structure engineered to allow for a galloping horse up there," notes Kirk, "so we built Promontory Summit against a series of sea containers and put an engineered wood deck on top of that. And then there are clear Plexiglas planks in between the wood, which allow the horse to look as if it is jumping from building to building." As with everything else in *The Lone Ranger* involving horses and the other animals, the company worked closely with representatives of the ever-present American Humane Association to ensure their safety.

BELOW: A lavish re-creation of the historic ceremony at Promontory Summit, Utah, where the Transcontinental Railroad was fully joined together from East and West.

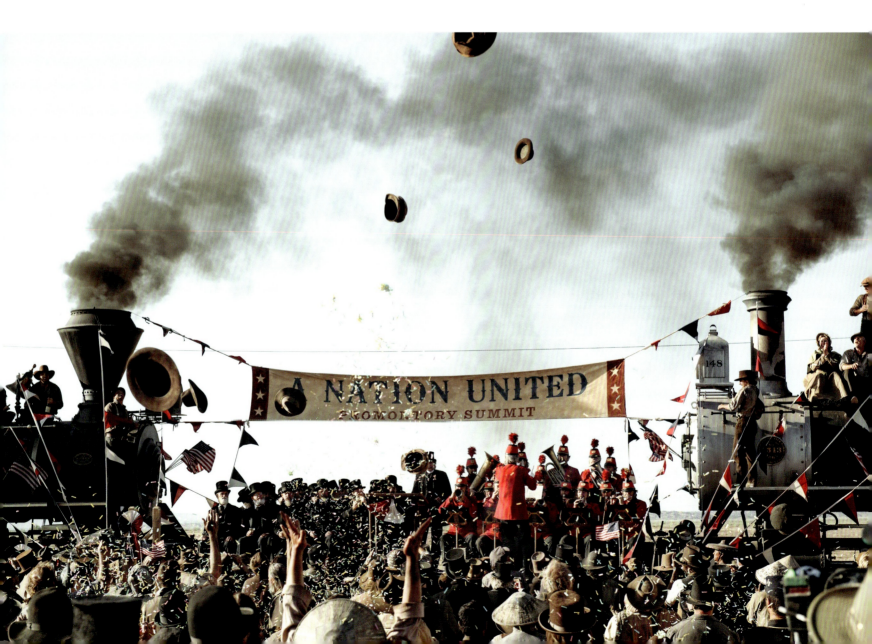

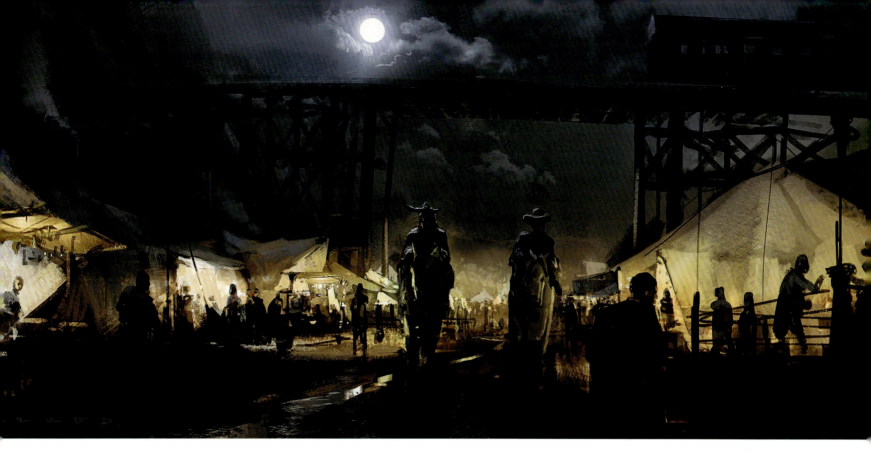

ABOVE: Conceptual illustration by artist John Park depicting the Lone Ranger and Tonto riding into Hell on Wheels.

HELL ON WHEELS

THE WILDER SIDE of Crash McCreery really got a workout with his designs for "Hell on Wheels." A movable tent town which follows the workers building the Transcontinental Railroad, Hell on Wheels was inspired by numerous pop-up towns that actually existed in the nineteenth century, and more than lives up to its name. The tent town's highlight is the lavish interior of its largest and most important establishment, Red's Traveling Entertainments. As Tonto tells the Lone Ranger when they ride into the town, "The iron horse carried you west . . . Here is where it lifts its tail."

"Hell on Wheels was like a Fellini film; probably the closest thing to actually walking into Gore's imagination," recalls Armie Hammer. "It was just bedlam. We shot in Hell on Wheels for a long time, I think partially because everybody was having so much fun on set. They were like, 'This is awesome, let's stay here.'"

The colorful and wonderfully bizarre Hell on Wheels set was prefabricated in the art department warehouse in Albuquerque for five weeks and then, over the course of another six weeks, assembled in the rolling hills of Lamy, New Mexico. The end result is a fantastical cornucopia that's akin to a traveling carnival on Wild West steroids and populated by a splendid and weird combination of snake charmers, human oddities, fire eaters, tea merchants, intestinal complaint medics, makeshift dentists, religious fanatics, and railroad workers. All this debauchery is set against a backdrop of lavish tents, stages, and booths anchored by the imposing exterior of Red's Traveling Entertainments.

"Hell on Wheels was kind of the embodiment of every spectacle and every fantasy about the Old West," says McCreery. "No matter what you wanted and what your desire was, you could find it here. And Cheryl Carasik's set dressing was spectacular, filling the street from one end to the other with every item imaginable."

"That was really fun," recalls Carasik, "I couldn't put enough on that set. I started prepping it eight months earlier because I knew it was going to be the one that got the most attention from me."

The set for the expansive interior of Red's was actually built and shot months earlier on an Albuquerque Studios soundstage—a colorful, textured vision of sinful opulence, replete with fine period detail and a touch of surrealism. The ramshackle walls of Red's riotous saloon are festooned with authentic 1860s postcards, advertisements, and bottles of liquor, along with a sign displaying RED'S HOUSE RULES (curious, since it seems that anything goes) and a painting of a reclining nude judiciously draped by Carasik so as not to shock PG-13 audiences. Posters trumpeting the charms of Red's establishment promise "MANY ORIGINAL SIGHTS AND ASTOUNDING WONDERS! BEAUTIFUL DANCING GIRLS! NOVEL AND ORIGINAL BEYOND ALL PRECEDENT!" For a change, truth in advertising! "When I first walked in there," says Armie Hammer, "I walked right up to Crash and asked him, 'Dude, will you please design my next birthday party?'"

Upstairs in the two-story set are Red's personal chambers, with their glorious Victorian clutter. "That was a really great set to dress," says Cheryl Carasik, "and again, there was a limited amount of time but a huge amount of resources. I came to New Mexico with miles and miles of set dressing specifically picked for that set." For Red's, Carasik actually collaborated with Helena Bonham Carter, who had her own ideas in mind for how her character's environment should look. "She's just tremendous," says Carasik. "I got a cryptic e-mail from Gore a couple of nights before we started, saying 'a couple of notes from Helena,' and there were some interesting requests . . . like a pair of period handcuffs and riding crops. When Helena came to see the set, she was incredibly gracious and loved it. We showed her around, and she requested some period-correct 1860s books on medicine and some risqué books that showed little more than exposed shoulders."

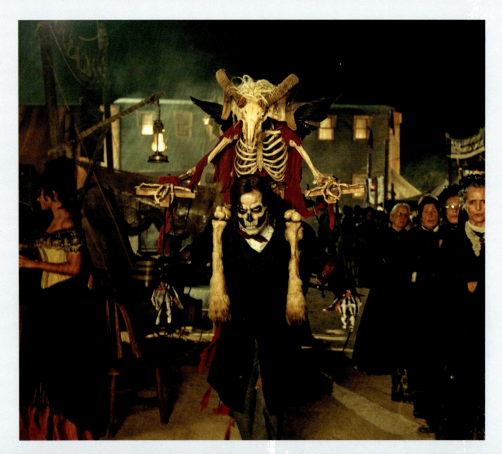

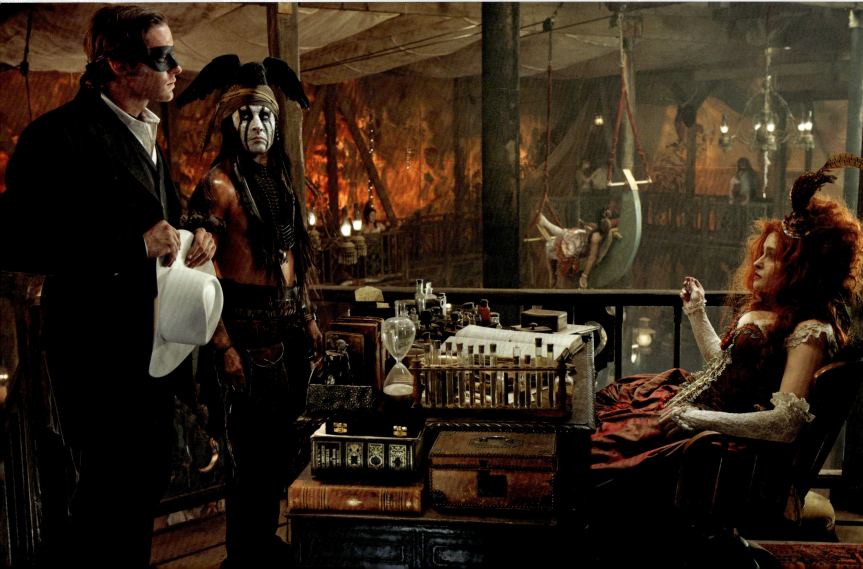

SLEEPING MAN MINE

ANOTHER OF MCCREERY and company's most impressive sets was the Sleeping Man Mine, constructed in mountainous Creede, Colorado. The set was designed to blend in with the historic town's actual nineteenth-century silver-mine buildings, but with elaborate new structures. These included a two-hundred-foot-long train tunnel with a forty-foot-tall faux rock front, a mile of railroad track, elevated tracks and trestles for ore carts, plus mining shacks that, although newly built, looked aged enough to fall apart at any moment. Constructing a set that large at nine thousand feet elevation presented challenge enough for the workers who had to catch their collective breath due to the rarified, oxygen-deprived air up there. Recalls McCreery, "When we first scouted the location, looking at what we had to do there—building bridges across the river, a trestle here and a wall with a tunnel there—I was amazed that there were all these really great mining buildings right around the corner that just didn't fit where we needed to shoot. I thought, 'We're here, why can't we shoot that?' And so we moved a scene in which Cavendish is being shaved to a different place where the mining buildings were still standing. We had a lot of great reference with the structures that we built, and I think it's one of the coolest sets, especially for the night scenes we shot there."

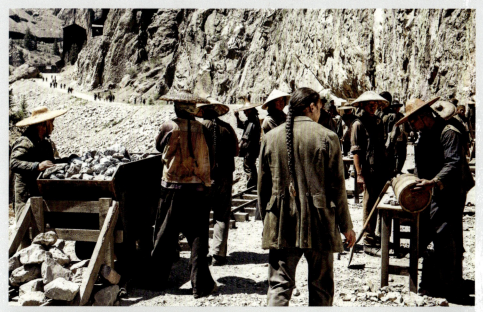

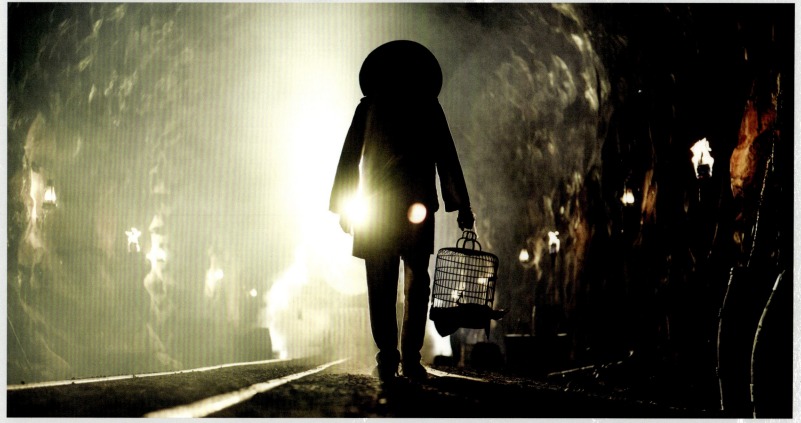

OPPOSITE TOP: One of makeup department head Joel Harlow's more exotic creations for Hell on Wheels. That's Harlow himself carrying the goat skeleton!
OPPOSITE BOTTOM: The Lone Ranger and Tonto question tent saloon owner Red Harrington about Butch Cavendish's whereabouts.
LEFT: Chinese workers toiling over railway construction in the Silver Man Mine.
BELOW: Dressed as a Chinese railroad worker, Tonto carries a birdcage into the Sleeping Man Mine train tunnel.

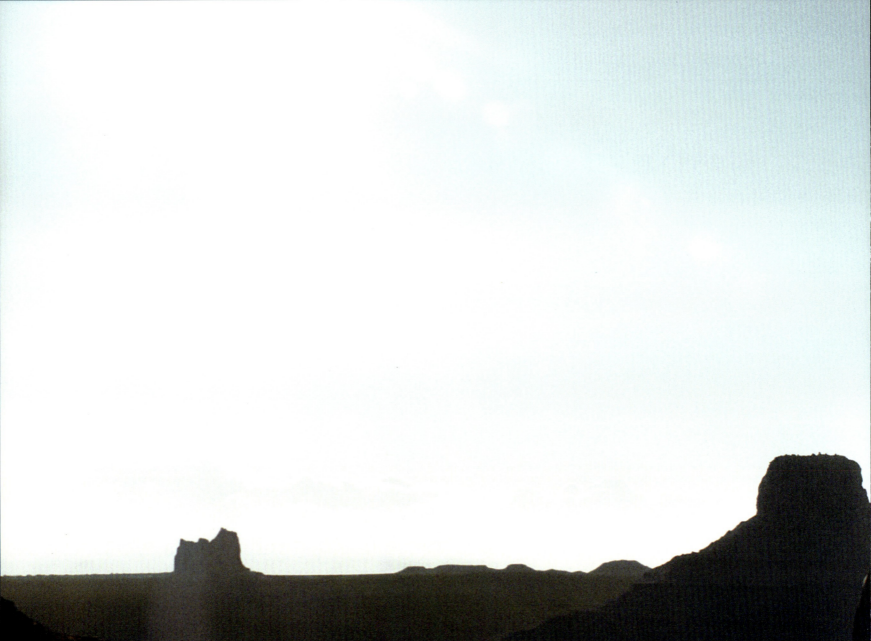

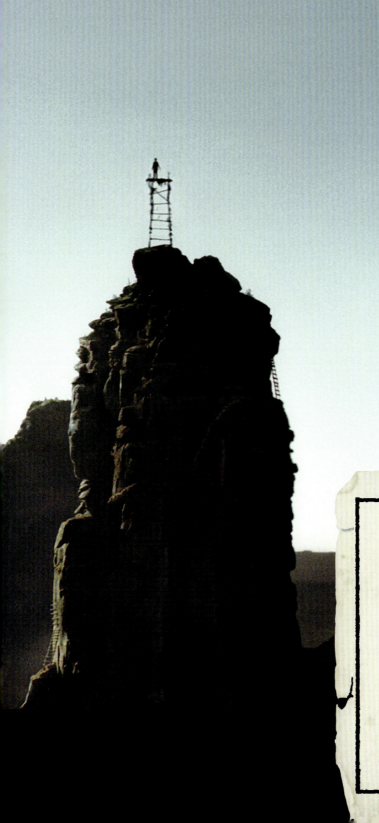

THE SPIRIT PLATFORM

The task of building a rickety wooden eighteen-foot-high "spirit platform" for a crucial scene with Armie Hammer was particularly daunting. Eighteen feet is bad enough to give an actor with a fear of heights the heebie-jeebies. Although the fearless Hammer has none of that, this platform was built on a boulder literally at the very edge of Dead Horse Point in Moab, Utah, with a nearly two-thousand-foot drop down to the valley floor and Colorado River far, far below. "I personally never stepped on that boulder," confesses Kirk, "because my knees would get a little shaky every time." In fact, although the spirit platform looks like shaky wood and timber, for safety's sake it was actually a steel structure that the art department dressed to appear more feeble.

PROPS FROM THE PAST

SUPPLYING THE CHARACTERS with a formidable arsenal and a huge number of accoutrements was prop master Kris Peck and his associate, armorer Harry Lu. From the Lone Ranger's famous pearl-handed pistols loaded with silver bullets to Red Harrington's ivory leg and Latham Cole's pocket watch, these beautifully crafted objects all played crucial parts in the story. "I was somebody who grew up with *The Lone Ranger*," notes Peck, "so for me it wasn't about putting my own fingerprint on it, but knowing which way Gore wanted to go. One of the first things I did was call up Colt and ask if they were interested in making some guns for the Lone Ranger, and so they built us a single-action army five-and-a-half-inch barrel with ivory grips." Peck also wanted to make certain that key "hero" props were properly aged, consistent with Verbinski's approach to the film's entire rustic design scheme. "The history is in the prop when you look at it," notes Peck. "Gore told me up front that there would be four or five props that we're going to see eighty feet across the screen, and the Lone Ranger's badge and silver bullet are two of those. They had to look as if they were made by hand, and not in a prop house. You need to see the sediment that was used in making the silver bullet to give it a roughness."

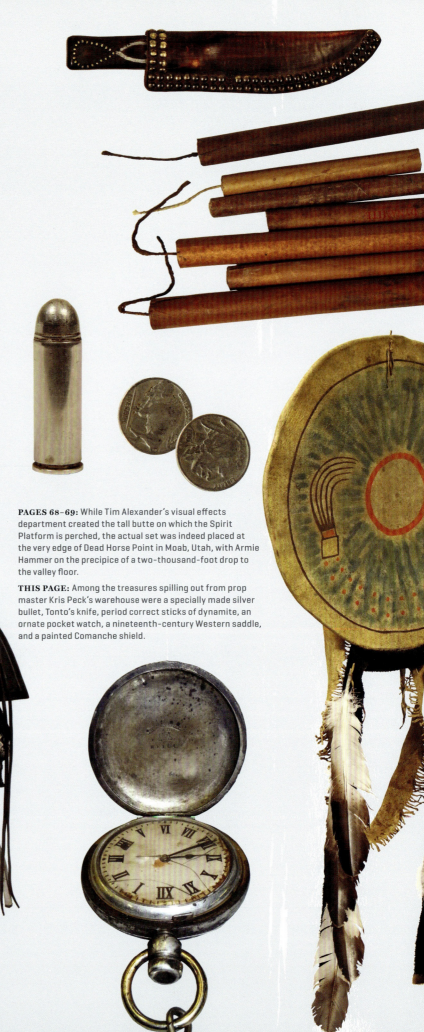

PAGES 68–69: While Tim Alexander's visual effects department created the tall butte on which the Spirit Platform is perched, the actual set was indeed placed at the very edge of Dead Horse Point in Moab, Utah, with Armie Hammer on the precipice of a two-thousand-foot drop to the valley floor.

THIS PAGE: Among the treasures spilling out from prop master Kris Peck's warehouse were a specially made silver bullet, Tonto's knife, period correct sticks of dynamite, an ornate pocket watch, a nineteenth-century Western saddle, and a painted Comanche shield.

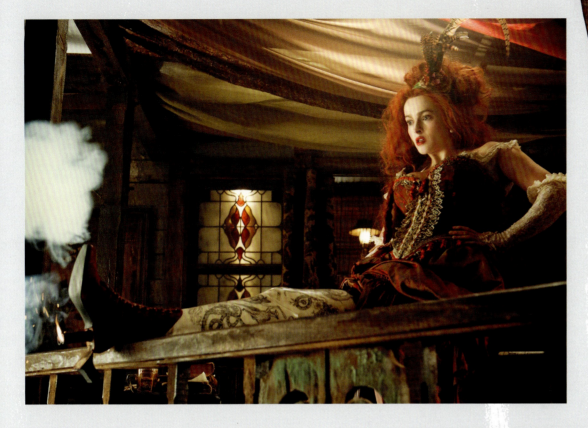

Curiously enough, Tonto's main prop is probably the beaded leather bag in which he keeps various totems and, even more important, seed for the crow that adorns his headdress. He carries no firearms, just two knives, one of which is fashioned—ironically enough—from a railroad spike, as if Tonto is turning his enemy's tool against him. But very possibly, Peck's most remarkable prop—certainly the most original—is Red Harrington's ivory prosthetic leg, which includes some hidden firepower. "Red is the living definition of how to turn a minus into a plus," says Red herself, Helena Bonham Carter. "Put a gun in your prosthetic leg and protect your girls. She's empowered by her loss, not disabled by it." Bonham Carter, for all intents and purposes, fell in love with her fake leg. "It's really the best prop I've ever had," she beams. "It is a thing of beauty. I thought it would just be any old peg leg, but it's really beautiful and decorative and also a beautiful shape. A piece of sculpture, really."

Red's ivory leg was designed by Crash McCreery and illustrator Jim Carson, while Peck was charged with getting it manufactured. "I really lucked out with the artist I found to do the artwork on the leg," says Peck, "a scrimshaw artist in Texas named Linda Capstone. She needed about three weeks to work on it, and there are never three weeks in our world, so there was concern about the timeline. But it's amazing what she pulled off. The leg you see in the movie was all hand done from photographs of artwork that we had, and it's absolutely spectacular. Truly one of the greatest props I've ever been involved with." There were ultimately three different versions of Red's leg that needed to be fabricated, and one was even outfitted by the special effects department, with a moveable gun barrel, fire, smoke, and pneumatic controls. "That one is a good fifty pounds," explains Bonham Carter. "It's got these little see-through tubes, and Kris Peck and Harry Lu are at the controls watching my moves just to make sure we're all in sync whenever I pull my garter. The heel drops, this double-barrel shotgun pops out, and then I fire. It's great fun. I've never had to shoot a gun before in a film, let alone a gun inside an ivory leg!"

TOP: Red Harrington fires a round from her ivory leg at an unruly patron.

RIGHT: Wonderfully detailed illustration by Crash McCreery of Red Harrington's artfully artificial leg.

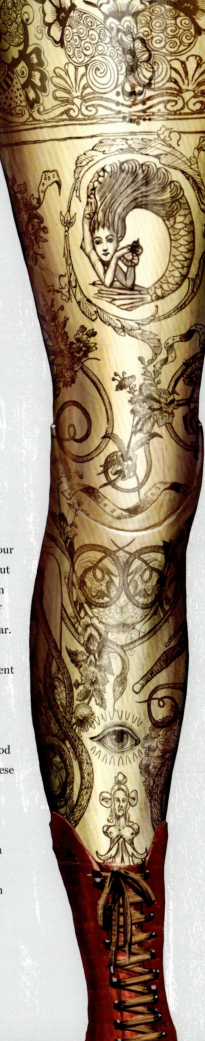

BUCKSKIN, BREECHES & SILK: COSTUME DESIGN

FOR BRITISH COSTUME DESIGNER PENNY ROSE, THE DEVIL IS IN THE DETAILS, AND NO DETAIL IS TOO SMALL TO ESCAPE HER DISCERNING, UNCOMPROMISING EYE. ROSE MAY HAVE HELPED CREATE THE DISTINCTIVE THREADBARE THREADS OF CAPTAIN JACK SPARROW IN ALL FOUR *PIRATES OF THE CARIBBEAN* MOVIES, THE GLAMOROUS COSTUMES OF THE ARGENTINIAN DICTATOR IN *EVITA*, AND THE BATTLE GEAR OF THE ROMAN AND NEAR EASTERN WARRIORS IN JERRY BRUCKHEIMER'S *KING ARTHUR* AND *PRINCE OF PERSIA: THE SANDS OF TIME*, BUT SHE HAS NEVER BEFORE TACKLED A WESTERN. "IT WAS QUITE A CHALLENGE," SAYS ROSE, "AS I ALWAYS DO THE COSTUMES AS AUTHENTICALLY AS POSSIBLE AND THEN GIVE THEM A BIT OF FUN."

Although Rose was well aware that the iconic Lone Ranger and Tonto costumes from the classic television show had been seared into the public's mind, neither she nor Bruckheimer nor Verbinski had any inclination to revive the charmingly campy, powder-blue ensemble Clayton Moore wore. "One of the things I observed watching Westerns from the 1950s and '60s was that they were quite often indicative of the time in which they were made," observes Rose, "whereas we decided that we were definitely going to make this as authentic to 1869 as possible." Rose's gigantic wardrobe department operation would include upwards of fifteen hundred costumes, and hundreds of hats, shoes, and other accessories, either created especially for the film or rented and altered according to need. Ensconced in a gigantic warehouse at Albuquerque Studios, Rose worked alongside small armies of costumers, cutter/fitters, seamstresses, stitchers, and agers/dyers, creating and assembling some fifteen hundred costumes for *The Lone Ranger*.

Joining Rose were numerous longtime collaborators, including assistant costume designer Charlotte Finlay, associate costume designer John Norster, and costume supervisor Stacy Horn, all attuned to the designer's whirlwind style of working. "I like to call her Hurricane Penny," says Jerry Bruckheimer, who utilized the formidable designer on six previous films. "There's really no one like Penny in her field; she's incredibly creative and has a supernatural energy level." Rose would need that energy level for *The Lone Ranger*, as at one point she and her crew needed to do an astonishing seven hundred fittings in one day for a scene with a large number of background players.

Rose's obsessive attention to detail means that "no polyester passes through me"—and certainly not for a period film, in which the designer, as much as possible, tries to use fabrics authentic to the time and place. "I don't like anything man-made," she confesses, "so everything is wool, cotton, and silk. I might cheat a little and use a fabric that looks like wool but would be more comfortable for the actors in the kind of extreme heat we've been filming in, but I never use anything fake. There are no zippers, the buttons have only two holes per that period, and every single female background player is wearing a corset. I don't let them off the hook. It makes people stand better, and gets them in the mood." And to age those costumes, Rose notes, "I've been lucky to always work with Gil Tobon, who has done at least ten films with me as head textile artist. We use all sorts of techniques for aging materials, including putting pebbles in a new cement mixer to break down the leather, and of course the cheese grater is a favorite tool." Rose's crew utilizes other unorthodox methods to accomplish their goals, occasionally taking blowtorches to materials to age them.

OPPOSITE: Tonto and the Lone Ranger determined to right the wrongs of the Old West.

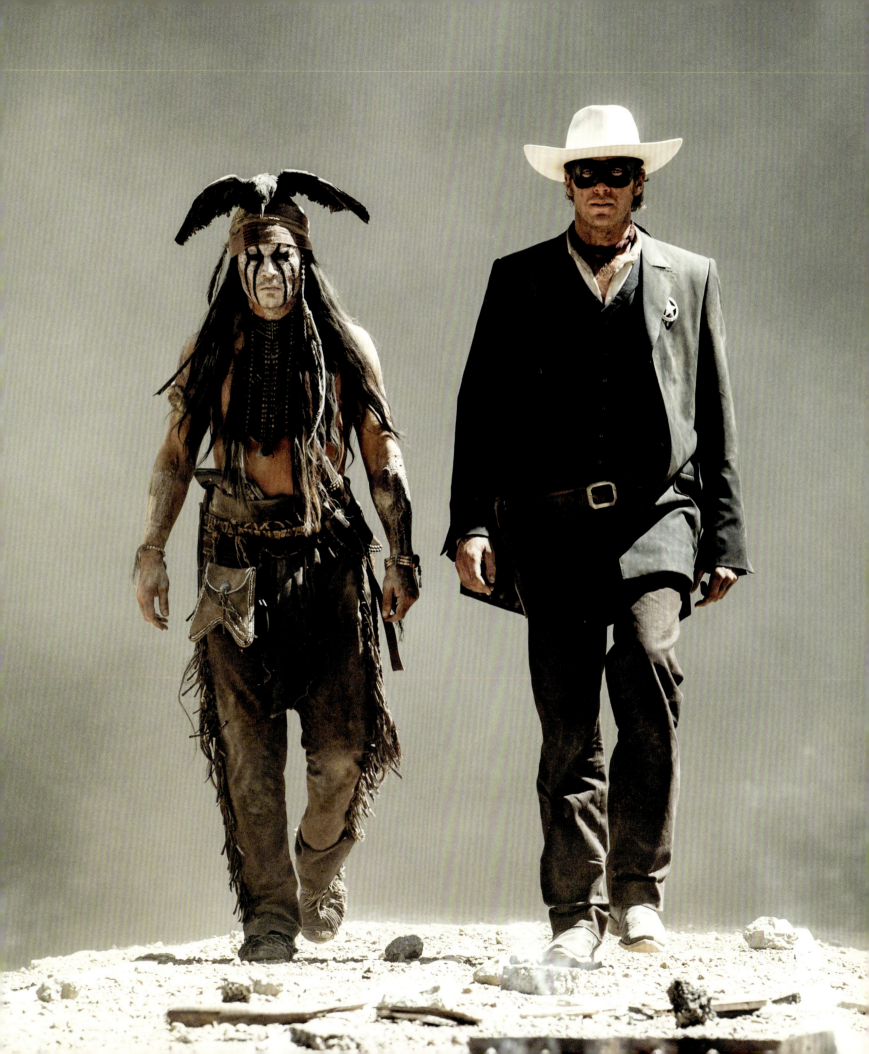

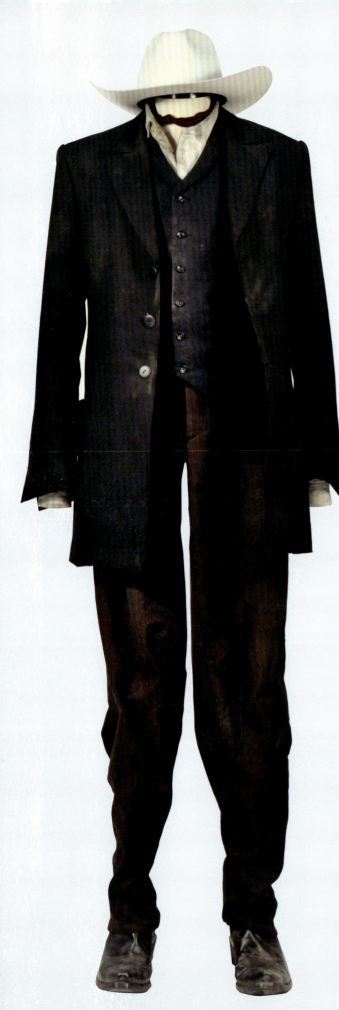

NEVER TAKE OFF THE MASK

There are basically two costumes for the Lone Ranger, one early in the film when he's introduced as young law school graduate John Reid, the second when he's made a Texas Ranger by his brother, Dan, and joins the posse in search of Butch Cavendish. "John Reid is a lawyer coming from a big city in the East in a three-piece suit, very proper, so when he morphs into the Lone Ranger, we decided that he shouldn't just become an instant cowboy," says Rose. "There should be a kind of transition between the two. Also, when you are given an actor who is six-foot-five-inches tall, as Armie is, it kind of changes things. He couldn't wear chaps, or a duster coat; he had to have an iconic look of his own. That's why we've gone for a really quite smart, tailored look, although throughout the film it becomes more and more distressed.

"He's a kind of a *GQ* Lone Ranger," continues Rose. "This guy's naturally got style." Rose designed period correct pants, a linen vest, a jacket of English wool, a white linen shirt, and, in a subtle nod to Clayton Moore's costume, a neckerchief and white hat, which was custom-made by Stetson and authentic right down to the period label inside the brim. "They very kindly gave us more than thirty hats," notes Rose, "which is a good thing because of all the wear and tear in the action scenes."

LEFT: The Lone Ranger's "hero" costume as designed by Penny Rose.

RIGHT: The Lone Ranger's mask went through numerous versions before Verbinski and Bruckheimer settled on one which looked appropriately weathered.

BELOW: Penny Rose's design for John Reid's three-piece suit, which instantly marks him as out of place in the rough, tough Old West.

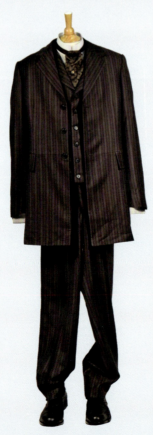

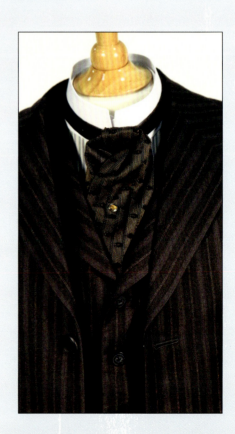

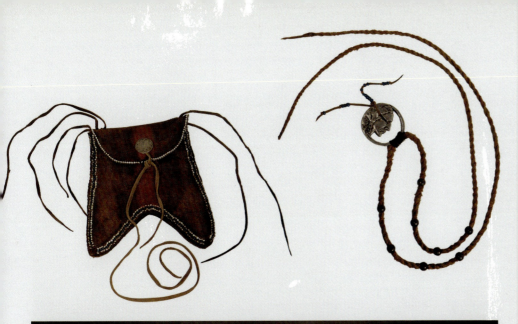

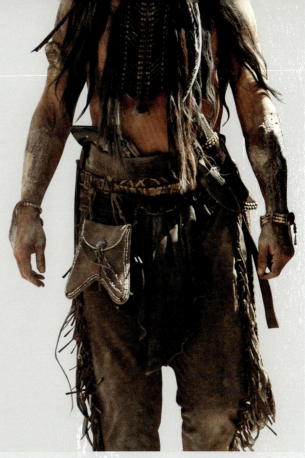

ABOVE AND LEFT: Johnny Depp's costume for Tonto is marked by clothing and accoutrements he's obtained through years of wandering, including his beaded leather pouch containing bird seed that he's constantly "feeding" the crow that adorns his head.

NATIVE STYLE

Penny Rose's long association with Johnny Depp meant that another exciting collaboration was at hand for his Tonto costume. "We have quite a good shorthand at this point, and Johnny is really good about costume," she says. "He knows immediately what works and what doesn't, so there aren't long-winded sessions. I offer him up a selection of things, and the decision making goes quite quickly. The story indicates that Tonto is a sort of rogue member of the Comanche tribe," she notes, "wandering around by himself for years. Joel Harlow, the key makeup designer, developed the crow on Tonto's head and Johnny's wonderful body makeup, so my work has really been from the waist down, except for the native breast piece I've given him. The concept is that Tonto has picked up different pieces on his journey, bits and bobs of his own personal history."

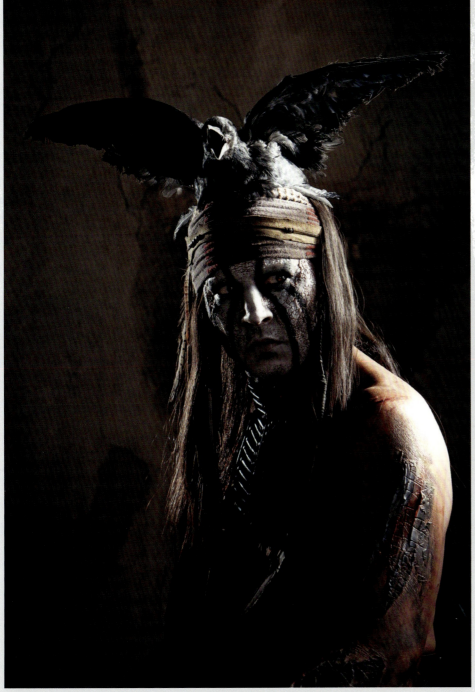

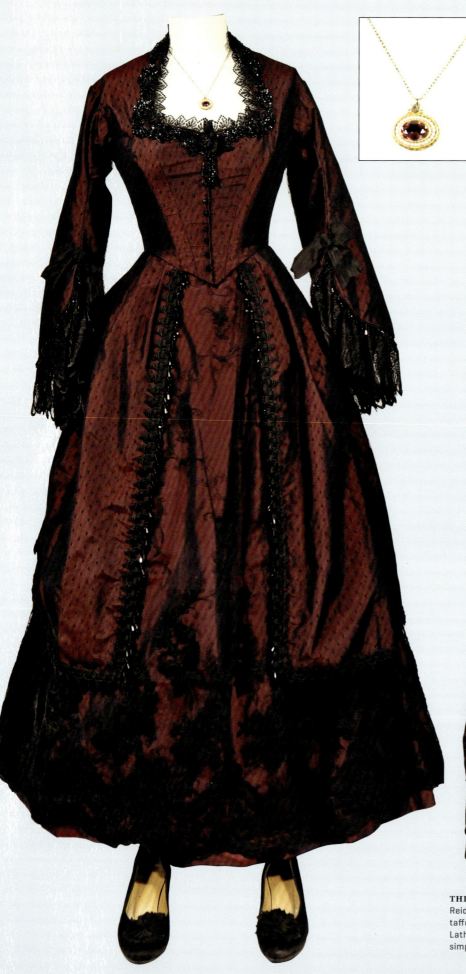
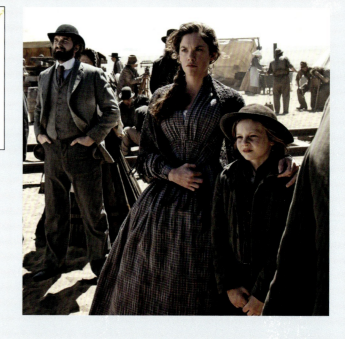

FRONTIER FASHION

For Rebecca Reid, the frontierswoman played by Ruth Wilson, Rose notes, "I designed her authentically as a frontier wife, which rather has a *Grapes of Wrath* flavor, but luckily, later on in the story she's given a gown that is a beautiful purple silk taffeta; so for a good portion of the film Ruth is looking really glorious."

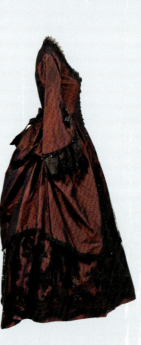
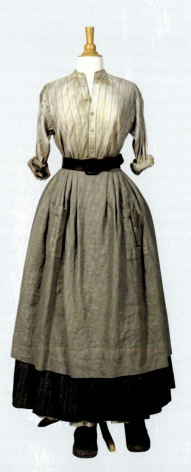

THIS PAGE: Ruth Wilson, as Rebecca Reid, is decorously adorned in the taffeta gown, which is given to her by Latham Cole, but prefers to wear a simpler frontier dress.

DRESSING BUTCH

Butch Cavendish, as played by William Fichtner, is "a bit of a dandy," according to Rose, although a particularly terrifying one. "William is just spectacular because he's such a wonderful actor," she says. "Once Joel had designed Bill's facial makeup, we just immediately got the essence of the man. We put silver epaulets on his shirts, because it says something about how Cavendish sees himself."

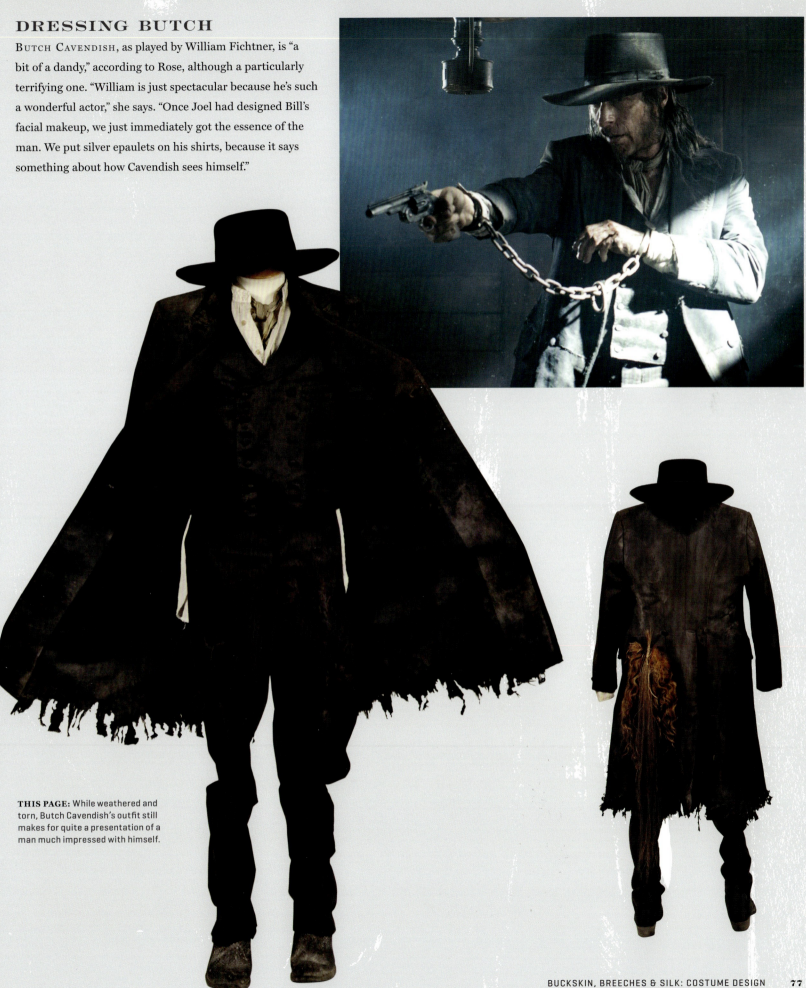

THIS PAGE: While weathered and torn, Butch Cavendish's outfit still makes for quite a presentation of a man much impressed with himself.

BUCKSKIN, BREECHES & SILK: COSTUME DESIGN

SEEING RED

ROSE DESCRIBES the deliciously extravagant Red Harrington as "obviously, the most fun. Nothing can be too over-the-top when you're designing for Helena Bonham Carter! There is not enough ribbon and beading and embroidery or anything else for Helena. I decided that she should be dressed in red, and Helena was happy about that." To accommodate Red's ivory leg, Rose and her team "made a rather amusing pair of bloomers that is sort of thigh-high-length on one side, and knee-length on the other." Red's girls, Rose notes, "are rather glamorous in that period and had to look welcoming to the gentlemen of the railway, so I did them all slightly tongue-in-cheek. A few of them have wonderful sort of dressing gown peignoirs on, with lots of feather and lace. And others are in once-glorious evening gowns that had sort of lost their glamour and were rather faded and slightly shredded. With the wonderful makeup from Joel Harlow's department, and fabulous wigs from Gloria Casny's hair department, it was a good collaborative moment between the three teams.

"I didn't know that the dancing girls in Red's were supposed to be butterflies until the last minute," continues Rose, "so we whipped up some wings. Gore has a wonderful imagination, and for the stage plays he kept coming up with ideas, such as the stage actor in a bumblebee costume. You have to be on your toes with Gore. He gets marvelous ideas, quite often at the last minute, and he's very observant. So you can't get away with anything, you can't cheat, but it's always very exciting."

Finally, Penny Rose says that the Hell on Wheels sequence "was almost like the film's gift to the creative team, because we could just really let go, and we did! I did Hell on Wheels almost exclusively with fabrics, which was very challenging because there were acrobats, contortionists, and little people, but it was all great fun. I know that it was a bit cheeky for a Brit to do a Western, because it's not my culture, but it was exhilarating to try something new."

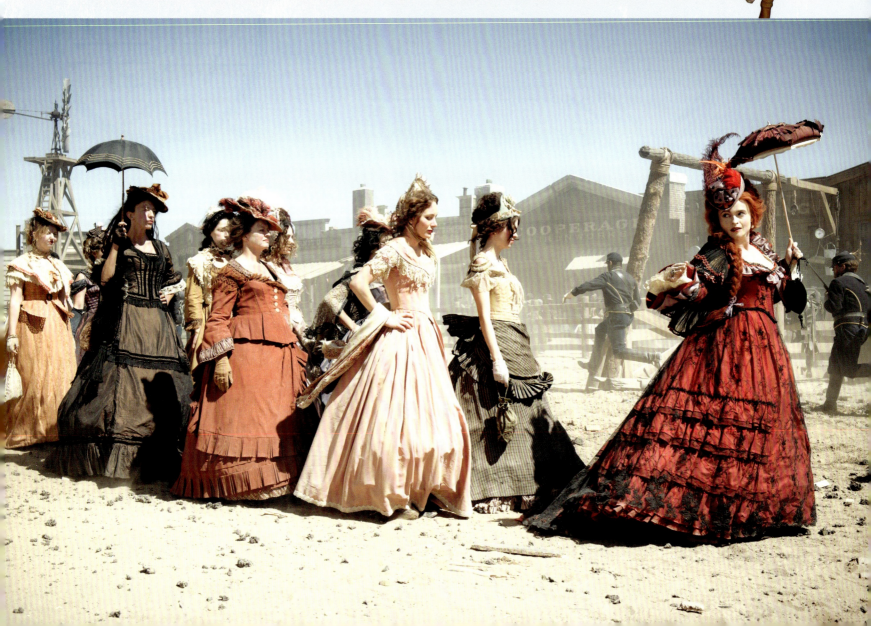

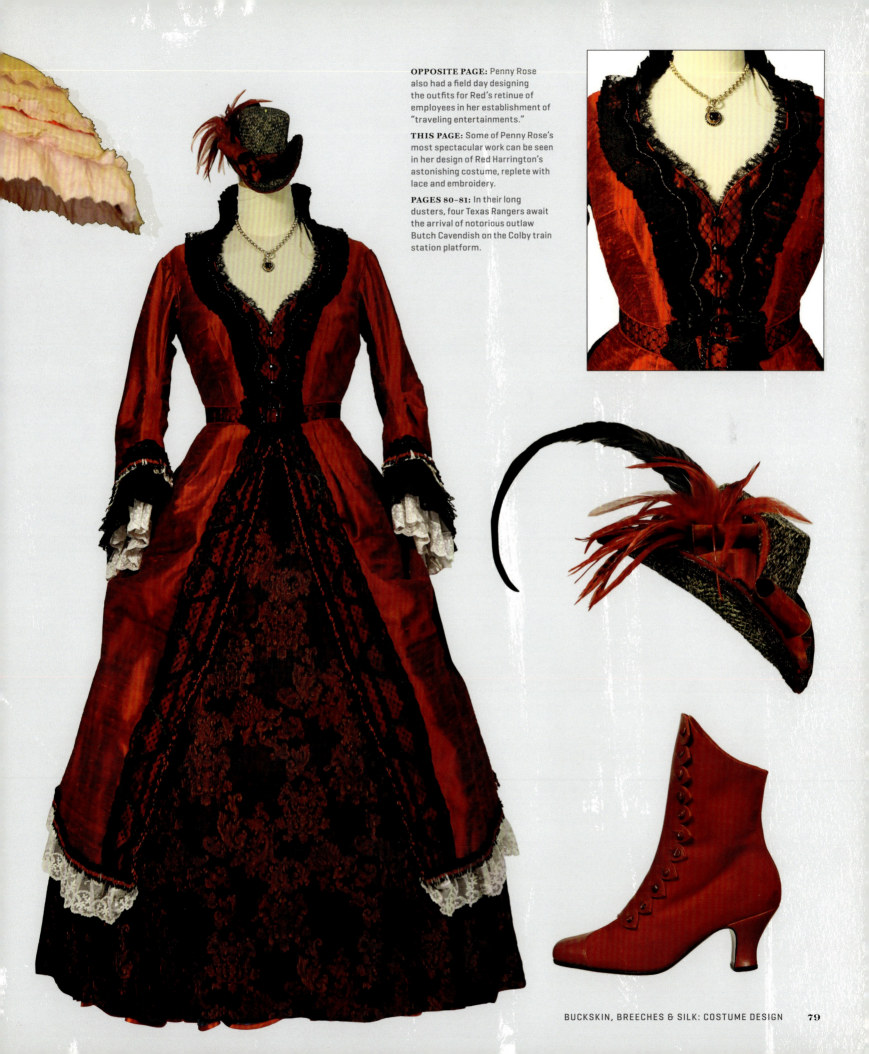

OPPOSITE PAGE: Penny Rose also had a field day designing the outfits for Red's retinue of employees in her establishment of "traveling entertainments."

THIS PAGE: Some of Penny Rose's most spectacular work can be seen in her design of Red Harrington's astonishing costume, replete with lace and embroidery.

PAGES 80–81: In their long dusters, four Texas Rangers await the arrival of notorious outlaw Butch Cavendish on the Colby train station platform.

BUCKSKIN, BREECHES & SILK: COSTUME DESIGN

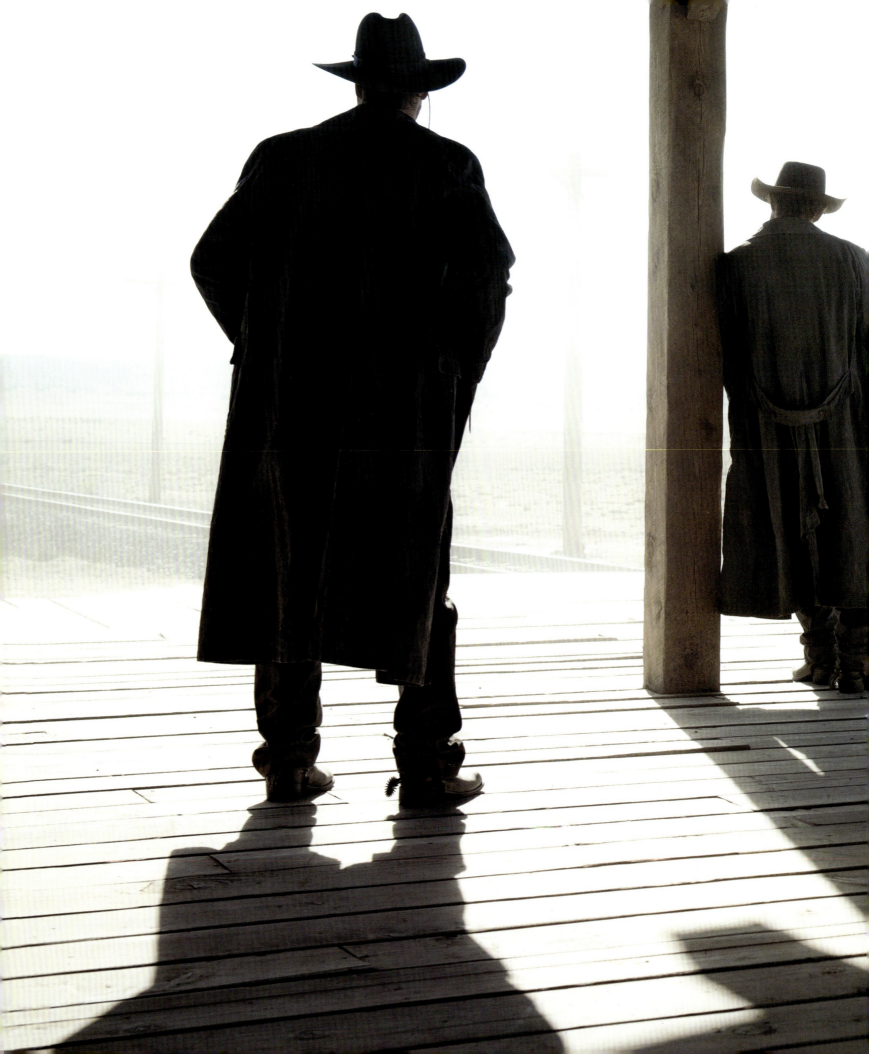

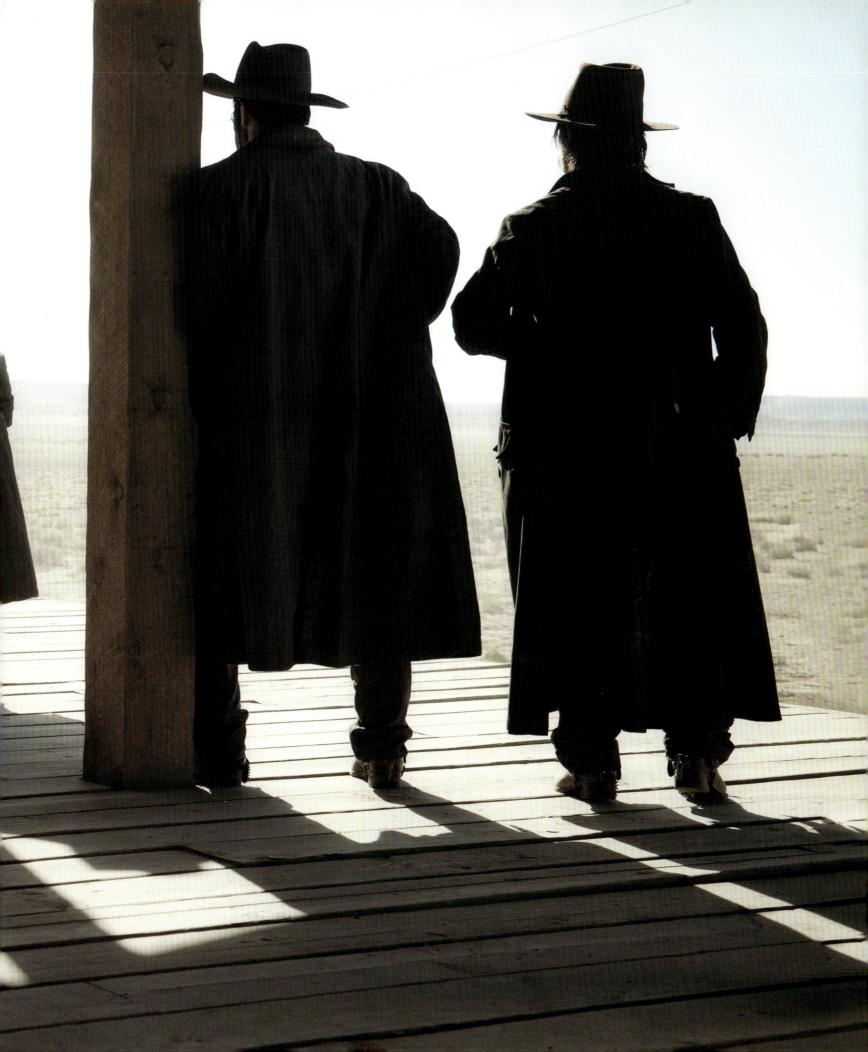

7

BETWEEN HEAVEN & HELL: FILMING IN THE AMERICAN SOUTHWEST

IT'S FEBRUARY 17, 2012. FOLLOWING A TYPICALLY CHILLY NEW MEXICO WINTER MORNING WHERE THE MOISTURE ON CAR WINDSHIELDS BECAME THIN ICE OVERNIGHT, AN EVEN MORE TYPICAL SUNNY AFTERNOON RAISES THE TEMPERATURE BY MORE THAN THIRTY DEGREES. IN WHAT IS ESSENTIALLY A HUGE PARKING LOT WITHIN THE WALLS OF ALBUQUERQUE STUDIOS—AN INCONGRUOUSLY PROTECTIVE SETTING CONSIDERING THAT 90 PERCENT OF THE FILM WILL BE FILMED ON WEATHER-BEATEN EXTERIOR LOCATIONS—DIRECTOR GORE VERBINSKI AND PRODUCER JERRY BRUCKHEIMER OVERSEE THE FIRST CAMERA TEST OF JOHNNY DEPP AND ARMIE HAMMER. THE TWO ACTORS, WHO WILL BE SPENDING THE BETTER PART OF THE NEXT YEAR WORKING TOGETHER, MET FOR THE FIRST TIME ONLY THE DAY BEFORE AT A TABLE READ OF THE SCREENPLAY. ALREADY, HOWEVER, THE TWO REVEAL A CHEMISTRY THAT MAKES IT SEEM AS IF THEY'VE WORKED TOGETHER FOR MONTHS. PRINCIPAL PHOTOGRAPHY IS JUST ONE WEEK AWAY, FOLLOWING BRUCKHEIMER'S SEVEN-YEAR EFFORT TO GET THIS FRESH VERSION OF THE CLASSIC TALE ONTO THE BIG SCREEN.

With shooting scheduled to begin on February 28, 2012, the Lone Ranger and Tonto will indeed ride again. And they will continue to do so for seven-plus months of arduous filming across four adjoining states of the great American Southwest plus Southern California. Throughout, Bruckheimer, Verbinski, Depp, Hammer, and the assembled cast and crew will experience a full range of production and environmental challenges and somehow find a way to overcome them all. They have already endured a two-month production shutdown commencing on August 12, 2011, while financial and creative concerns were negotiated by all parties with Talmudic precision. "I've never seen Jerry more on fire," says Verbinski of Bruckheimer's Herculean effort to keep the project on track. "I mean, this movie was dead, and he resuscitated it. Jerry was phenomenal. You know, in Hollywood, people lose track of what a producer is and does. Jerry is a *producer*, and I got to see him like I had never seen him before, really fighting for this movie when nobody else believed in it. And in the end, it was healthy that it fell apart when it did, because we were originally going to shoot in winter, which was impossible for a script with ninety percent exteriors." This is hardly the first time that Bruckheimer and Verbinski experienced such a halt in production, as the same thing happened on *Pirates of the Caribbean: The Curse of the Black Pearl* nearly a decade before. This sort of disruption, however, is par for the course when creating an epic of this magnitude and Bruckheimer and Verbinski aren't only filming a great adventure—the filming of *The Lone Ranger* is a great adventure in itself.

RIGHT: The crew, along with the actors playing Butch Cavendish's gang, film a particularly adventurous scene while precariously perched on the edge of a Monument Valley cliff.

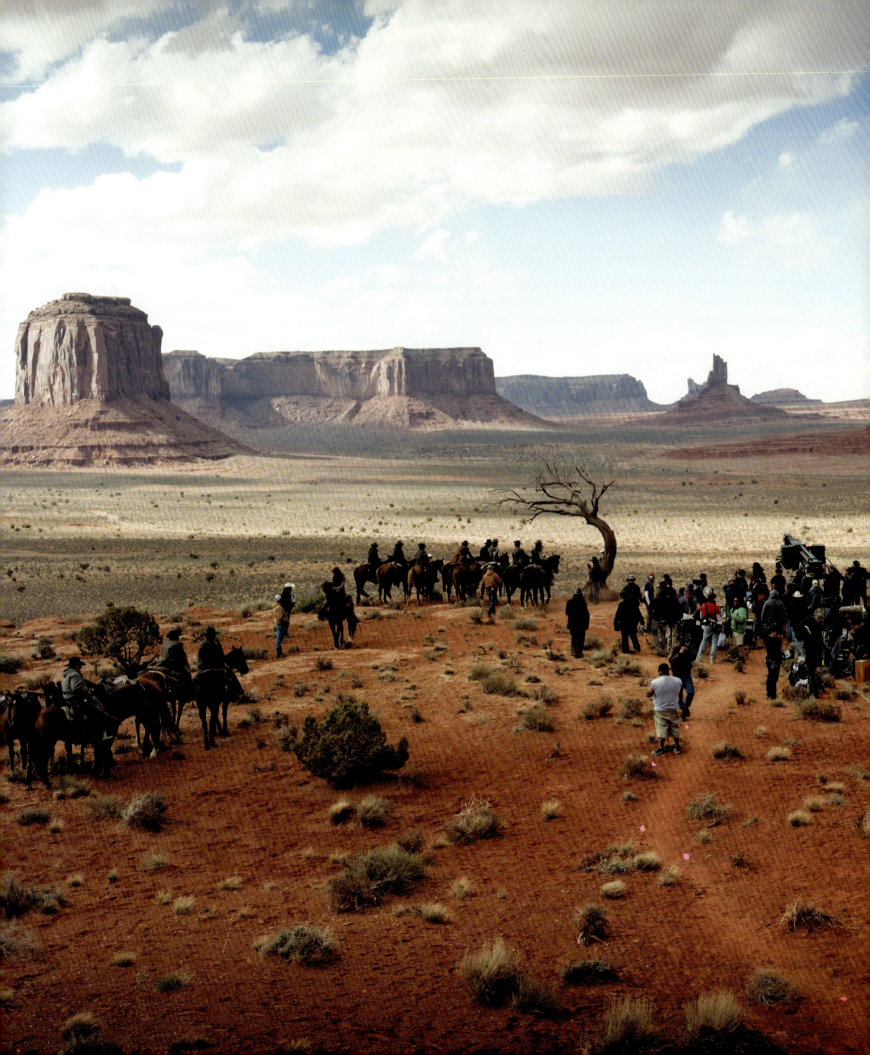

LOCATION, LOCATION, LOCATION . . .

IF THERE'S ONE CERTAINTY, it's that when seeking locations for his films, Gore Verbinski will always find a trail that has not yet been blazed. Recalls Tom Hayslip, production supervisor and veteran of the *Pirates of the Caribbean* movies, who dealt with a myriad of issues on *The Lone Ranger* alongside unit production manager Mark Indig: "One of my fondest memories of Gore from *Pirates of the Caribbean 2* and *3* was when he said about a certain location, 'If it was easy, everyone would have shot there already.' He likes to go to places that have been untouched or hardly filmed to get the true essence of a location. I think that, mentally, Gore has to approach a location as its own character. What I've seen on *The Lone Ranger* is that every single shot is the perfect shot, every scene is the most important scene in the movie, and every location is the most important location. Gore is adamant about the aesthetic he wants for his vision, and we're here to serve it to him regardless of how difficult that may be."

The Lone Ranger was a film for all seasons—literally. By the time the company wrapped principal photography in Lone Pine, California, on September 29, 2012, the crew had experienced every type of weather imaginable. This journey put forty-two thousand miles on the odometer of supervising location manager Janice Polley, as she, Verbinski, and McCreery scouted sites that would become the background canvas for the film. "I think the biggest challenge," says executive producer Eric McLeod, who as line producer took care of the nuts and bolts of daily production, "was not only getting into Gore's head on what he wanted, but also coming up with interesting locations that portray his very specific vision. We had to find some places that had never been shot before." The wildly inconsistent weather conditions, of course, drove McLeod mad. "The craziest was when we'd just been filming in Albuquerque for a little over a month. Monday, April 2, was beautiful. Then we wake up the next day, and it was a full-on snowstorm. Cars and trucks were getting stuck, and we ended up having to shut down production for two days so we could clear the road and pull them all out. We also had numerous complete brownouts because of the sandstorms. It's just part of the joy of working on a big exterior film."

The battle-hardened crew members who worked on Verbinski's *Pirates of the Caribbean* films more or less knew what to expect, but as costumer Scott Hankins pointed out late in the production: "If this were the Ironman triathlon, *Pirates* was the swimming portion, but *The Lone Ranger* is the race!"

> **E-MAIL FROM PRODUCTION TO CREW, APRIL 30, 2012:**
> Rattlesnakes have been sighted at base camp and on set. Now that it is getting warmer, they will be much more active. Please be aware of your surroundings. If you see a snake, please bring its location to the attention of the assistant directors. DO NOT ATTEMPT TO REMOVE OR KILL ANY SNAKES YOURSELF.

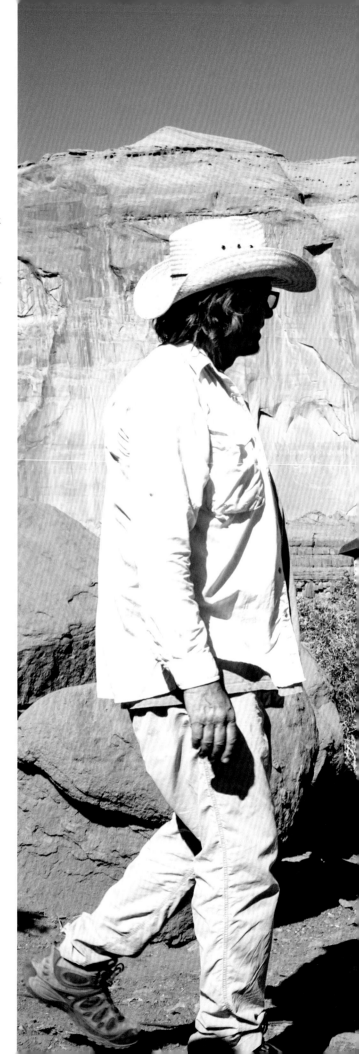

RIGHT: Gore Verbinski (middle) and his team, including camera operator Martin Schaer (foreground far left) and first assistant director Simon Warnock (to right of Verbinski) embark on a day's work in Canyon de Chelly.

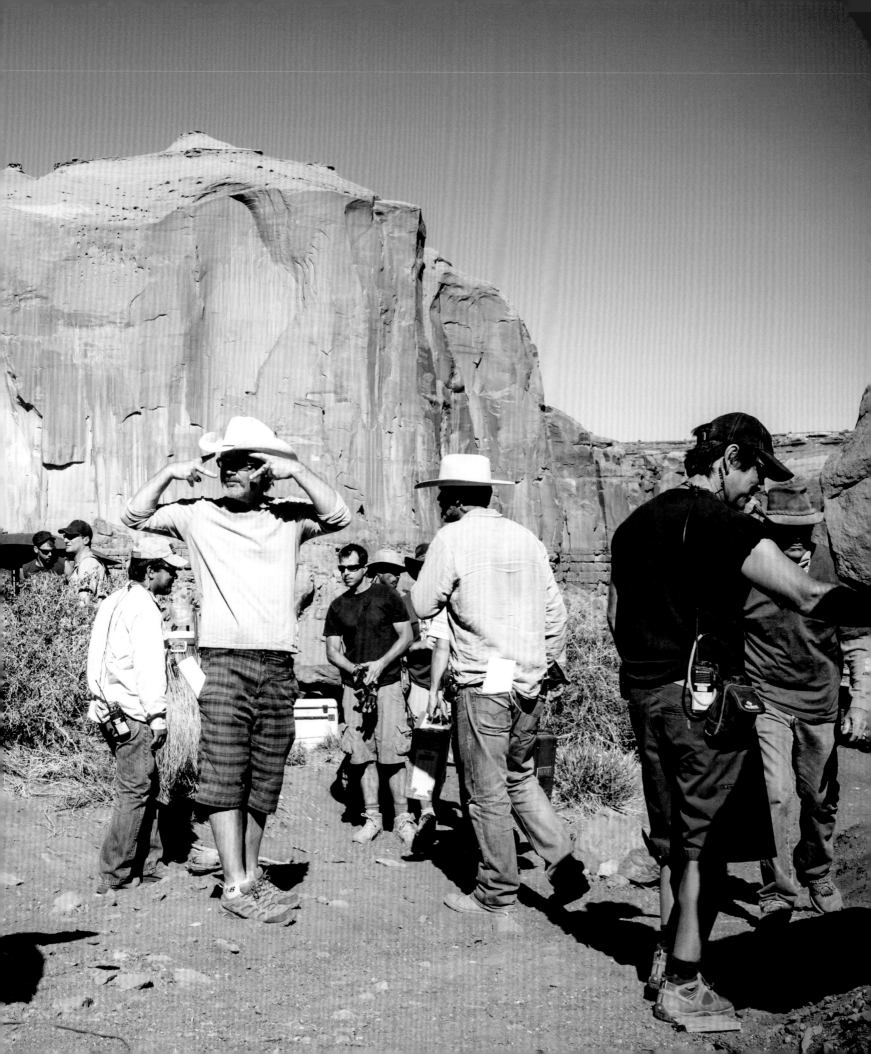

BLESSED BEGINNINGS

BEFORE THE CAMERAS turned for the first time on *The Lone Ranger*, the film's Comanche adviser, Wahathuweeka-William Voelker and his associate Troy "The Last Captive" performed a traditional blessing ceremony on the grounds of Albuquerque Studios. Confirming the sanctity of birds in Comanche spirituality, Bill Voelker and Troy had brought with them a magnificent two-and-a-half-year-old Golden Eagle named "Nue Pi" ("Tornado"), which they raised at Sia, their ethno-ornithological facility in Cyril, Oklahoma. To the Comanche, the Golden Eagle is the only bird noble enough to be an intermediary between humans and the Creator.

The beginnings of *The Lone Ranger* shoot were deceptively mild, taking place within the protective walls of Albuquerque Studios. Inside three soundstages, the sequences involving railroad cars, a Wild West Exhibition tent, and the lavish interior of Red's Traveling Entertainments were filmed, although outside, the howling winds and occasional lashings of snow were a reminder of the elements that would soon dominate the shoots. This became more apparent on March 5, during the studio backlot shoot of the 1933 San Francisco fairgrounds sequence, when gusts of Albuquerque wind nearly swept Verbinski and several of his key associates, including director of photography Bojan Bazelli, first assistant director Simon Warnock, key grip Mike Popovich, and gaffer (chief lighting designer) Raffi Sanchez, off the top of a shipping container being used to mount a camera crane. This was the company's first indication that March really had roared in like a lion, and this intemperance was further confirmed once they headed beyond the safety of the studio on March 20. The short journey took them approximately thirty-six miles west of Albuquerque, where they would make a right turn at the gas station proudly serving up "Laguna Burgers" before heading eight miles down a dirt road that production had specially improved in order to withstand the traffic of thousands of vehicles during three months of filming.

A TRIP TO RIO (PUERCO)

THIS WAS RIO PUERCO, site of the built-from-ground-up sets of Colby and Promontory Summit. Complete with five miles of railroad track laid just for the movie plus newly constructed period trains to run on them and a base camp big enough to qualify as a village in itself, the location was a sight to behold. Sharing the same space were dozens of trailers, massive tents housing hair, makeup, and catering (with the team from Tony's Food Service sometimes feeding as many as five hundred people twice a day) and around one hundred equipment trucks.

With the exception of sojourns to Monument Valley and Canyon de Chelly in the Navajo Nation, Rio Puerco would provide the base of operations for the company for the next three months. Although not an easy place to fall in love with, it fulfilled its functions brilliantly but not without cost to the company. "The Devil's Sandbox," as production assistant Quinton Bender dubbed it (other company members had less polite nicknames for the site after a few weeks), with its flat, brown desert landscape and very fine dirt, was a testing site for nature's worst excesses—most notably brutal gusts of wind that blew anywhere from twenty-five to seventy miles per hour.

Cast and crew soon learned to keep their faces covered with scarves, bandanas, and goggles, but that didn't prevent them from literally eating dirt on a daily basis, ending the day with gritty mouths and dusty from head to toe. Says screenwriter Justin Haythe, who was on set nearly every day of the shoot, "You learn a lot about each other in those circumstances when you're picking sand out of your teeth and trying to give a note about a performance. They might not want to hear it."

But Rio Puerco was the site of numerous sequences of tremendous scope, as witnessed by William Fichtner when he visited the Colby set for the first time. "It was the scene where the train blows right through the station," he recalls. "They had these massive fans and all these folks dressed in period costumes on the train platform. When the train rushed past the station at full speed, and I saw the dust it whipped up along with the fans, blowing people over, I just stood there and thought, 'Wow.' That was just one little shot, and believe me, I think we had scenes like that every day!"

Capturing the sweeping canvas of *The Lone Ranger* was director of photography Bojan Bazelli, with whom Verbinski had previously worked on several commercials

OPPOSITE: Gore Verbinski lines up a shot on a Transcontinental Railroad worker, as director of photography Bojan Bazelli (white cap) observes with his camera team.

PAGES 88–89: Corralled horses escape from their confines, creating total chaos amidst both the citizenry of Colby and the United States Cavalry, allowing the Lone Ranger and Tonto to carry out their plans for justice.

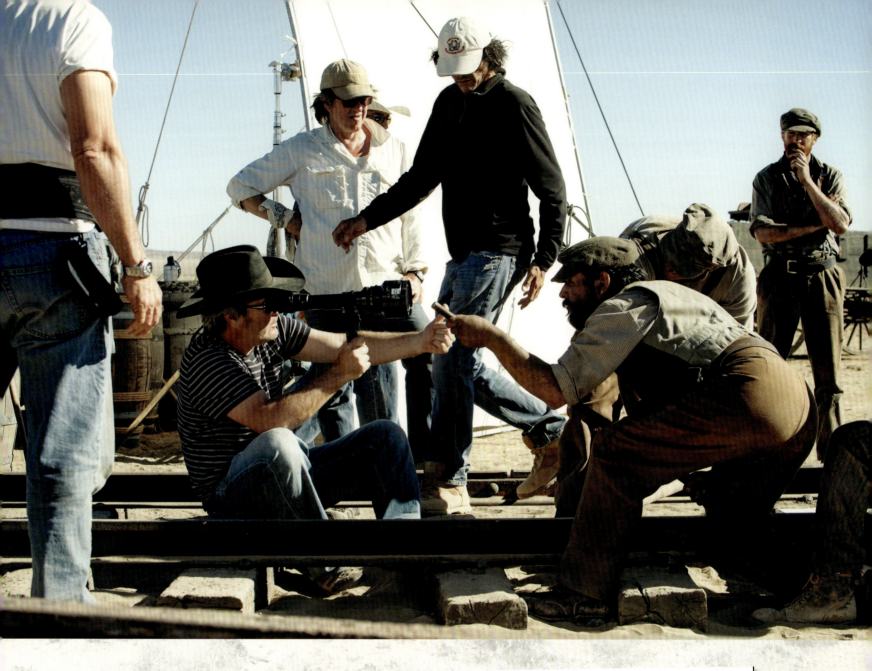

and his hit horror film *The Ring*. Bazelli had also previously been summoned to shoot both *G-Force* and *The Sorcerer's Apprentice* for Jerry Bruckheimer. Says Verbinski of the wiry, Montenegro-born Bazelli, with his wild shock of curly hair and endearingly manic energy: "Bojan is the crazy brother you've got to embrace. Nobody understands the photochemical process better than Bojan. He understands what happens to your eye when you light a room, he understands what's happening at the back of the lens when it hits the emulsion, and now, digitally, when it hits the chip. I think he has a better understanding of that than anybody I've ever worked with." To aid Bazelli in the mammoth task he was facing, Verbinski enlisted Raffi Sanchez and Mike Popovich, who over the years have developed a kind of telepathic communication with the filmmaker.

> PLEASE NOTE: THERE WILL BE AN EXPLODING PICKLE CART DURING THE DAY AS WELL AS 20 HORSES RUNNING THROUGH THE SET. PLEASE PAY ATTENTION AND LISTEN TO THE AD DEPARTMENT REGARDING CORRECT SAFETY PROCEDURES.
> THANK YOU VERY MUCH.

"We wanted to keep it hot and raw," says Verbinski of the visual approach that he and Bazelli brought to *The Lone Ranger*. "We didn't want to make it so pretty that it felt theatrical. We already have an inherently theatrical tale, like an opera, but if we started to put creams and sauces on the meats I think you lose some sense of integrity."

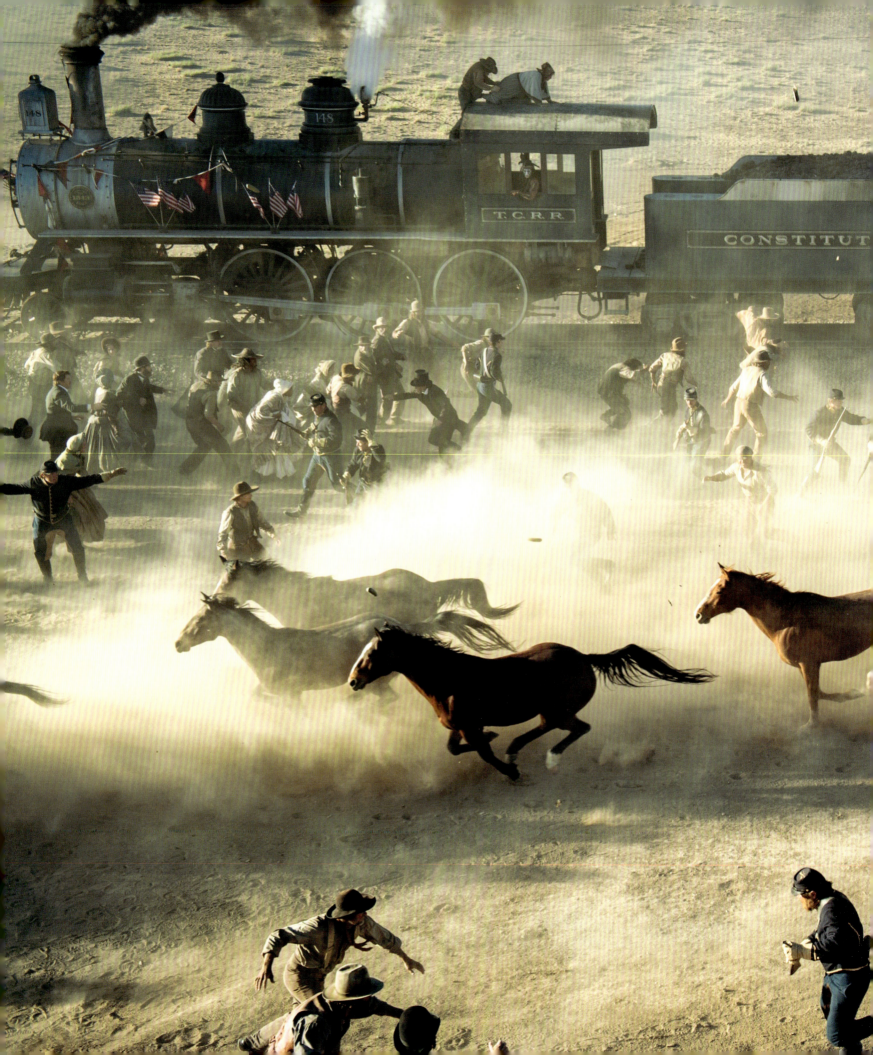

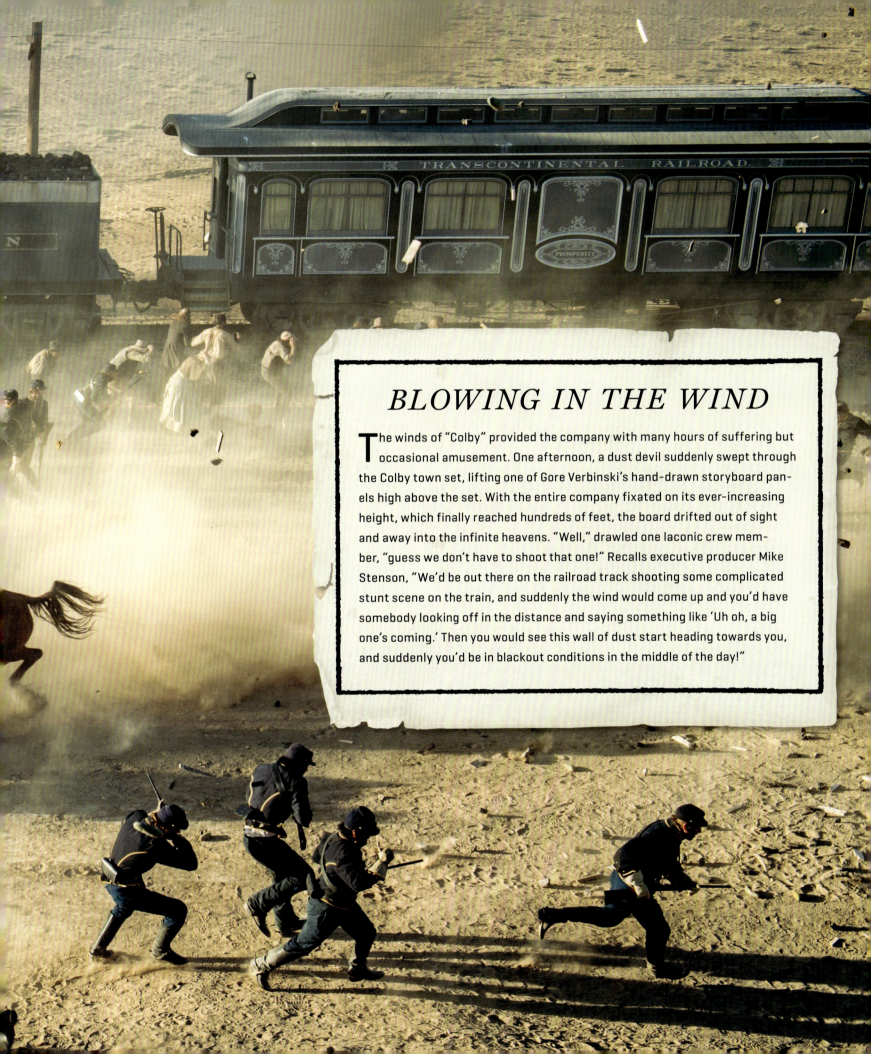

BLOWING IN THE WIND

The winds of "Colby" provided the company with many hours of suffering but occasional amusement. One afternoon, a dust devil suddenly swept through the Colby town set, lifting one of Gore Verbinski's hand-drawn storyboard panels high above the set. With the entire company fixated on its ever-increasing height, which finally reached hundreds of feet, the board drifted out of sight and away into the infinite heavens. "Well," drawled one laconic crew member, "guess we don't have to shoot that one!" Recalls executive producer Mike Stenson, "We'd be out there on the railroad track shooting some complicated stunt scene on the train, and suddenly the wind would come up and you'd have somebody looking off in the distance and saying something like 'Uh oh, a big one's coming.' Then you would see this wall of dust start heading towards you, and suddenly you'd be in blackout conditions in the middle of the day!"

BELOW: The Cavendish Gang rides hell bent for leather through the rocky desert terrain.

ON THE ROAD

Following the first stage of work at Rio Puerco, the Great Lone Ranger Road Trip was about to commence. As Eric McLeod points out, "There was no flying. Every place was too small, no major airports. So we just all packed up the hundred-plus trucks that we had, people jumped in their rental cars, and we bussed people, just like a traveling circus." When the entire *Lone Ranger* armada of 220 vehicles drove more than three hundred miles northwest to Monument Valley and the awe-inspiring Navajo Tribal Park straddling both Arizona and Utah in the vast and beautiful Navajo Nation, ferocious winds gusting to more than fifty miles per hour greeted them. For Bruckheimer, Verbinski, Depp, and much of *The Lone Ranger* company that had worked on the first three *Pirates of the Caribbean* movies, it was par for the course. After all, they had previously survived hurricanes, tropical storms, rough seas, vicious insects, and other natural catastrophes.

Filming in Monument Valley began before sunrise on the morning of Thursday, April 12, preceded by a blessing by two distinguished Navajo medicine men elders. The sun rose on cue above the ridge known as John Ford Point for a shot of the Lone Ranger and Tonto on horseback, right at the edge of the rim. At the area of Monument Valley known as North Window, the company was honored with a visit of Navajo Nation leaders, including president Ben Shelly and vice president Rex Lee Jim, all of whom warmly welcomed the first major feature film to shoot in Monument Valley in more than a decade, presenting gifts of Pendleton blankets to Depp, Hammer, Bruckheimer, and Verbinski.

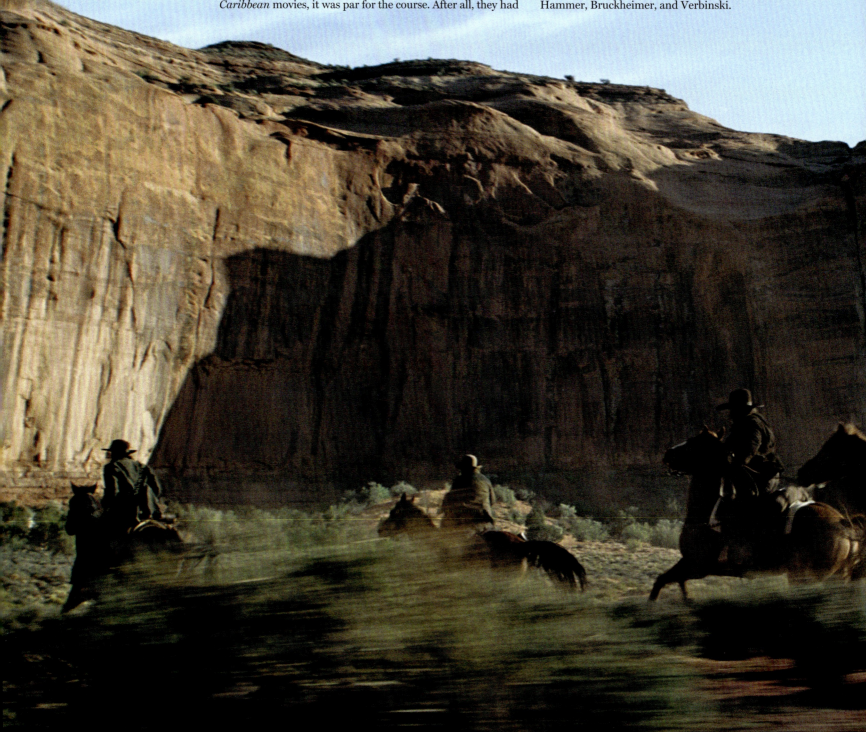

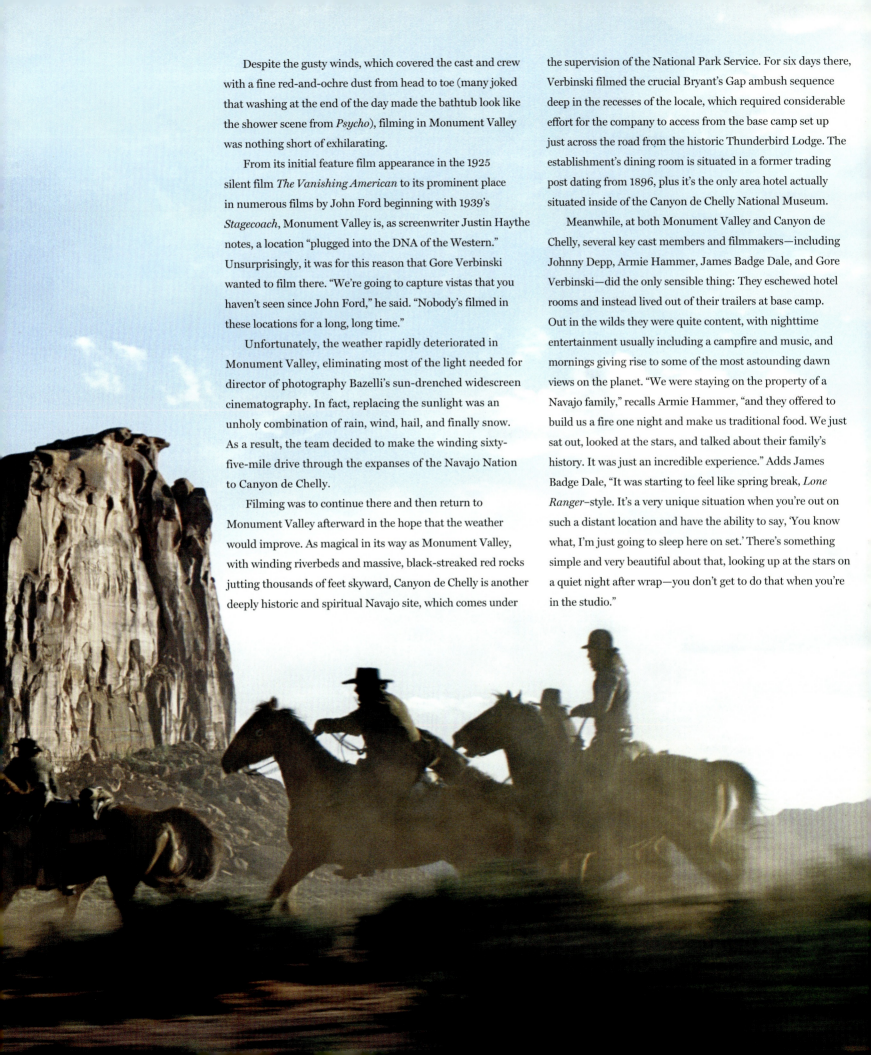

Despite the gusty winds, which covered the cast and crew with a fine red-and-ochre dust from head to toe (many joked that washing at the end of the day made the bathtub look like the shower scene from *Psycho*), filming in Monument Valley was nothing short of exhilarating.

From its initial feature film appearance in the 1925 silent film *The Vanishing American* to its prominent place in numerous films by John Ford beginning with 1939's *Stagecoach*, Monument Valley is, as screenwriter Justin Haythe notes, a location "plugged into the DNA of the Western." Unsurprisingly, it was for this reason that Gore Verbinski wanted to film there. "We're going to capture vistas that you haven't seen since John Ford," he said. "Nobody's filmed in these locations for a long, long time."

Unfortunately, the weather rapidly deteriorated in Monument Valley, eliminating most of the light needed for director of photography Bazelli's sun-drenched widescreen cinematography. In fact, replacing the sunlight was an unholy combination of rain, wind, hail, and finally snow. As a result, the team decided to make the winding sixty-five-mile drive through the expanses of the Navajo Nation to Canyon de Chelly.

Filming was to continue there and then return to Monument Valley afterward in the hope that the weather would improve. As magical in its way as Monument Valley, with winding riverbeds and massive, black-streaked red rocks jutting thousands of feet skyward, Canyon de Chelly is another deeply historic and spiritual Navajo site, which comes under the supervision of the National Park Service. For six days there, Verbinski filmed the crucial Bryant's Gap ambush sequence deep in the recesses of the locale, which required considerable effort for the company to access from the base camp set up just across the road from the historic Thunderbird Lodge. The establishment's dining room is situated in a former trading post dating from 1896, plus it's the only area hotel actually situated inside of the Canyon de Chelly National Museum.

Meanwhile, at both Monument Valley and Canyon de Chelly, several key cast members and filmmakers—including Johnny Depp, Armie Hammer, James Badge Dale, and Gore Verbinski—did the only sensible thing: They eschewed hotel rooms and instead lived out of their trailers at base camp. Out in the wilds they were quite content, with nighttime entertainment usually including a campfire and music, and mornings giving rise to some of the most astounding dawn views on the planet. "We were staying on the property of a Navajo family," recalls Armie Hammer, "and they offered to build us a fire one night and make us traditional food. We just sat out, looked at the stars, and talked about their family's history. It was just an incredible experience." Adds James Badge Dale, "It was starting to feel like spring break, *Lone Ranger*–style. It's a very unique situation when you're out on such a distant location and have the ability to say, 'You know what, I'm just going to sleep here on set.' There's something simple and very beautiful about that, looking up at the stars on a quiet night after wrap—you don't get to do that when you're in the studio."

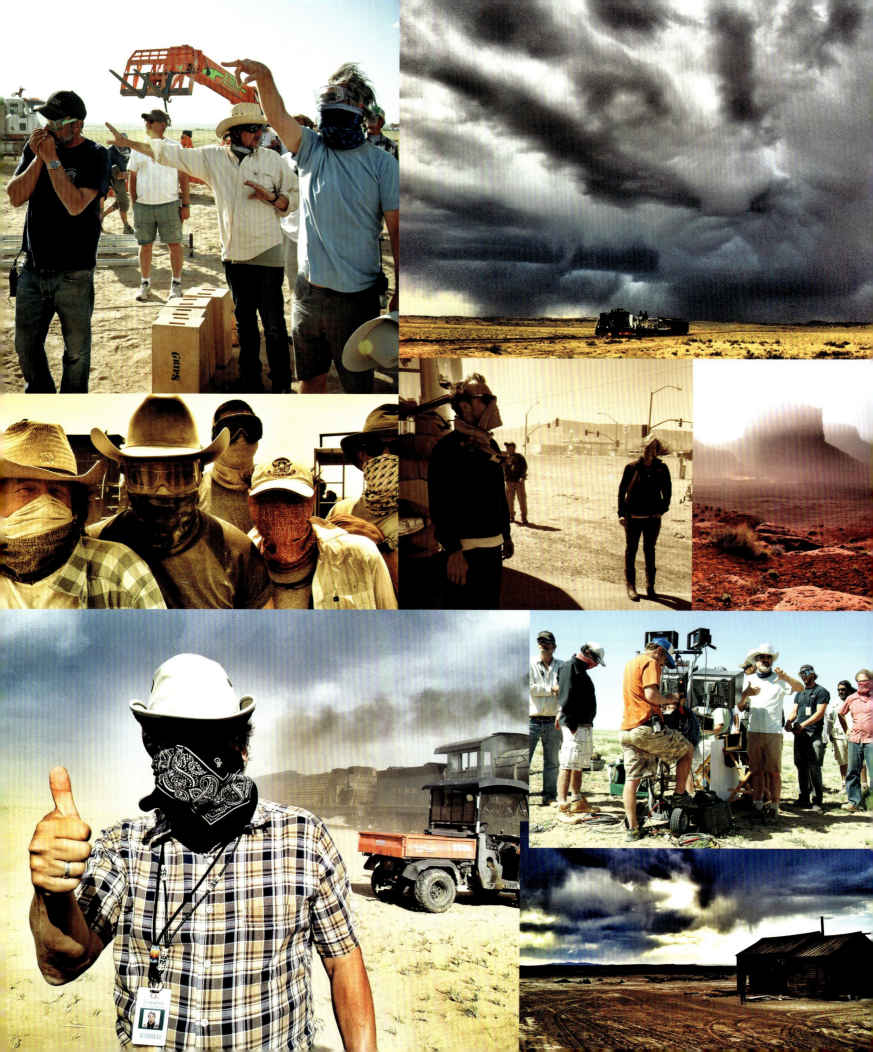

BACK TO THE WIND

WITH FILMING COMPLETED at Monument Valley, more than one member of *The Lone Ranger* company was thankful for the copious sunshine in which they were able film. On the company's first day back at Rio Puerco, however, a storm blowing in from Southern California created blinding sandstorms of biblical proportions. Nonetheless, the unstoppable company pushed on, and instead of shooting a planned sequence featuring two hundred background players, Verbinski took his cameras inside one of the Constitution's railroad cars for a scene with William Fichtner, Ruth Wilson, and Bryant Prince. Adding to the sand and dust devils raised by the winds, by Friday, May 25, Rio Puerco was also besieged by smoke drifting from the giant Whitewater-Baldy fires, which the day before had merged to burn across more than 110 square miles of the Gila National Forest.

The Lone Ranger continued filming in Rio Puerco until Monday, June 4, in temperatures often in the mid-nineties and the winds still blowing. Then followed a dramatic change of scenery as production moved 270 miles north from Albuquerque to the tiny mountain town of Creede, Colorado, for three weeks of filming. With a population of only 290, Creede's elevation of 8,852 feet presented a literal breath of fresh air to the heat-besotted *Lone Ranger* company, although that air did contain a little less oxygen than they were accustomed to.

Perched beneath craggy peaks dotted with pine trees, the historic and picturesque Creede was the last silver-mining boomtown of late nineteenth-century Colorado. The village has a fascinating rough-and-tumble history, attracting such unsavory characters during its mining heyday as Soapy Smith and Robert Ford. It was in Creede in June 1892 that Ford, the man who shot Jesse James, was himself gunned down in the tented saloon he operated for the rowdy townsfolk of the time. Creede is now dedicated to more genteel tourism and the arts, with many galleries as well as the nationally famed Creede Repertory Theatre peppering its charming Main Street. *The Lone Ranger* took advantage of Creede's storied past by building its own Sleeping Man Mine just north of downtown, amid the ruins of the real-life Amethyst Mine. The community welcomed the new infusion of energy the film brought to the town; there was barely a storefront in Creede that didn't have signs out front to welcome *The Lone Ranger* cast and crew.

"It's really authentic," notes Jerry Bruckheimer, "just a beautiful part of Colorado. But to get all our equipment here, including an entire train, wasn't easy. It's never easy in small towns to move around and find housing for this big of a company. Some of the crew have to stay an hour away because of that. But when you see the picture, you'll see the authenticity, and that's what's wonderful about this movie. We're in the real locations, not using a lot of CGI. In a lot of films these days, the environments are artificially created. This is the real deal."

It was on the stunningly beautiful Highway 149 that connects Creede with South Fork that train "road rig" work began. During this leg of the shoot, railroad cars were mounted and towed on flatbed trucks along the road in order to capture footage that could be blended with sequence shot on the specially built train tracks back in Rio Puerco.

After wrap on the final day of shooting in Creede on Friday, June 22, Johnny Depp situated himself inside the tiny city hall and proceeded to sign autographs and meet locals for nearly four hours. Interestingly, despite the fact that no more than three hundred people live in Creede, nearly a thousand souls turned up, getting news of the unexpected occasion through word of mouth and social media.

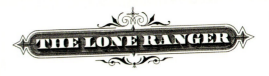

OPPOSITE PAGE: Crew members chronicled some of the day-to-day challenges of shooting, particularly the wildly changing weather. Author Michael Singer can be seen with his thumb up in the middle of a Rio Puerco sandstorm.

PAGES 94–95: The Lone Ranger has to traverse the burning hot desert to bring the vicious Butch Cavendish to the law.

LOCATING CREEDE

It was almost by accident that the company discovered Creede at all. "We were scouting some train track outside of Alamosa, Colorado," recalls executive producer Eric McLeod, "and I was looking through a travel magazine at a local hotel. I saw a little two-by-two picture in the magazine, and I thought, 'Hey, this looks interesting.' It was just a picture of a rock wall with a mine building on it, and we went and looked at it the next day. When we showed pictures to Gore, he said, 'This is what I've been looking for all this time.'"

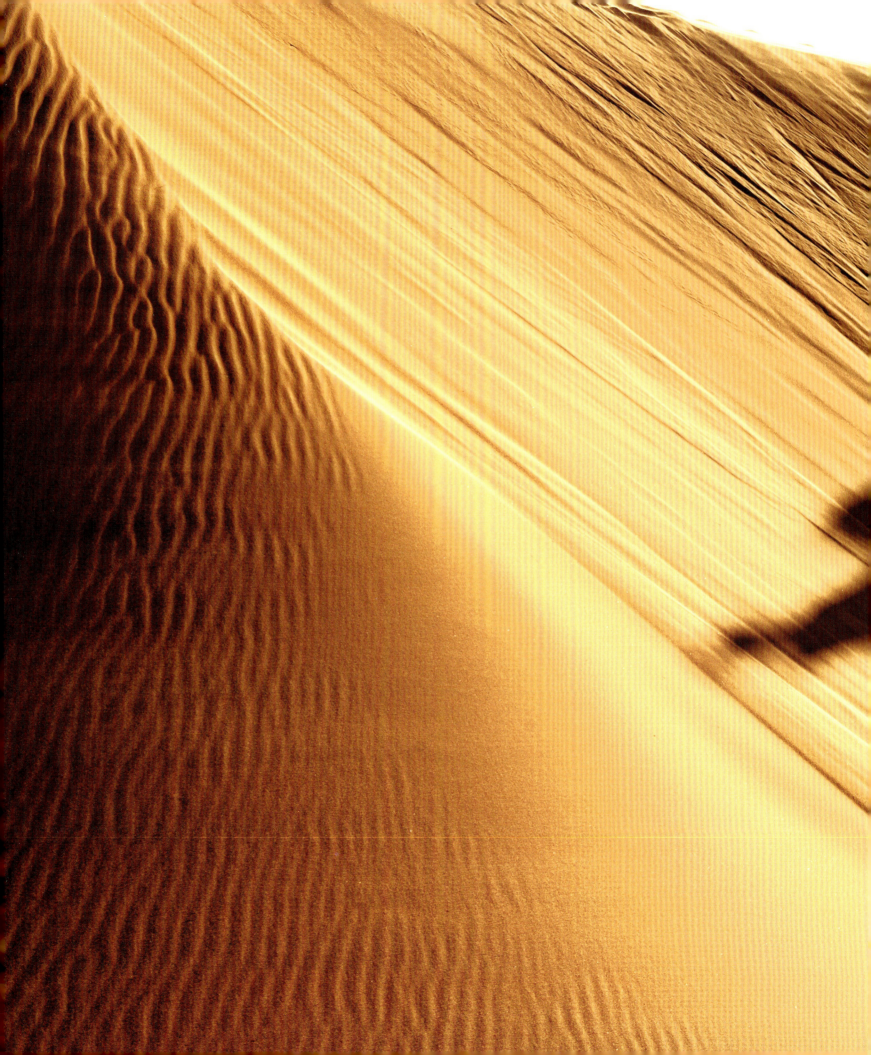

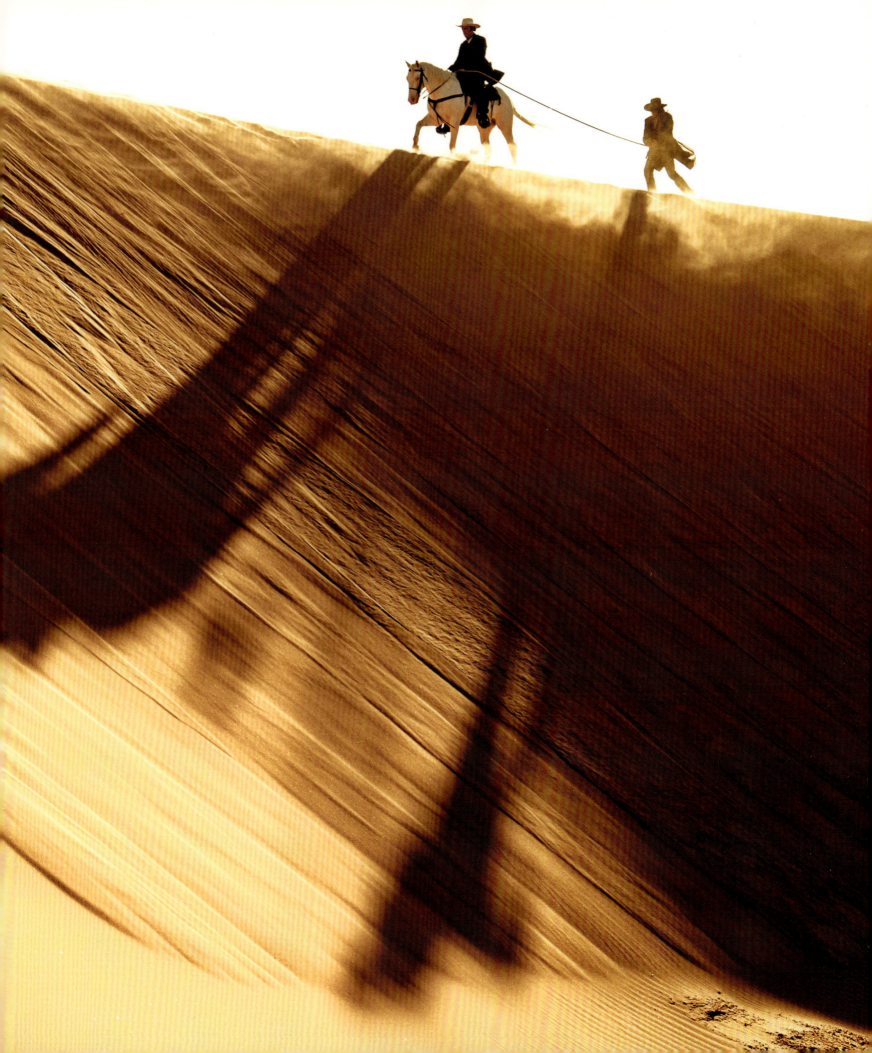

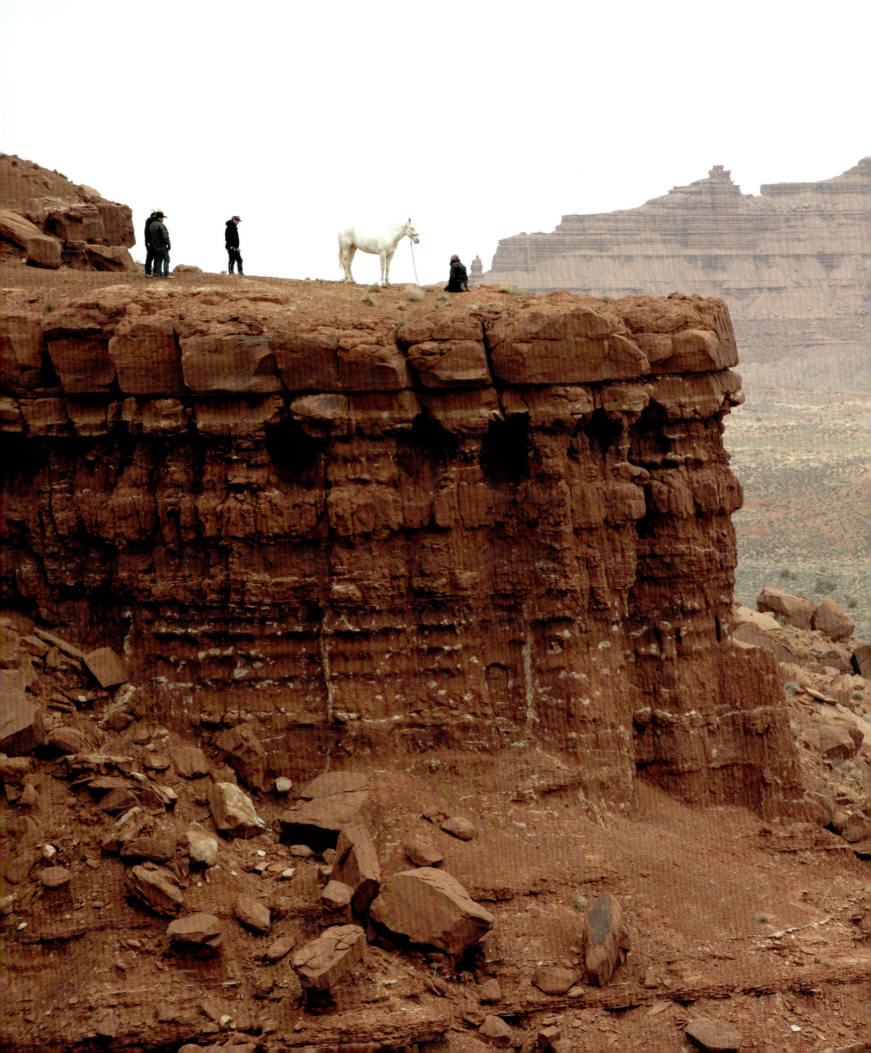

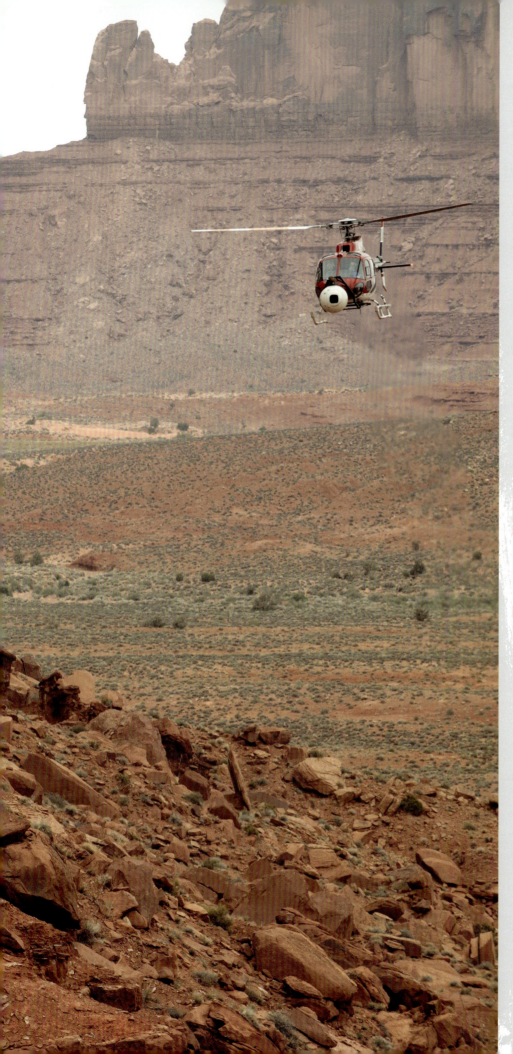

JUST DESERTS

FROM THE COOL HEIGHTS to the beautiful, burning desert, *The Lone Ranger* company next moved on to the red rock mountains, valleys, canyons, mesas, and rivers of Moab, Utah, described by Ruth Wilson as "a land made by giants." For three weeks of filming on a varied range of locales, the crew added yet another form of transportation to an ever-lengthening list—dune buggies—as they filmed at White Wash Sand Dunes, an hour's drive from town. And in the established tradition, the company was greeted by sirocco conditions, with gusts up to forty-five miles an hour hurling tons of sand at the cast and crew. Following two days of shooting in the dunes with Depp and Hammer, the company moved to a deep canyon that required twenty minutes of terrifying driving on Kane Creek Road, a perilous red rock mountain pass with no guardrails, nauseating switchbacks, and a potential plunge of hundreds of feet into the abyss.

The Colorado River in Moab would provide the next location, with Johnny Depp, long familiar with water work from the *Pirates of the Caribbean* movies, getting drenched again (along with the crew). Then back up to the heights, with shooting at two of Moab's most stunning locations, Fossil Point and Dead Horse Point. And while Fossil Point is also known as Thelma & Louise Point, where the two outlaws drove off a cliff at the finale of the famed Ridley Scott film, the addition of a full-size train, workers' camp, and 154 costumed extras made it virtually unrecognizable. Dead Horse Point was the site of the rickety, edge-of-the-cliff spirit platform on which John Reid awakens after being saved by Tonto. "It was a rinky-dink structure about eighteen feet tall," recalls Armie Hammer, "and while I was standing on top of that thing, the platform would sway about three feet. Then, looking down, I realized that it would be a two-thousand-foot drop to the bottom of the canyon floor. That was a trip. Then we also shot my recovery scene, which unfortunately involved about three days of me walking barefoot through the desert with the temperatures hitting about 120 degrees." Hammer notes that, in Moab, "heat was the main obstacle we all had to overcome." Also in Moab, the Harley Bates Ranch and Highways 279, 128, and 313 (the roads used for road rig train work) would provide even more picturesque shooting locales.

Following a one-day shoot back in New Mexico at Shiprock, a stunning 1,583-foot-high rock formation known to the Navajos as Tse'Bit'Ai ("rock with wings"), the company drove for more than six hours until they reached their next base of operations, Santa Fe, New Mexico. Along with shooting the Hell on Wheels and Reid Farm scenes in

MOAB R&R

Moab, a mecca for outdoors tourism attracting visitors from all over the world, presented a perfect opportunity for *The Lone Ranger* cast and crew to spend their weekends in the Great Outdoors (as if their time spent there during the workweek wasn't enough). "We've ridden horses, played in the river, gone on hikes, swam in waterfalls, gone base jumping," said Armie Hammer. "You feel like a lazy ass if you sit on your couch all day during the weekend." But for those who just wanted to hang out in town rather than risk their lives on weekends, the sole sushi restaurant in Moab, patronized by many cast and crew, honored its visitors by creating specials during the film's shoot such as "Tonto-maki" and "Kemowasabee Roll" and a drink called "Kemo-sake Mojito."

nearby Lamy, Verbinski found other ways to utilize the varied and often astounding topography of the region.

The forbidding, jagged, moonscape-like rocks of Plaza Blanca were appropriately selected as the "Valley of Tears" location for scenes with Ruth Wilson, William Fichtner, and the Cavendish Gang. Meanwhile, the magnificent Valles Caldera National Preserve, a huge twelve-mile-wide grass valley in the crater of a volcano, was utilized as the setting of a Comanche warriors' village that "welcomes" the Lone Ranger and Tonto in a rather unique way and is then attacked by the United States Cavalry. Also utilized were the Gilman Tunnels, tucked into a dramatic gorge and an ideal site for more train road rig work. And the high elevations of Pajarito Mountains provided the dramatic site of a last stand of courageous Comanche warriors.

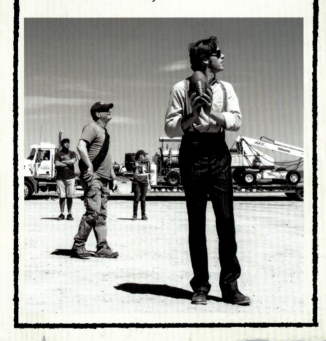

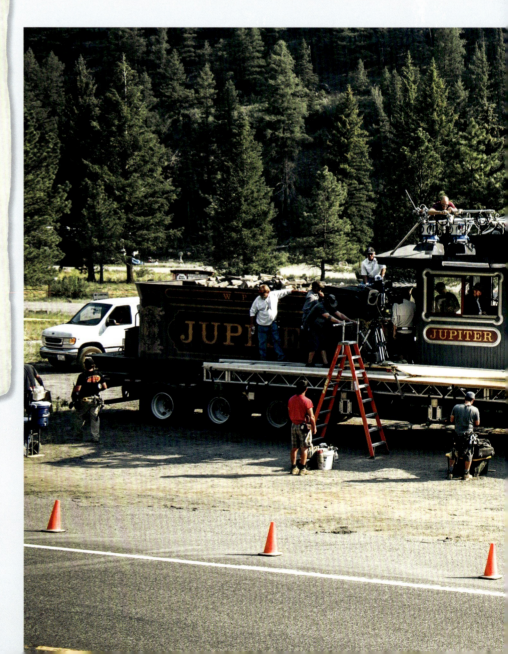

PAGES 96–97: In Monument Valley, Silver wranglers wait while a helicopter mounted with a camera gets into position for a shot featuring the magnificent horse.
ABOVE: Armie Hammer tosses the pigskin between scenes in the desert.
RIGHT: The Jupiter locomotive and coal car mounted on a road rig in the heights of Angel Fire, New Mexico.

CAMPED OUT IN ANGEL FIRE

In mid-August, the company once again packed their kits and returned to Albuquerque for one week more of shooting, before traveling 154 miles northward, beyond Taos, and 8,600 feet up in the mountains of Angel Fire, New Mexico, for seventeen final days of location shooting. This last leg was almost entirely made up of alpine train road rig work as well as a spectacular crash engineered by special effects coordinator John Frazier and his team. Filming also took place on miles of road in nearby Cimarron Canyon State Park, a location chosen for its staggering cliffs and thick groves of pine trees perched like eagles on its sheer inclines. Fifty production assistants from the area were hired to work on the scene, and apart from the rainy weather, their only problem was the bears that occasionally wandered out of the wilderness for a "visit." Thankfully, they all remained peaceable. The weather, as usual, was anything but, with drenching thunderstorms and showers on a nearly daily basis, much to the increasing frustration of the filmmakers. Says Morgan Des Groseillers, Verbinski's indispensable right hand, "If we have sun, we have to shoot through the day before the thunderstorms begin in the late afternoon. We have to shoot through lunch to beat the afternoon storms and at wrap have to huddle up to discuss how everything moving around has affected the schedule."

The company finally decided that, in order to finish the extensive backlot work that was required, much of which would utilize exterior green screen for visual effects, filming would need to move to the more dependable summer weather of the Los Angeles area.

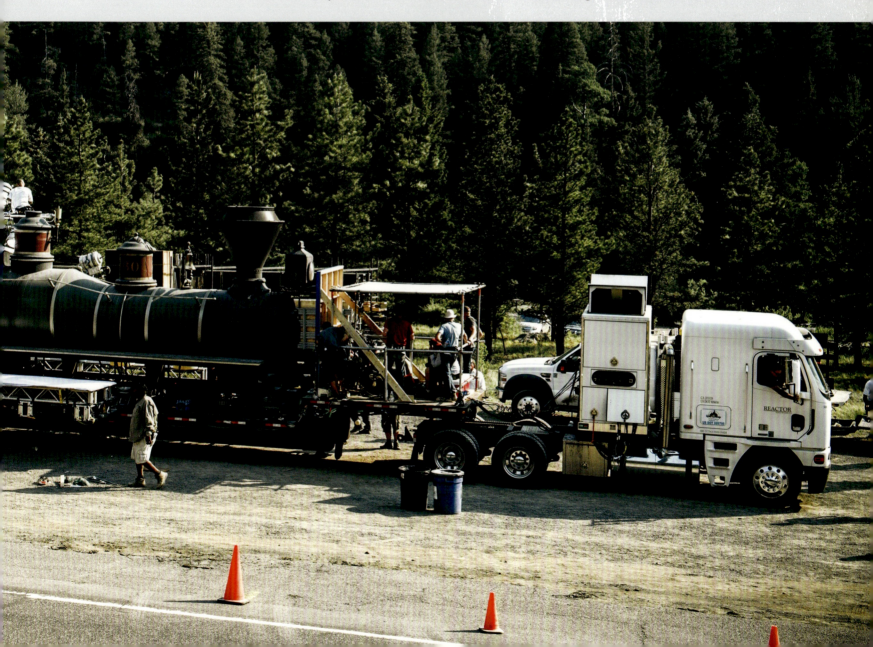

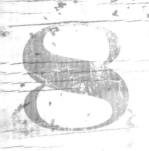

THE HARPER GANG: STUNTS

THERE WAS A GOLDEN AGE OF WESTERN MOVIE STUNT WORK THAT SAW LEGENDARY STUNT PERFORMERS LIKE YAKIMA CANUTT, DAVE SHARPE, AND LOREN JANES PERFORM FEATS OF DARING ON SCREEN THAT DEFIED BELIEF AND GRAVITY. FOR *THE LONE RANGER*'S STUNT COORDINATOR, THOMAS ROBINSON HARPER—BETTER KNOWN AS TOMMY—THE TASK WAS ONCE AGAIN TO SHOW AUDIENCES THINGS ON SCREEN THAT, LIKE THOSE GREAT STUNTS OF YESTERYEAR, COULD NOT BE ACCOMPLISHED WITH MODERN TECHNOLOGIES LIKE CGI. VERBINSKI ATTEMPTED TO SHOOT AS MANY FULLY BUILT SETS AND DRAMATIC LANDSCAPES "IN CAMERA" WITH AS LITTLE TRICKERY AS POSSIBLE— THE SAME RULE APPLIED TO STUNT WORK. MORE OFTEN THAN NOT, IT WAS THE REAL DEAL.

OPPOSITE: William Fichtner's perilous train-to-horse transfer in *The Lone Ranger*'s first big railroad action sequence.

BELOW: Concept illustrator John Park created this action-packed rendering of John Reid and Tonto's spill from the crashed Colby passenger train.

But considering that Harper comes from a family with multiple generations of Hollywood stunt players, that mandate was right up his alley. "Growing up around the business," he says, "I knew that the Lone Ranger was an iconic character, and to be able to be a part in bringing that back was fantastic." To do so, Harper brought together a crack team of associates, including stunt co-coordinators Casey O'Neill and Tad Griffith, an eight-man team of stunt riggers, and three hundred of the best stunt players in the business.

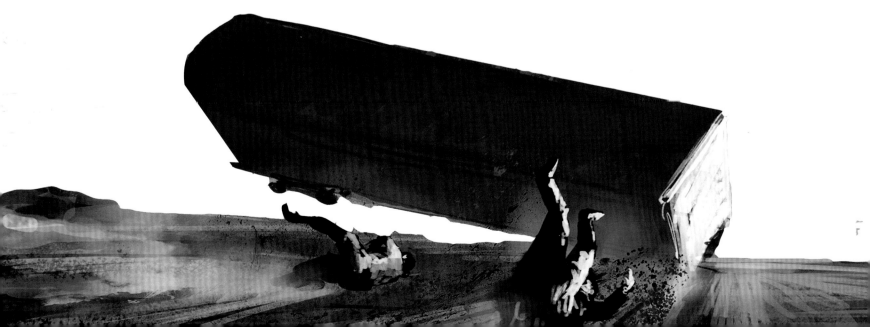

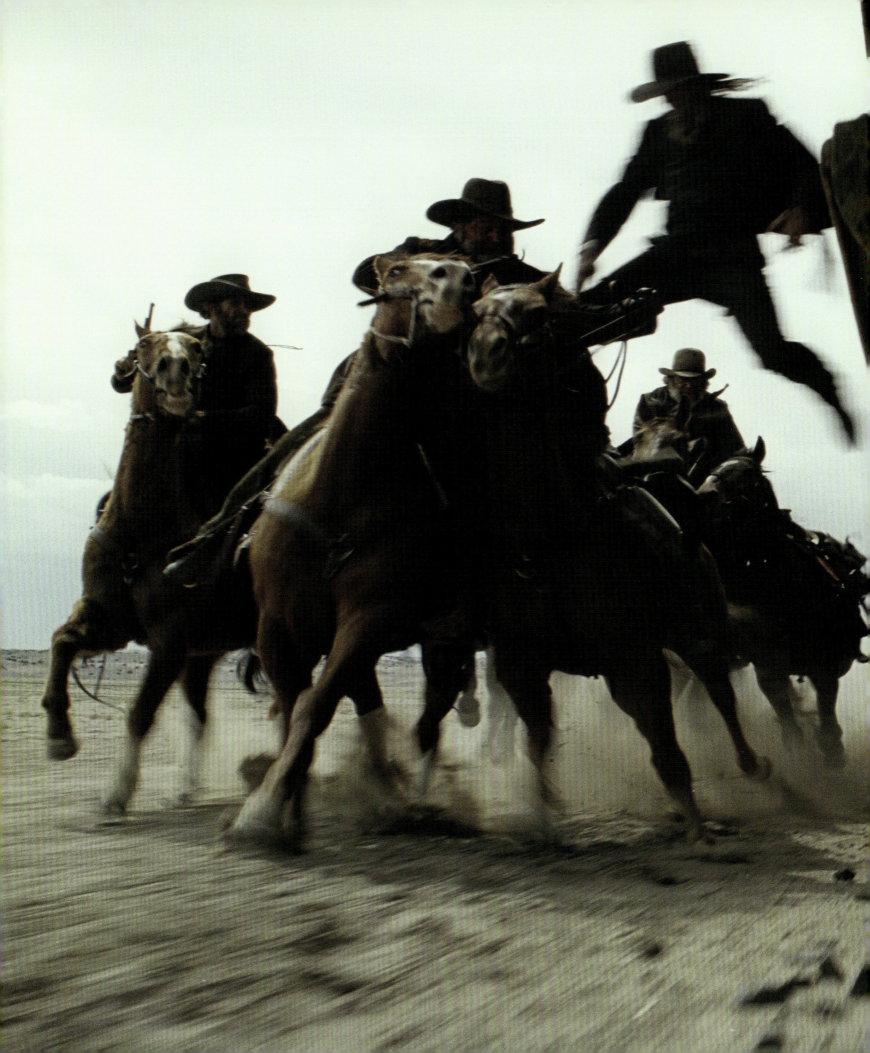

TRAIN TO WIN

The seven months of filming would see Harper and his team accomplishing impossible stunts, many of them inside and on top of trains for the spectacular action sequences that bookend the film. The bar that had been set for these breakneck scenes by classics like *The Great Train Robbery* (1903), Buster Keaton's *The General* (1926), *Butch Cassidy and the Sundance Kid* (1969), and *The Wild Bunch* (1969) would be raised ever higher at Verbinski's command. "I don't even know if there's dialogue in this film," jokes Harper, who looks, sounds, and even walks like a classic cowboy. "It feels like it's just pure action. Gore has this movie in his head, and he doesn't waver from that. When we feel we've got something tacked down, Gore will say, 'Great, but can we do *this* instead?' Then we've got to rethink and take it to the next level. He likes everyone to really push and get the most out of it.

"The trains are amazing in that they're real," continues Harper. "We never did anything on those trains slower than thirty miles per hour, and usually somewhere around forty miles per hour. We put special tracks on the top of the train cars so that the stunt players could run along the top but always be tethered to the train on a limit line, which you can't see, so that if something should happen, they wouldn't fall off." Harper and his team were constantly doing safety checks and ensuring that, to the best of their abilities, the action, though inherently perilous, would be within certain boundaries. "This is one of the most dangerous movies I've ever worked on," confesses Harper. "We literally have to watch each other's backs on a movie like this. The trains, the horses, the speed, the conditions—whether wind, dust storms, snow, hail, 115 degree temperatures—we've been through everything on this movie, and it's been one heck of an adventure."

OPPOSITE: Gore Verbinski plans another thrilling shot on top of a section of railroad car mounted on a road rig.

BELOW: The camera vehicle dubbed "The Edge" captures the action as William Fichtner, Tom Wilkinson, and Ruth Wilson pull off a daring stunt on the Jupiter locomotive.

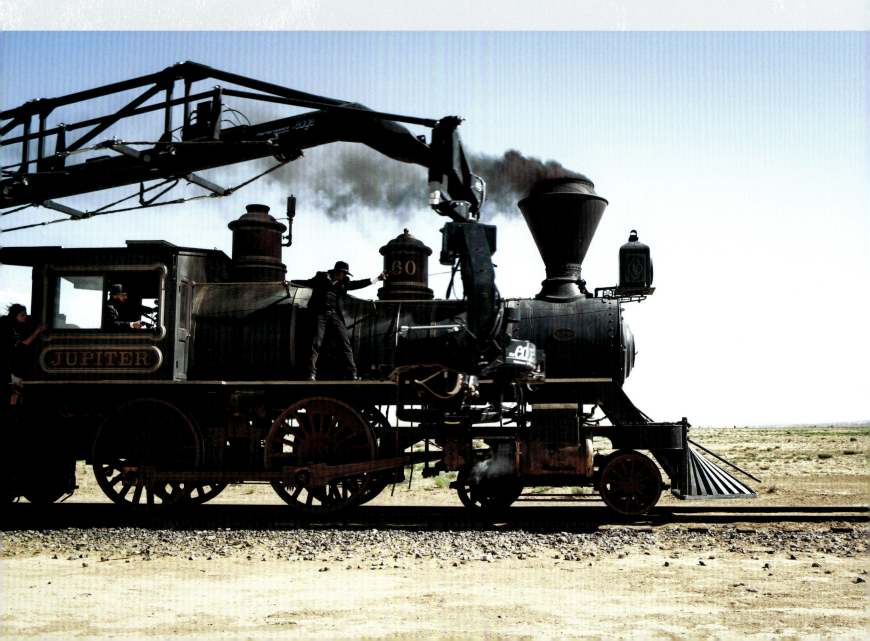

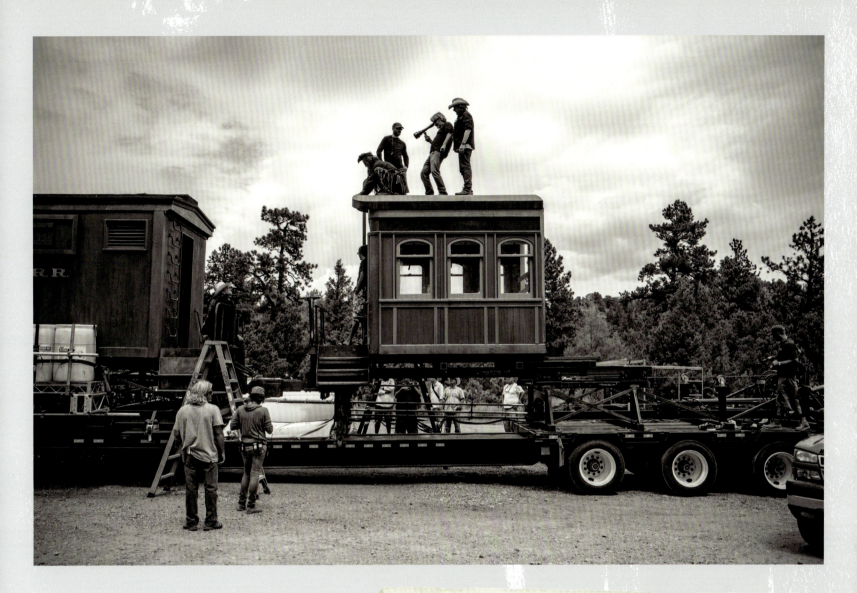

"And the road rigs were actually more dangerous than the real trains on tracks because the turns, starts, and stops on the trains were a little softer," Harper continues. "When you have a diesel truck pulling those cars down a mountain road with trees going by, you can't always see what's going on up there. You have to just feel what's happening."

The dust alone created challenges for Harper and his department. "We have very precise equipment," he says, "and when dust and dirt get in them, as they did in Rio Puerco, we had to take them completely apart to be inspected and cleaned. We had two fifty-three-foot trailers that were packed with all kinds of specialty gear just to accomplish what we needed to do on the movie."

ROAD RIG RISK

"I think I'm the only actor who really liked being on top of the trains," laughs Armie Hammer, "but if you're the guy facing backward on the road rig, you can't see the turns coming. It's hard to keep your composure and stay in character when you're thinking, 'I'm gonna fall off this thing.'"

Tom Wilkinson also admits to the challenge of standing atop moving railroad cars: "Sometimes you think, 'I want to stay on the rails, I don't want this to fall over,' and there are chasms on either side of the road when you're doing road rig. But you do think that people actually did ride in these trains across America in uncomfortable weather conditions, and it was easier for me, I'm sure, than it was for them."

JOHNNY TAKES A SPILL

Despite Johnny Depp's surefooted approach to stunts, there was a moment during filming at North Window in Monument Valley that made the stunt teams' hearts drop. In the scene, cameras were capturing the Lone Ranger on Silver and Tonto on Scout at full gallop through desert brush, when the brown-and-white paint horse on which Depp was mounted suddenly found himself without a rider. "Horses, no matter how well trained, are unpredictable animals," says Harper. "When a horse is galloping through bushes, it can suddenly change its path, and that's exactly what happened. Unfortunately, Johnny did fall; luckily, the horse didn't step on him and it was a soft, sandy spot." To the incredible relief of the entire company and a few dozen Navajo onlookers, Depp immediately got up, laughed off the spill despite some abrasions and bruises, and cheerfully continued on with his work.

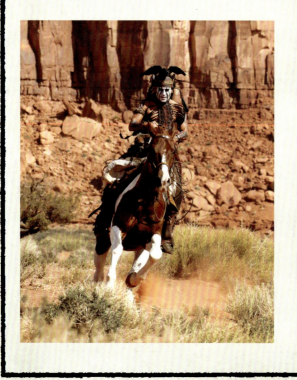

WILD WEST DAREDEVILS

In addition to his great team of stunt players, Tommy Harper was blessed with two stars and several supporting players who absolutely loved doing as many of their own stunts as possible. For Johnny Depp, that meant running on top of moving train cars and plenty of work on horseback. "Johnny's fantastic," says Harper. "What's so great about him is that you tell him something, and he says, 'Okay, yeah, I get that.' And Johnny will go and do exactly what you say. He doesn't change it at all but tunes in to what you tell him. We actually had him running along the top of the train and jumping off the side onto the car, decelerating him onto a crash mat using a wire. And Johnny trusted me and my riggers to protect him. Johnny knows what his comfort level is and will say when he prefers for Todd Warren, his double, to do the stunt. He understands that because he's been doing it for so long."

With his youth, athleticism, and adventurous spirit, Armie Hammer was pretty much up for anything as far as stunts and riding were concerned, and Tommy Harper took full advantage of the actor's enthusiasm. "I told him that if the whole acting thing didn't pan out, he could come work for me anytime because he did a fantastic job with all his stunts. Armie had one of the best stunt doubles in the business, Jeremy Fitzgerald, but so many times he just insisted on doing the stunt himself. I think we found his breaking point, though, in a scene where he had to slide down a banister and hit a piece of wood that catapults him into the saddle on Silver. He gave it a heck of a go for more than ten takes and was real sore the next day."

"That seemed like such a hard one at the time," says Hammer of the stunt, "but now looking back, it was kind of medium. I think we did something like twenty-five takes, and the reason is that I jump blind and just hope that Silver will be in the right spot. But the horse is thinking, 'Uh-uh, there's a two-hundred-pound dude who's gonna drop on me, I don't want that.'" Hammer, however, was game for much worse than jumping on a horse. "We've done a lot of stunts on ratchets, which are basically big air pistons that jerk you in a certain direction. They harness you up, push a button, and you basically go from being a stationary object to moving, very, very quickly, either straight up or diagonally. There were three days in a row when I was in the ratchet harness all day long doing stuff like getting ripped out of the train or swinging on a mail chain hook that swings you around in a circle. It looked like a carnival ride, but you have metal shackles on your wrist that start binding. Gore's saying, 'Yell more, yell more!' and I'm going, 'I'm yelling, this hurts!' That was a rough one."

LEFT: Johnny Depp at full gallop in Monument Valley astride Tonto's paint horse.
RIGHT: The cameras capture Armie Hammer performing a particularly daring stunt.

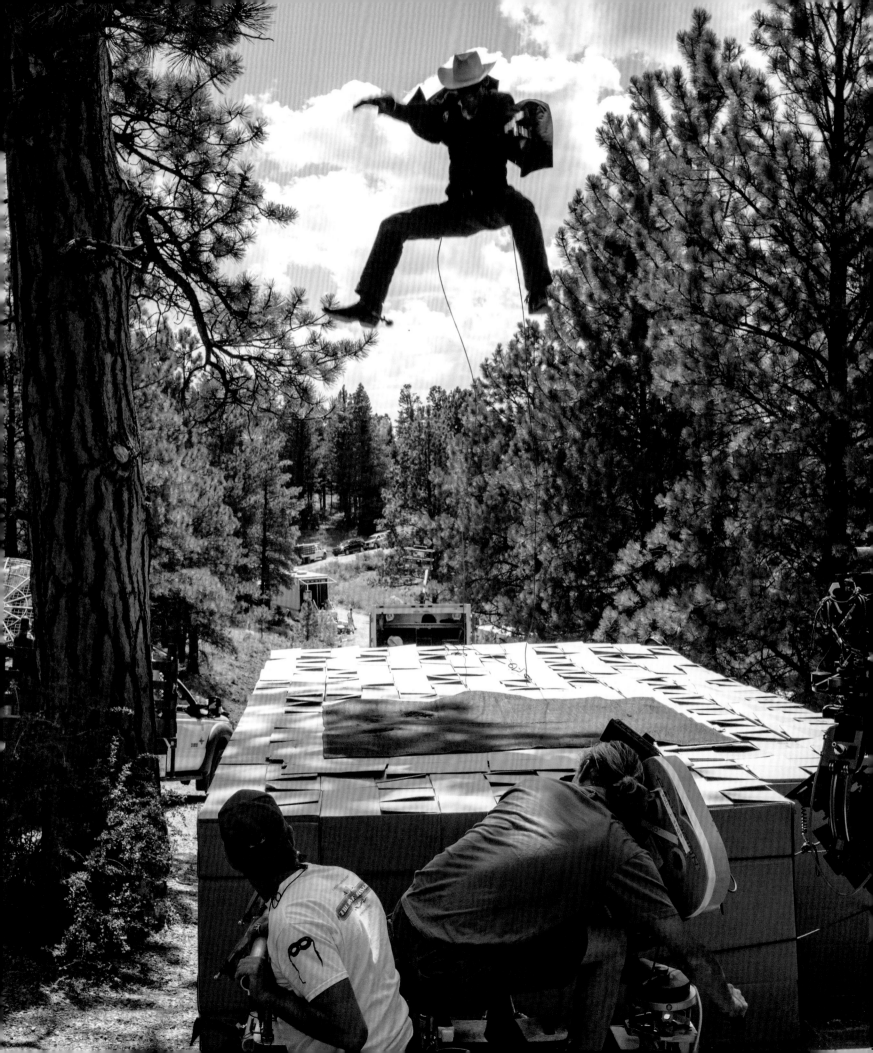

THE PERFECT TRAIN WRECK

ROUGHEST OF ALL was a scene in which special effects supervisor John Frazier, his coordinator Jim Schwalm, and their crew imaginatively turned a nearly impossible action in the script into reality by mounting a 25,400-pound locomotive on a 4,000-pound turntable, which, pulled by cables, twisted and turned its way down a 10,000-pound track, almost pulverizing the Lone Ranger and Tonto. Hammer explains: "They had a truck connected to the cable that would accelerate and pull the locomotive sideways on the ground. The truck had to hit a certain mark, and I'm not sure what happened, but the locomotive jumped off the safety track it was on, skidded at us, and ended up hitting the train car that Todd and I were leaning against. It took a good two minutes for the dust to settle, and all of a sudden Gore pokes in and says, 'Everybody okay?' We said, 'Yeah, we're good.' So he said, 'Okay, let's do it again.'"

Another principal actor who got a major stunt workout was William Fichtner as Butch Cavendish. "Bill really embraced that character," notes Harper, "one of the best movie bad guys I've ever seen. In one scene, he jumps from a

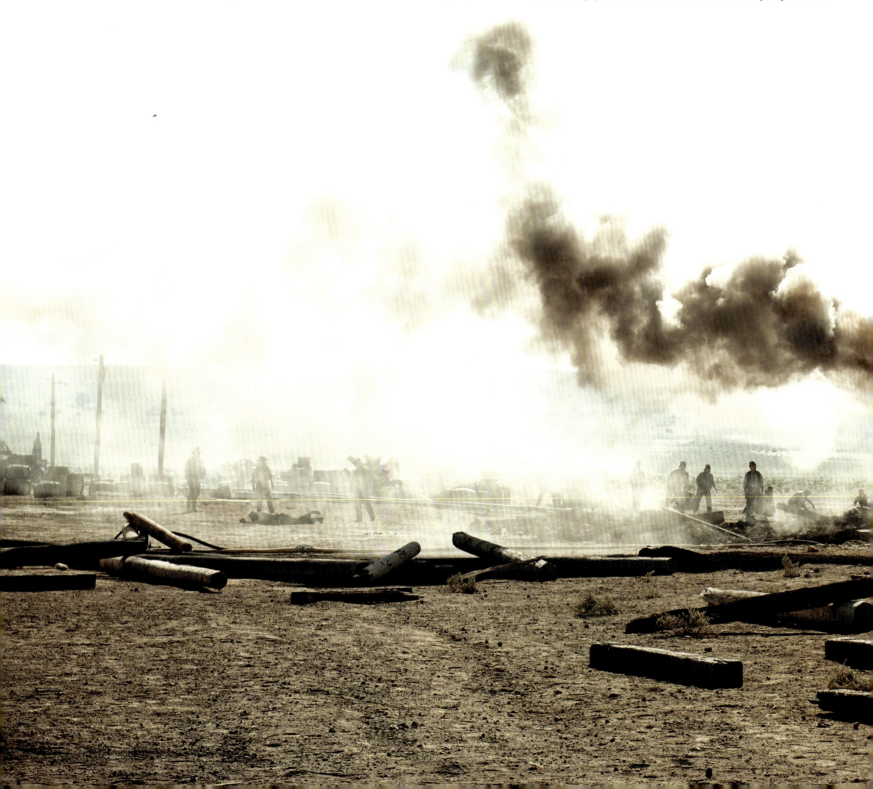

moving train onto his horse, and he really did that. We had a big overhead rig off the top of the train and hooked Bill onto a line. The train was going twenty-five or thirty miles per hour, with the horses running hard right next to it. We had to get Bill's horse to the right spot for him to jump onto it, but he had to commit to going because it's about six or eight feet out from the train to his horse. He really had to leap, because if he missed, he'd just be floating on the wire. Bill went for it the first time and landed on the back of the horse just behind the saddle and kind of bounced along until we saved him. Then the second time, Bill nailed it right there.

"He was excited because it was a big stunt for him," continues Harper, "and he did a great job. Tad Griffith, my lead coordinator for all the horse stunts, is an amazing third-generation stunt guy who's been around horses forever and helped train Bill."

Strangely enough, Fichtner found that incredible stunt considerably less intimidating than the road rig work: "All I can tell you is that jumping out of a twenty-mile-per-hour train onto a full galloping horse and landing on an empty saddle was not nearly as nerve-wracking as standing on top of a moving train when it's flying around the bend!"

Ruth Wilson, although a tomboy as a child, couldn't have imagined what was awaiting her during the shoot. "I'd never done any sort of stunt work in my life, so I was quite worried about it," she confesses. "I thought I would have to fake all sorts of reactions. But Gore tries to do things for real most of the time, so he got us up on top of the train going thirty or forty miles per hour and had me spinning, falling off, and hanging upside down. On *The Lone Ranger* I've done loads of the stunt work myself, which has been really exciting. It frees you up as an actor because you don't have to overthink a scene; you just have to do something. Your adrenaline really flows. Gore also likes to tease out character traits within the action, so rather than just having you jump from here to there, he'll actually focus on the character within the moment as well. It makes the action sequences much more fun to watch and to be part of because you're maintaining your character."

THESE PAGES: The incredible camera vehicle known as "The Edge" captures the crashed Colby locomotive's perilous slide.

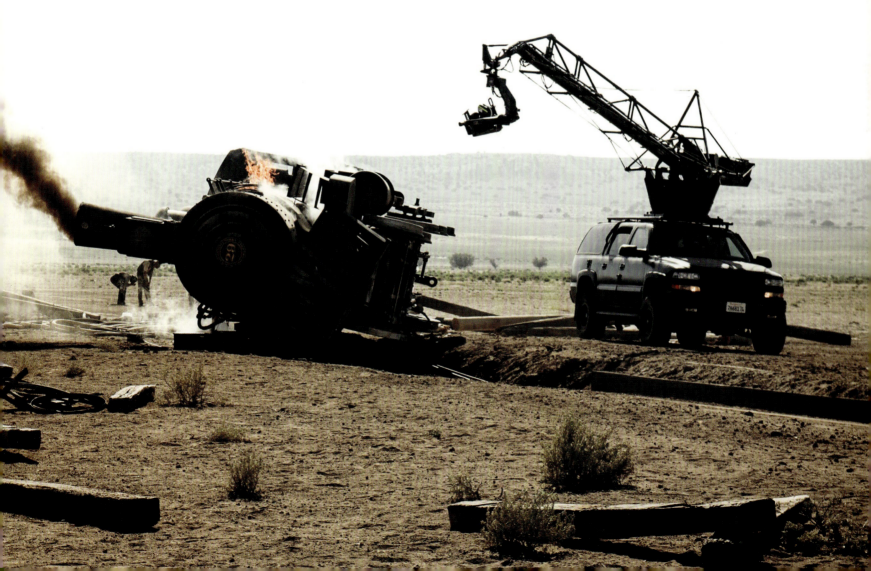

HORSEPLAY

Among the greatest stunt players featured in *The Lone Ranger* were forty famed Blackfeet Indian bareback riders from Montana, for years under the supervision of legendary wrangler, rodeo rider, and stuntman Alvin William "Dutch" Lunak. During chilly night shooting at Pajarito Ski Resort, these amazing horsemen, among the world's greatest, portrayed Comanche braves making one last, desperate stand against the U.S. Cavalry on a steep incline. Head wrangler Clay Lilley and stunt co-coordinator Tad Griffith worked with the riders for two weeks preparing the shoot, which was stunning in its impact.

One of the final days of filming, September 20, 2012, in the huge parking lot of Santa Anita Park, brought out an incredible assemblage of stunt legends to participate in a scene in which the Lone Ranger gallops through a railroad passenger car on Silver, firing his pearl-handled six-shooter at full speed while passengers duck for cover amidst the flying glass and debris. This noble company included the likes of Terry Leonard, Hal Burton, Mic Rodgers, Randy Hice, Mike Runyard, Donna Evans, and Lisa Hoyle, many of them second or third generation in their field and the descendants of stunt performers who would have worked in the Golden Age of Hollywood when the Western was at its zenith. It was a fitting way to celebrate the work of *The Lone Ranger* stunt team, honoring the long and thrilling traditions of their profession.

BELOW: Horsemen at sunset on location near Lamy, New Mexico.

RIGHT: Ruth Wilson performs one of her own stunts as Rebecca Reid on an Albuquerque Studios sound stage.

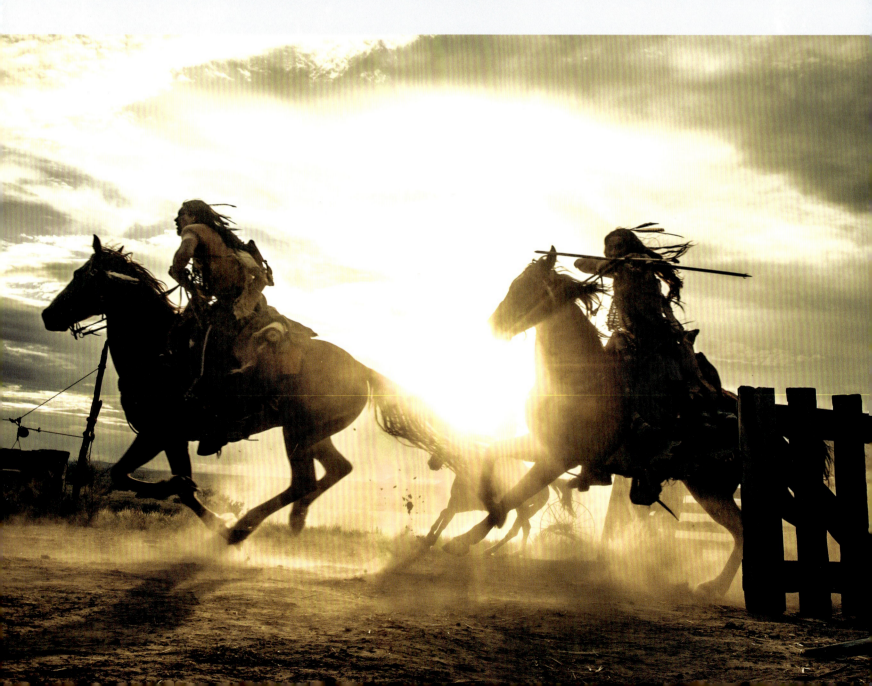

TRUE GRIT

It wasn't just the boys in the cast who were having all the fun. "Ruth Wilson is amazing," confirms Harper. "She's another one who could be a stuntwoman. She's fearless and very smart. She doesn't just throw herself out there but asks all the right questions. I had Ruth hanging off the side of the train upside down with her head right next to the wheels. She saw what the parameters were and felt safe with us rigging her. I was able to have Ruth do a lot of her own stunts, which Gore loved because he can shoot her in the middle of the action. All the actors on this film have done some of their own stunt work, and it's great to incorporate them because they're able to act and do the action as well."

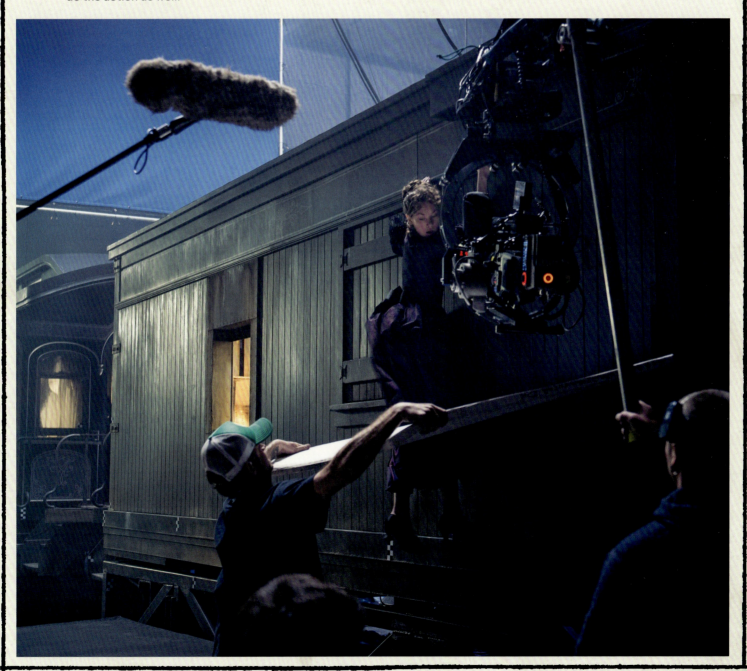

RIDING (& BUILDING) THE RAILS: THE TRAINS OF *THE LONE RANGER*

WHAT HAPPENS WHEN A PRODUCER AND DIRECTOR NEED THREE NINETEENTH-CENTURY AMERICAN TRAINS FOR SEVERAL OF THE MOST AMBITIOUS ACTION SCENES EVER COMMITTED TO FILM? "WE BUILD THEM," STATES JERRY BRUCKHEIMER, "JUST AS WE BUILT SEVERAL FULL-SIZE SHIPS FOR THE *PIRATES OF THE CARIBBEAN* MOVIES. THERE'S NO SUBSTITUTE FOR REALITY, AND GIVEN WHAT WE NEEDED TO DO WITH THOSE TRAINS, THE REAL THING WAS THE ONLY WAY TO GO."

The dilemma Bruckheimer and Verbinski faced in preparing *The Lone Ranger* was how to accomplish the mighty task of shooting what was in the screenplay—nothing less than some of the most complex and hair-raising train action ever devised. Possibilities included creating miniatures, using CGI, or utilizing extant period trains, but the trains in the screenplay were so well-defined and such an important element of the drama and action that only the real thing would do. "When you go into the exacting mind of Gore Verbinski, who knows camera angles, speeds, tilts, and duration of shots, then it becomes very technical and specific," explains production supervisor Tom Hayslip. "As the trains became a more important element of the movie, we started worrying about how they could do what they were needed to do. How can they go fast enough? How can they stop fast enough? In a way, the trains became characters, much like the *Black Pearl* did in the *Pirates* movies. They lived, breathed, worked, and failed us. Sometimes they would be great and other times not. There was a lot of head scratching as we got into the specificity of what Gore needed out of those trains."

OPPOSITE: Guarded by U.S. cavalrymen, the Constitution, belching steam, enters the Silver Man Mine.

BELOW: John Park's concept illustration of one of the film's period trains accentuates its brute force and strength as it cuts through the wilderness of the Old West.

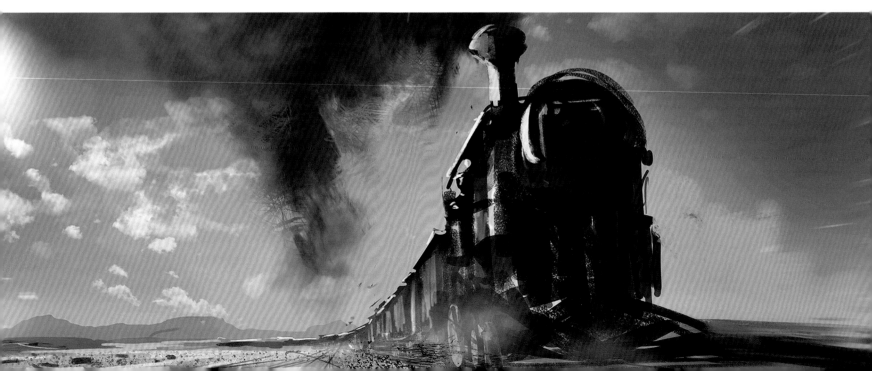

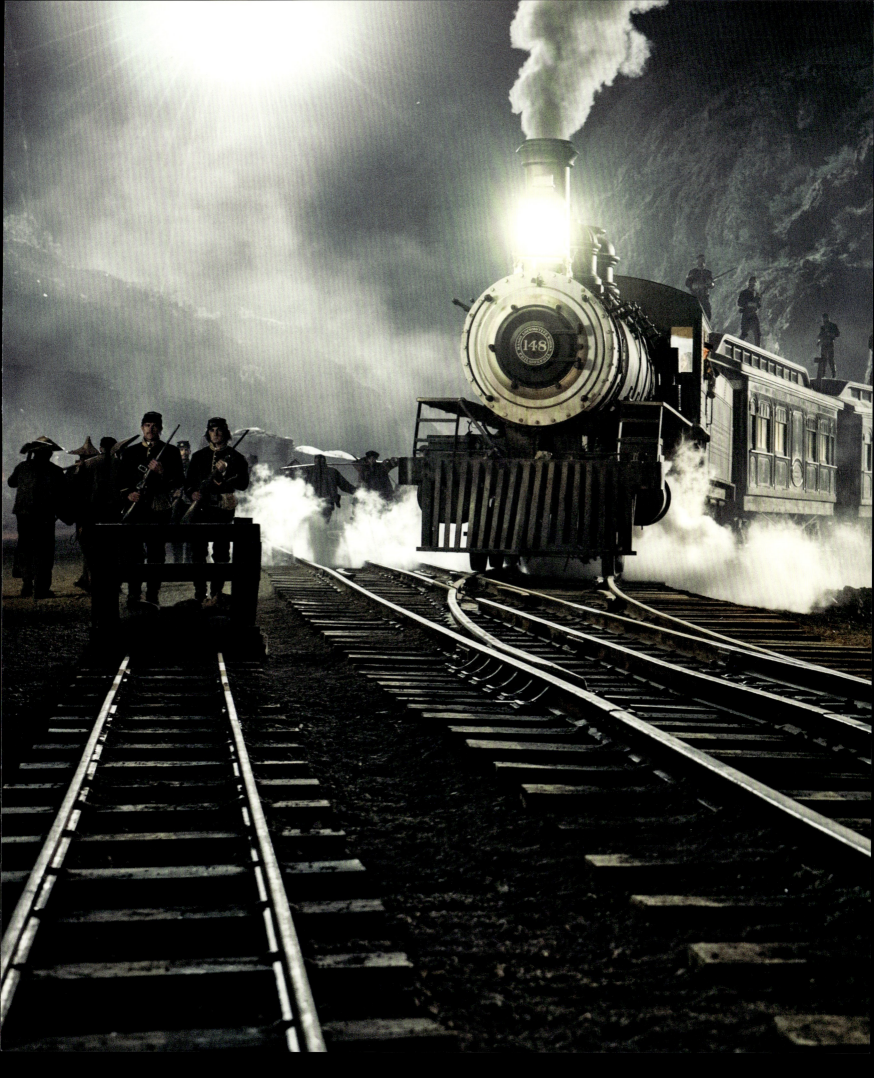

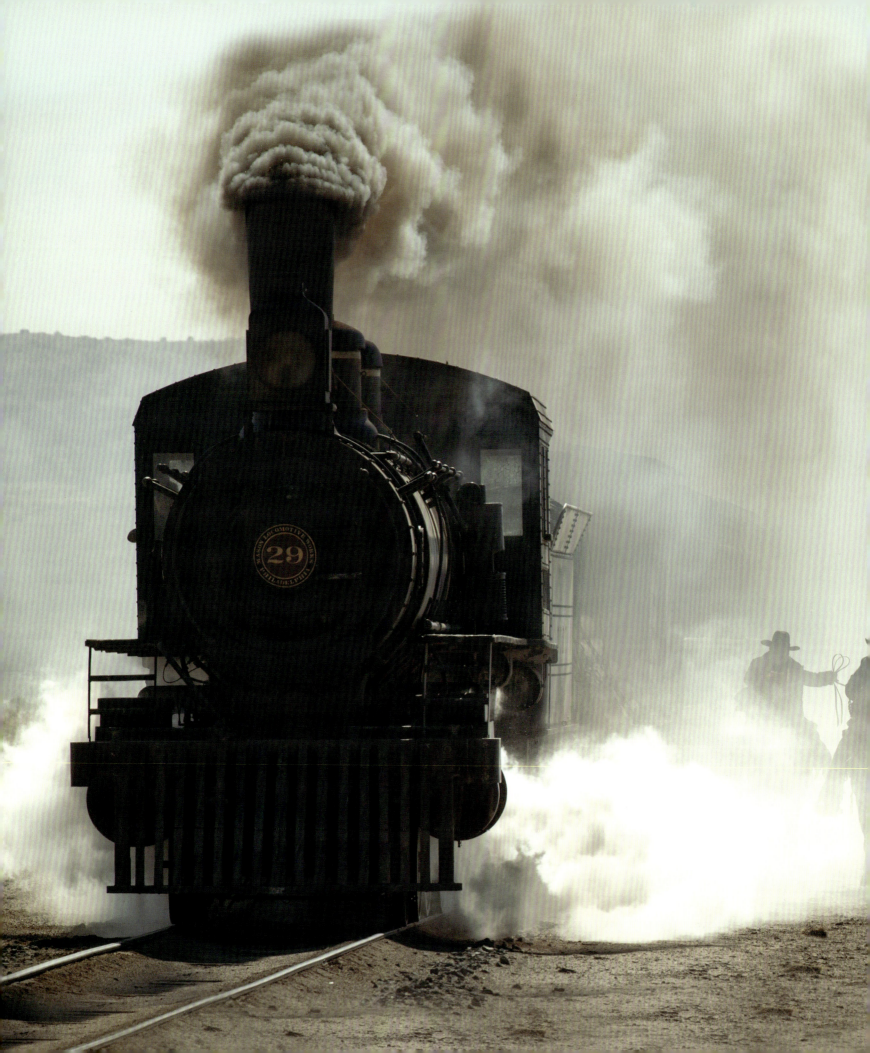

ON THE RIGHT TRACK

THE TRAIN DEPARTMENT of *The Lone Ranger* was coordinated first by Jim Clark, who brought years of traditional knowledge to the task, and then by Jason Lamb, alongside assistant coordinator Luke Johnson, with their contemporary engineering and logistics knowledge. The building of the two 250-ton trains, and the tracks on which they rolled, was a remarkable collaboration between several of the film's departments and a major engineering feat by any standard. Originally, the production planned to utilize existing track in a different part of New Mexico. Explains Hayslip, "They had already started construction on Colby down in the southern part of the state, which was chosen because there was already some railroad track there that could be used. But upon scouting it, we found that we would have to upgrade that track in order to travel up to thirty miles per hour on it, as well as build extra track and share it with the mining company that owns it. We immediately shifted gears and started the process of building our own track and trains."

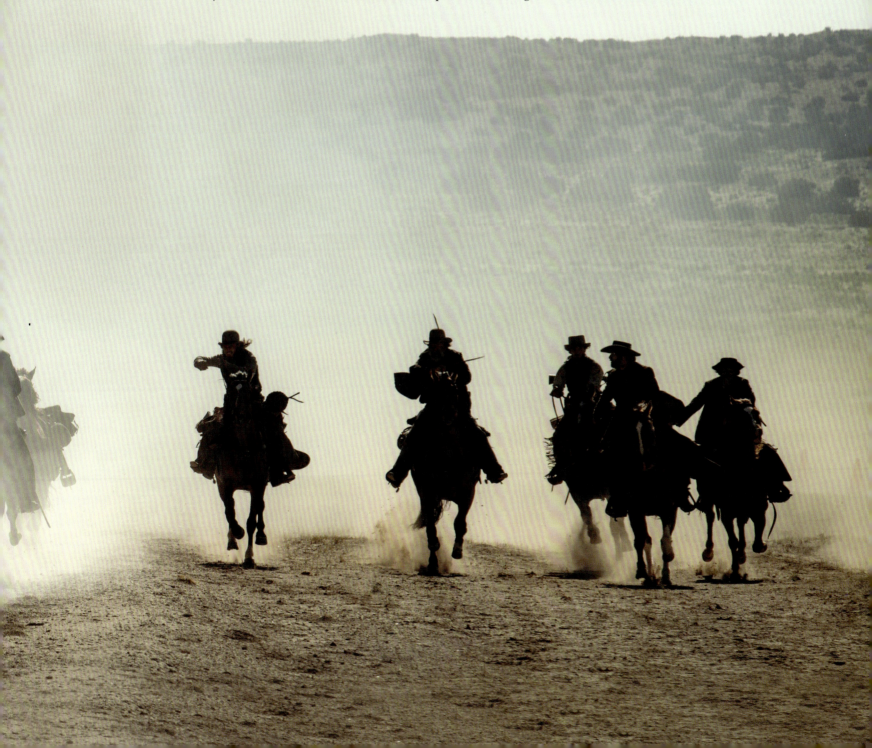

THESE PAGES: The Cavendish Gang gallops toward the Colby passenger train where Butch is imprisoned.

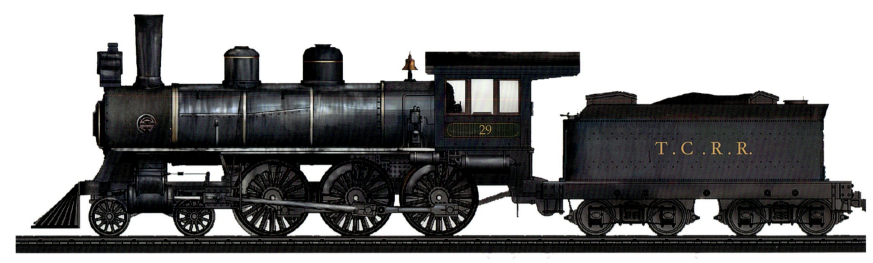

The towns of Colby and Promontory Summit were built with five miles of track surrounding them in an oval, along with a couple of miles of double track so Verbinski could shoot side-by-side train sequences. The construction of these tracks required sixteen weeks of building by Gandy Dancer, an Albuquerque-based railroad and excavating service company under the supervision of Joey Hutchens. Gandy Dancer hauled in 3,889,425 pounds of the thirty-three-foot rail, bars, tie plates, and ties on eighty-two flatbed truckloads from Blythe, California. A whopping 60,429 pounds of bolts, washers, and turnouts were sent on two flatbed trucks from Kansas City, and 402,000 pounds of ties and spikes from Stockton, California. Once the materials were collected, the company set to work building something akin to a whole new railway line in the dusty Rio Puerco desert, and another mile of track also had to be laid for the Sleeping Man Mine location in Creede, Colorado, for additional train work there.

UNDER THEIR OWN STEAM

Now all that was needed was the trains to go on the tracks. And back in a Sun Valley, California, workshop, nine-time Academy Award–nominated special effects coordinator John Frazier was doing exactly that, building two full-size trains, the historic Jupiter and what came to be known as the Colby train, which was later converted into Latham Cole's train, the Constitution. The trains were period authentic down to the last detail, save for two important things: First of all, the locomotives would work on modern hydraulic power rather than steam, and second, the railway cars were all built like shipping containers, so that they could be lifted on and off the train chassis or the flatbed trucks that comprised the road rigs. "The trains have hydraulic hoses going up into the coal cars, known as tenders, where we hide two one-thousand-horsepower Cummins diesel motors," explains Frazier. "We have special effect steam and black smoke to give the illusion that they're period trains." Frazier built the locomotives for the trains, while the art and construction departments designed and built the fifteen period railroad cars. Since the locomotives were not actually powered by steam, he had to be concerned about realistic smoke effects—and how to control them! "When we got into building the trains," Frazier explains, "it wasn't about just trains anymore; it was also about the smoke. When you use a real train, you can't control the smoke, and Gore wanted us to come up with a way to make and control black smoke so he could put it anywhere he wanted. That was a real challenge; nobody has ever been able to do that. You can burn rubber tires, like we did in the past before we knew how bad that was, or use black chemical smoke, but you can't control it. After months of testing, we were able to harness the beast. We took our big smoke generators and mounted them into a high-reach lift and put that on a train car moving on the tracks and blowing smoke in any which direction necessary so that even when we weren't using the locomotive on camera, we could still see the smoke drifting above the rest of the railway cars."

LARGER THAN LIFE

In terms of design, visual consultant Crash McCreery points out that the trains in *The Lone Ranger* are "built bigger than they actually were in that time period, because Gore wanted to give audiences a sense that these things were beasts tearing through the country. The Colby train was a utilitarian passenger train, but Cole's train, the Constitution, was much more elegant, and it was fun to design his lounge and dining cars. It had to be a very opulent, masculine environment." Art directors Domenic Silvestri and Naaman Marshall were assigned to work only on the trains, and they took their inspiration both from history and the needs of the fictional film. As such, they definitely took liberties with the two vehicles that met head-to-head at Promontory Summit for the Golden Spike ceremony on May 10, 1869. As Silvestri notes, the film's Jupiter train, aka Central Pacific No. 60,

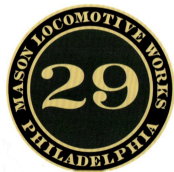

ABOVE AND OPPOSITE TOP: Concept illustrations of the film's trains, which, although period correct, were tweaked to emphasize their threatening, ironclad intrusion into the pristine American landscape.

RIGHT: One of the locomotives under construction in special effects supervisor John Frazier's workshop.

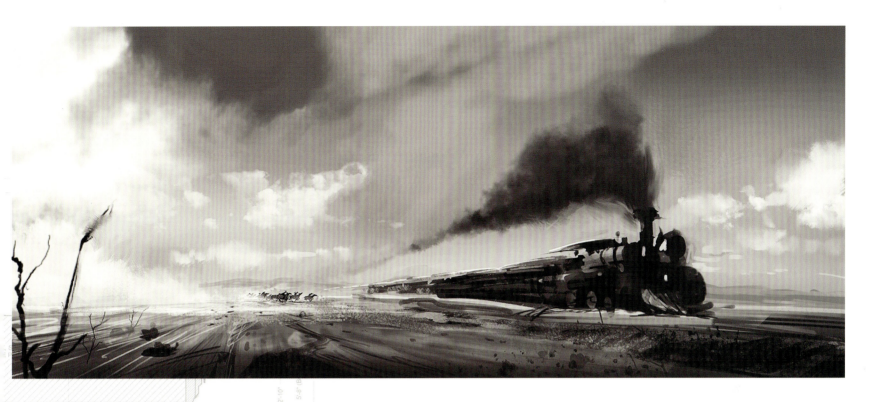
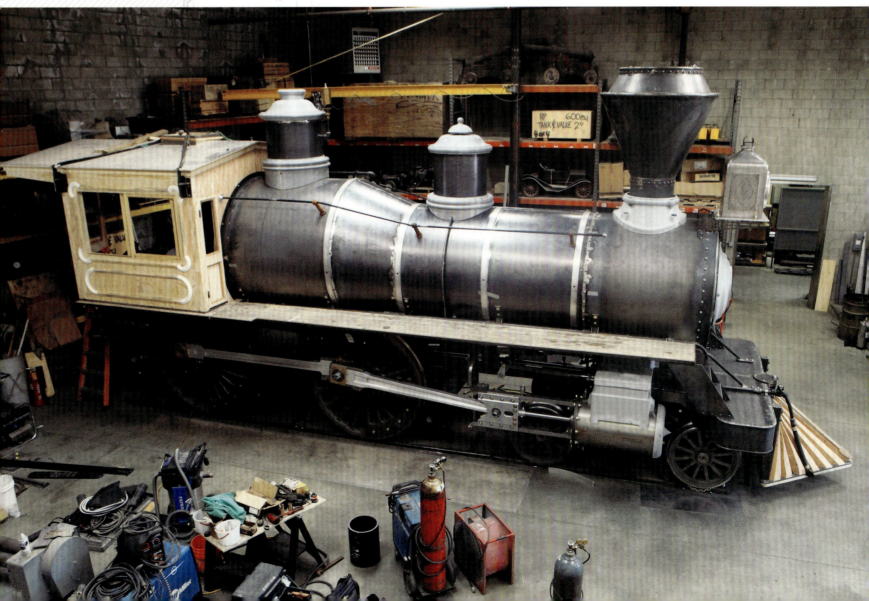

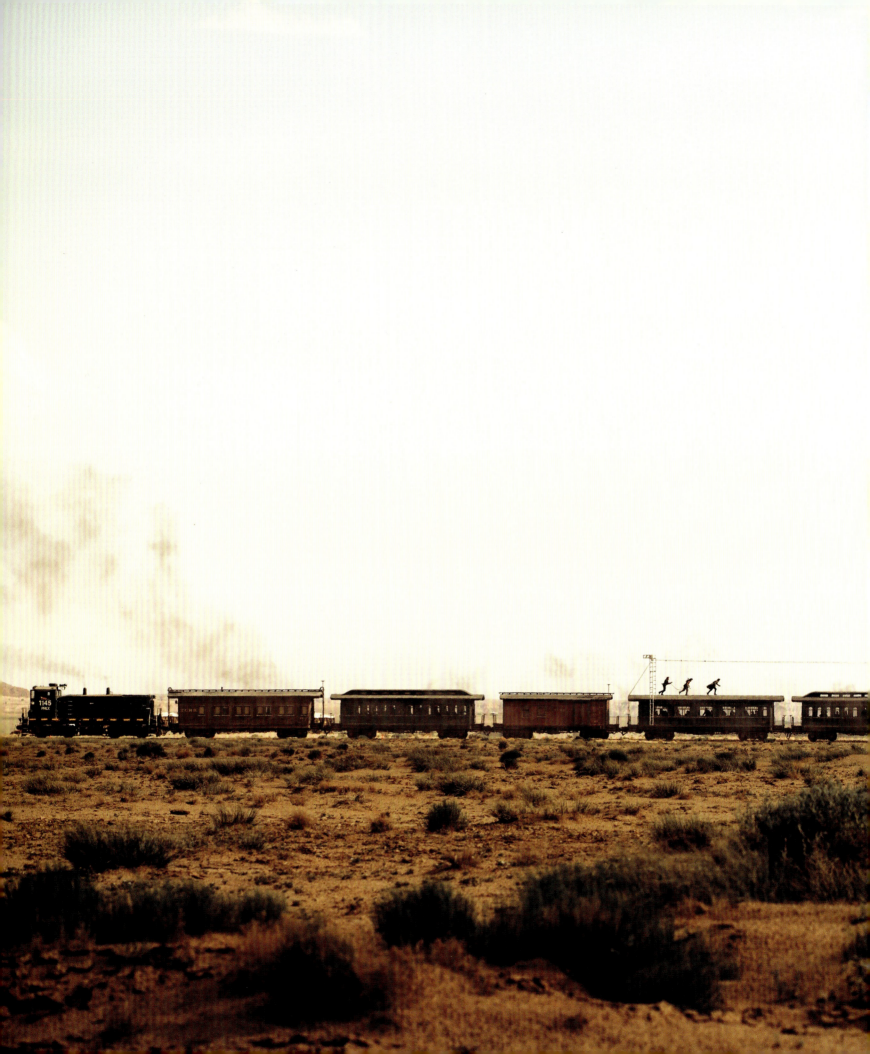

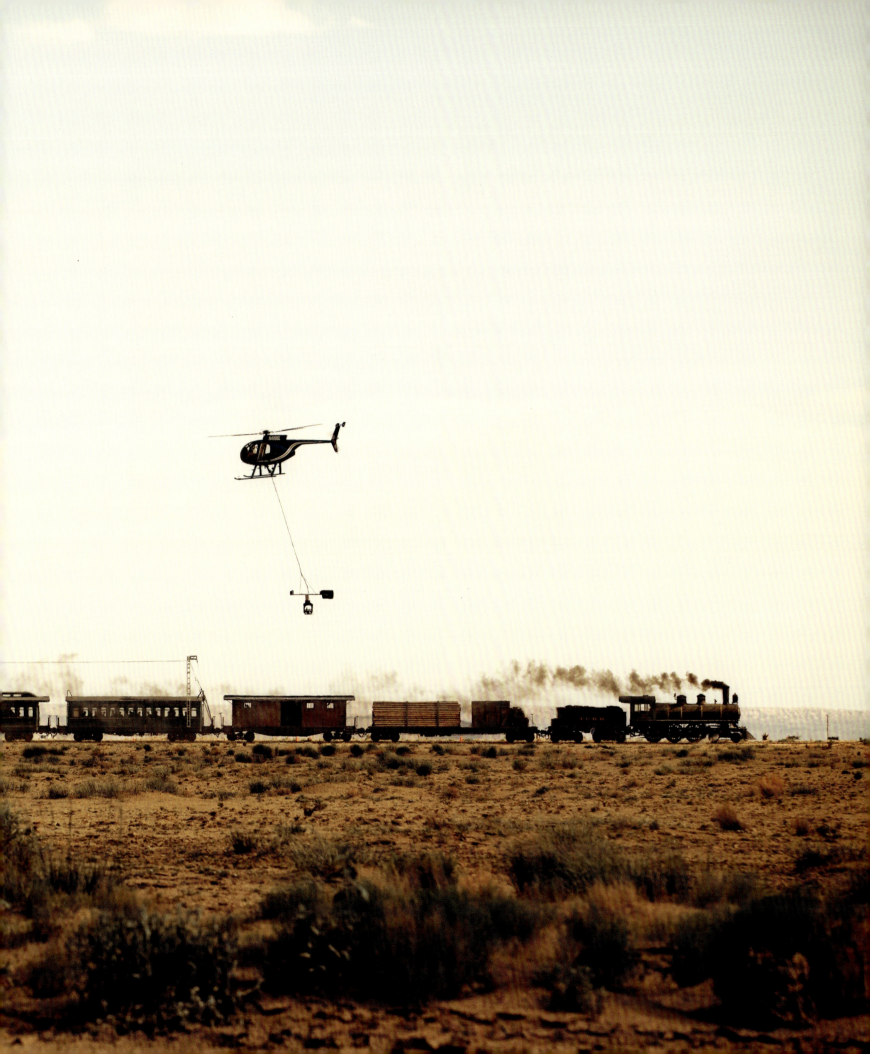

21ST CENTURY LOCOMOTION

The trains were driven from a computer inside of the cab, and if Gore Verbinski was filming inside of the locomotive, the controls were moved back into one of the cars. However, a real train engineer was needed to control the braking system, so that in case of an emergency he could override the safety brake, which was the only control not computerized. But all new, innovative, and basically experimental technologies are fraught with potential problems, and the locomotives were no exception. "Our own Jaws story," notes Verbinski, "is that sometimes, like Bruce the Shark, the trains just didn't work." So although Frazier engineered the trains to go thirty miles per hour, when the locomotives weren't functioning, or when it was necessary for them to provide more power than they were capable of, modern diesel locomotives were put in play to either tow or push the period trains.

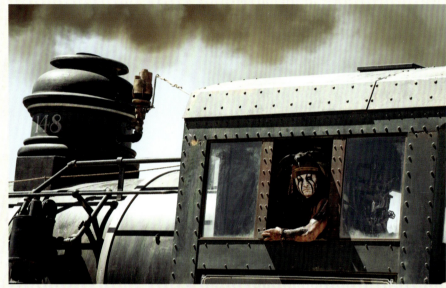

PAGES 118-119: Astounding view of a sweeping helicopter shot capturing action on the Colby train in the Rio Puerco, New Mexico, location.

TOP: Tonto at the controls of the Constitution.

OPPOSITE: Gore Verbinski oversees a remote controlled crane shot that involves Rebecca Reid struggling with Butch Cavendish atop a moving railway car.

PAGES 122-123: With its locomotive belching smoke like a monster from hell, the Constitution pulls into the Silver Man Mine on a less than savory mission.

"is relatively close to the real thing," but the Constitution diverges from the historic train simply known as Union Pacific No. 119. "The Constitution is tied to the character of Latham Cole, so it's more about his character than being historically accurate," he says. "We looked at a lot of photographs of the period when designing the Constitution, and Gore wanted it to be big and mean looking, a black and silver coal-burning villain as opposed to the wood-burning Jupiter." The locomotives of the Jupiter and Constitution were also remarkably authentic down to the last detail, including the plaques adorning their exteriors.

In constructing the trains, Naaman Marshall explains that "the first step was bringing in a train department headed by Jason Lamb and Luke Johnson, to tell us exactly what specifications are required in the building of railway cars. The practical train chassis was made to look old. But in designing and building the cars, we had to look at what was taking place inside of them, including shootouts and horses running through, so each one had its own set of parameters. We started out with a steel chassis, then built a steel frame that was designed to lift off the chassis. We also built "wild walls" in the cars, so that every wall of the train could be removed for lighting and filming."

Set decorator Cheryl Carasik made certain to decorate the interior of the railroad cars with objects that would swing to the motion of the train, even down to curtains with trim on the edge especially chosen for their movement. As for Latham Cole's personal train cars, Carasik admits that "they're a little over-the-top for a man, but Cole is over-the-top."

ENGINES OF DESTRUCTION

THE FINAL, MASSIVE ACTION SEQUENCE of the film also required specially designed trucks to tow railroad cars during the road rig work. "The third act train sequence traverses many different looks," explains Tom Hayslip. "It starts in the desert, then goes to high scrub, then down to low hills, then foothills, and on to alpine. Of course, we weren't able to find rail track traversing all those looks, so we thought early on that we could instead bring our train into those environments. The road rigs are our actual train cars, lifted off and placed onto flatbed trailers, some of them up to seventy-five feet long."

With extensive need for actors and stunt players to perform on the roofs of the trains, platforms had to be built on the sides of the railroad cars, with camera-mounted Technocranes capturing the action. "But once we got all that stuff on," Hayslip continues, "we still had to get down the road. So we've got a ten-foot-wide train, six-foot-wide Technocrane platform on one side, and ballast—usually big water barrels—to keep it steady on the other side. Meanwhile, some of those rural roads we shot on were only twenty-two feet wide, so we would be clearing the trees by maybe two inches."

To Armie Hammer, working or even observing the road rigs was nothing short of awesome. "When you see the rigs working their way down a highway, almost one hundred feet long and followed by support vehicles and police cars behind them, it's breathtaking. After about an hour of shooting, all the townspeople are lined up on the side of the road, never having seen anything like it. Just the magnitude of it is amazing."

All that was needed then were actors crazy enough to actually stand on top of trains moving upwards of forty miles per hour down mountain roads with hairpin curves and long drops below. Luckily for Gore Verbinski and Jerry Bruckheimer, they found them. Says William Fichtner, "I'll tell you one thing . . . it gets your heart rate going. It's great, thrilling, takes your breath away, but yeah, a little scary." In one scene, Ruth Wilson, as Rebecca Reid, is dragged by Fichtner's Butch Cavendish to the top of the train. "Bill spins me around and threatens to push me off the side of the train," she recalls. "So I've got one foot on and one foot off the train, going about thirty miles per hour. It was incredibly exhilarating!"

Adds Barry Pepper, who plays the film's eccentric Captain Fuller, "Just driving up and down through the mountains and forests, seeing this amazing scenery, doing all these gunfights as the trains are careening around these corners—it was absolutely incredible. You get the real rush of wind coming in, branches hitting the side of the train, people bouncing and rattling all over the place, lanterns swinging, and it's just alive and electric. It's something you just can't create on a soundstage. It was incredible what Gore pulled off. I mean, he had Johnny Depp running on top of the train, with me shooting at him through the ceiling. It was a testament, too, to what Disney was willing to do to change the paradigm of the cowboy movie. The Western will forever be changed after this. That's what Jerry, Gore, and Johnny do, and it's amazing to be a part of it."

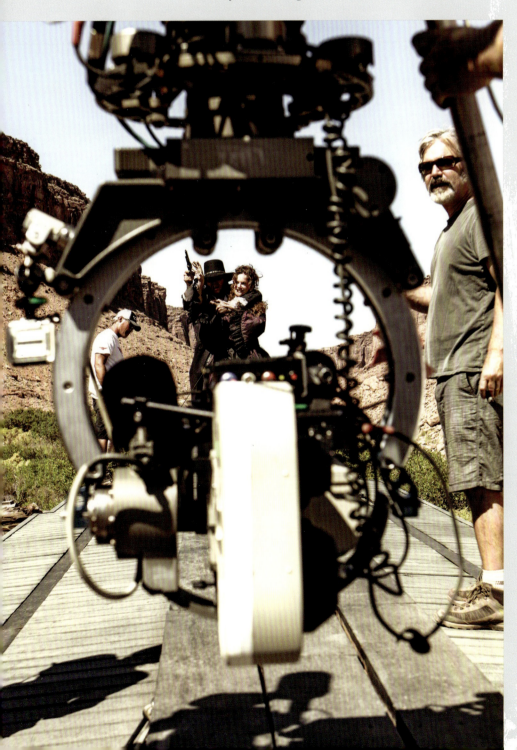

RIDING (& BUILDING) THE RAILS 121

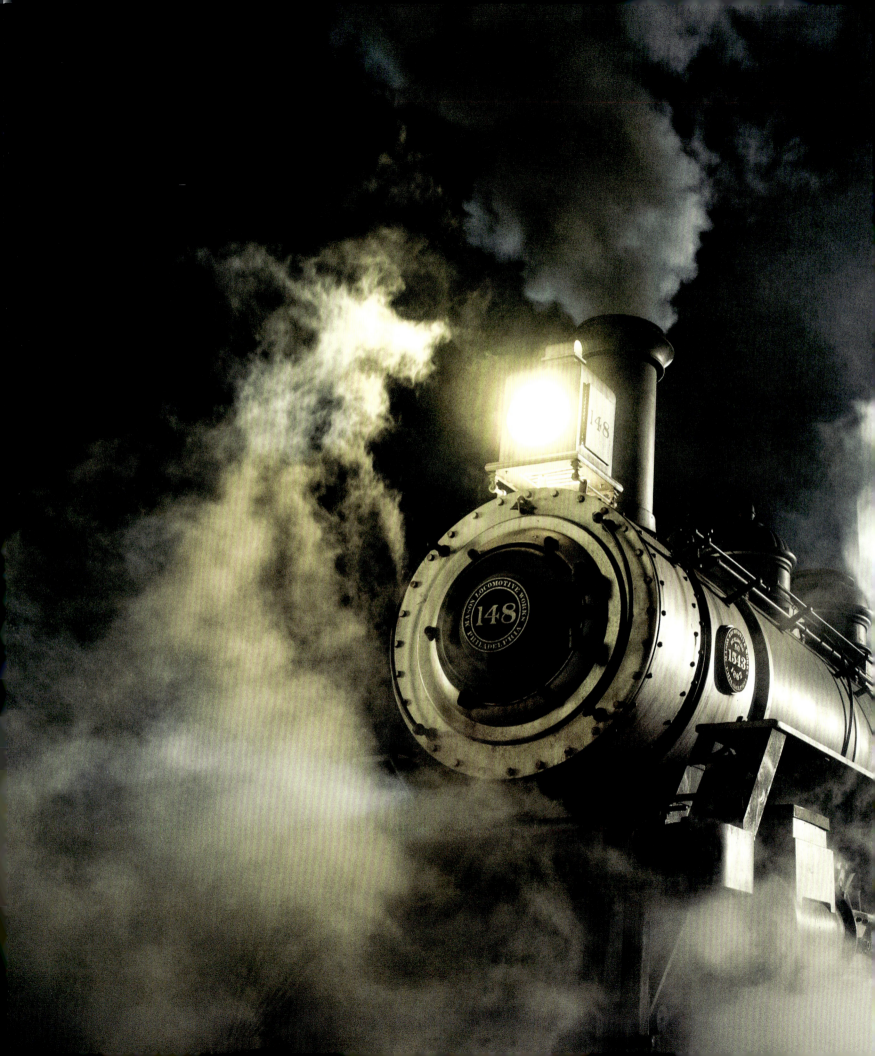

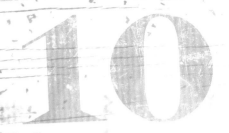

10

SILVER REDUX: THE EQUINE HERO RETURNS

THERE WAS TOM MIX'S TONY, ROY ROGERS'S TRIGGER, DALE EVANS'S BUTTERMILK, HOPALONG CASSIDY'S TOPPER, AND GENE AUTRY'S HORSE "CHAMPION," BUT ARGUABLY, NO EQUINE HERO OF CLASSIC WESTERNS EVER EQUALED THE FAME OF THE LONE RANGER'S SILVER. ALTHOUGH THAT "FIERY HORSE WITH THE SPEED OF LIGHT" WAS BELOVED BY MILLIONS ON THE RADIO PROGRAMS AND TELEVISION SHOWS, GORE VERBINSKI AND JERRY BRUCKHEIMER'S *THE LONE RANGER* GIVES THE HORSE SOMETHING HE DIDN'T REALLY HAVE IN PAST VERSIONS OF THE TALE: A DISTINCT PERSONALITY.

In fact, in the new movie, Silver possesses a beguiling combination of mystery, humor, majesty, eccentricity, and heroism. This Silver is a horse who suddenly appears in treetops and on the roof of a burning barn, a horse who recognizes something special about John Reid, even when he's already buried after being "killed" at Bryant's Gap. Silver is also a horse that drinks beer! "Something very wrong with that horse," notes Tonto to the Lone Ranger, puzzled by some of the animal's behavior. But Tonto also knows that the animal is John Reid's "spirit horse," a being that recognizes the young man as a "spirit walker," one who has been to the other side and returned. "Silver is a scene-stealer," confirms Gore Verbinski. "He shows up in the most unexpected places."

With Silver featured so prominently in the film, it was incumbent upon the production to find not only the best animal for the role, but also the best person to train it. In that respect, the path was absolutely clear, and it led straight to Bobby Lovgren, acknowledged as the finest in the world at his very specialized profession. The South African–born Lovgren, who grew up in an equestrian family, was a stable manager and rider in his home country before moving to Los Angeles and learning the ropes under legendary movie horse trainers Glenn Randall Sr. and Corky Randall. Lovgren is now perhaps best known as the head trainer on Steven Spielberg's *War Horse*, but previously he devoted his skills to the likes of *Seabiscuit* and *The Mask of Zorro*. The key to his success is that Lovgren loves and understands horses, and that feeling seems to be mutual. "We have to find out what horses understand," says Lovgren. "Are we communicating with them properly? And then making sure they're comfortable

OPPOSITE: Silver helps himself to a bottle of beer in Hell on Wheels.

BELOW: Anthony Leonardi III's artwork depicting the Lone Ranger dragging a roped Butch Cavendish to justice truly captures the atmosphere and spirit of the film.

PAGES 126–127: Sharing Silver, the Lone Ranger and Tonto (with frilly parasol) make their way through burning desert sands. This scene was filmed in the rugged White Wash Sand Dunes near Moab, Utah, with the crew getting from one location to another on dune buggies.

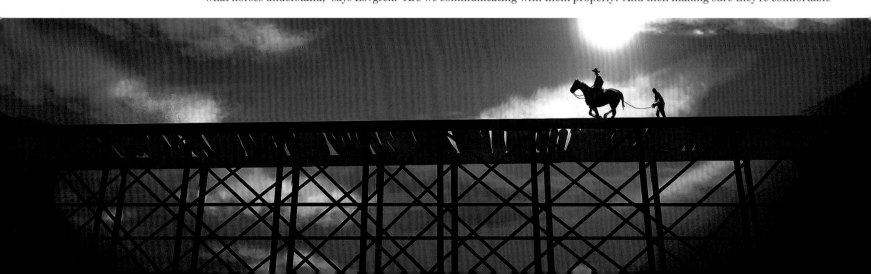

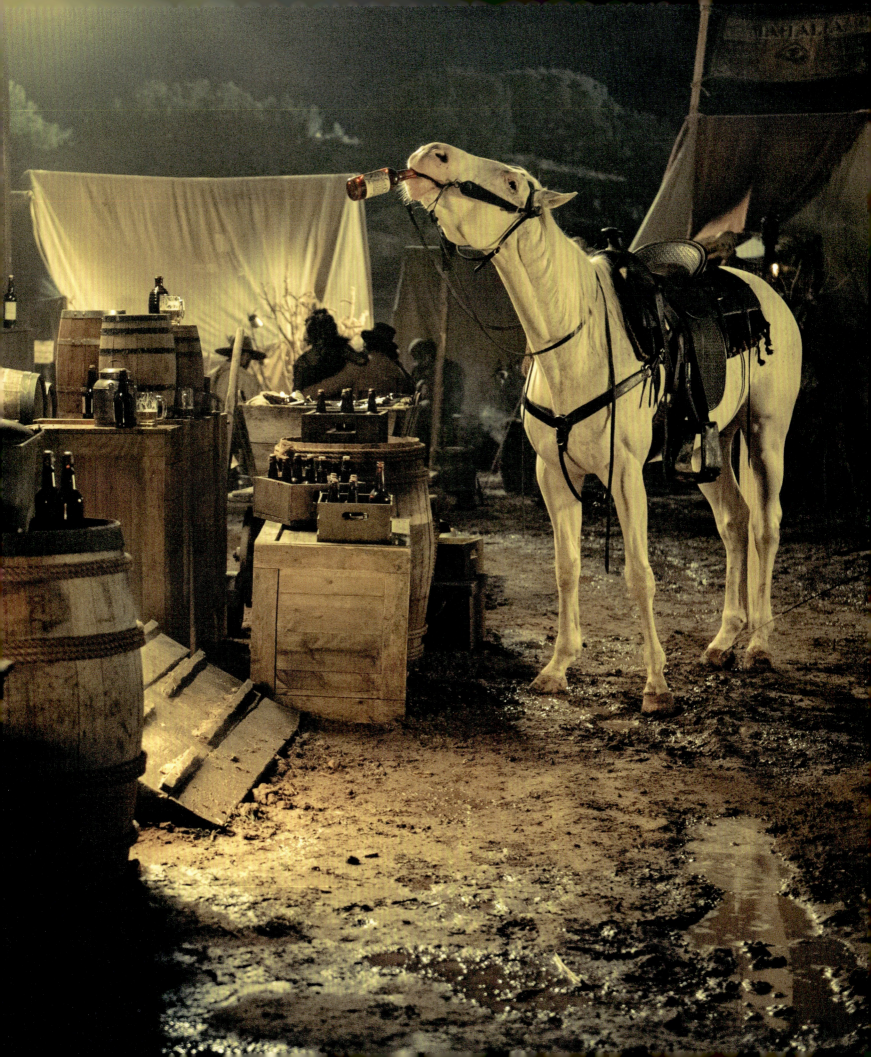

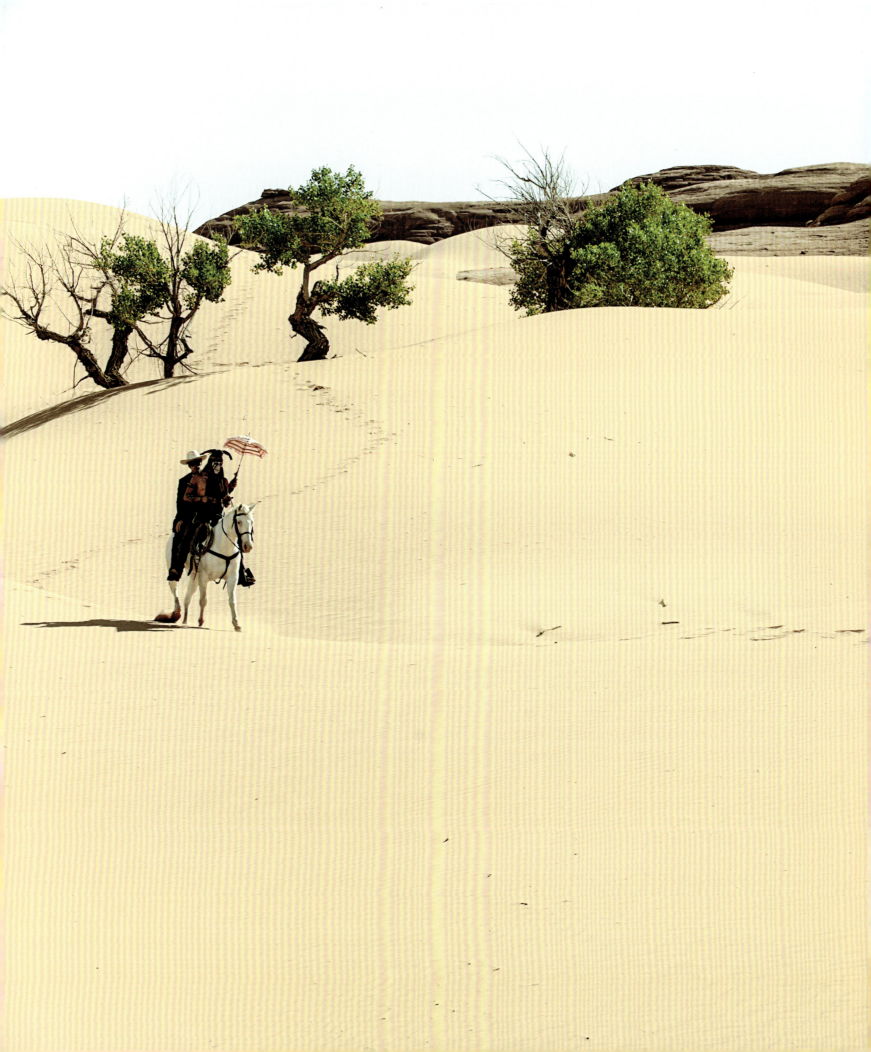

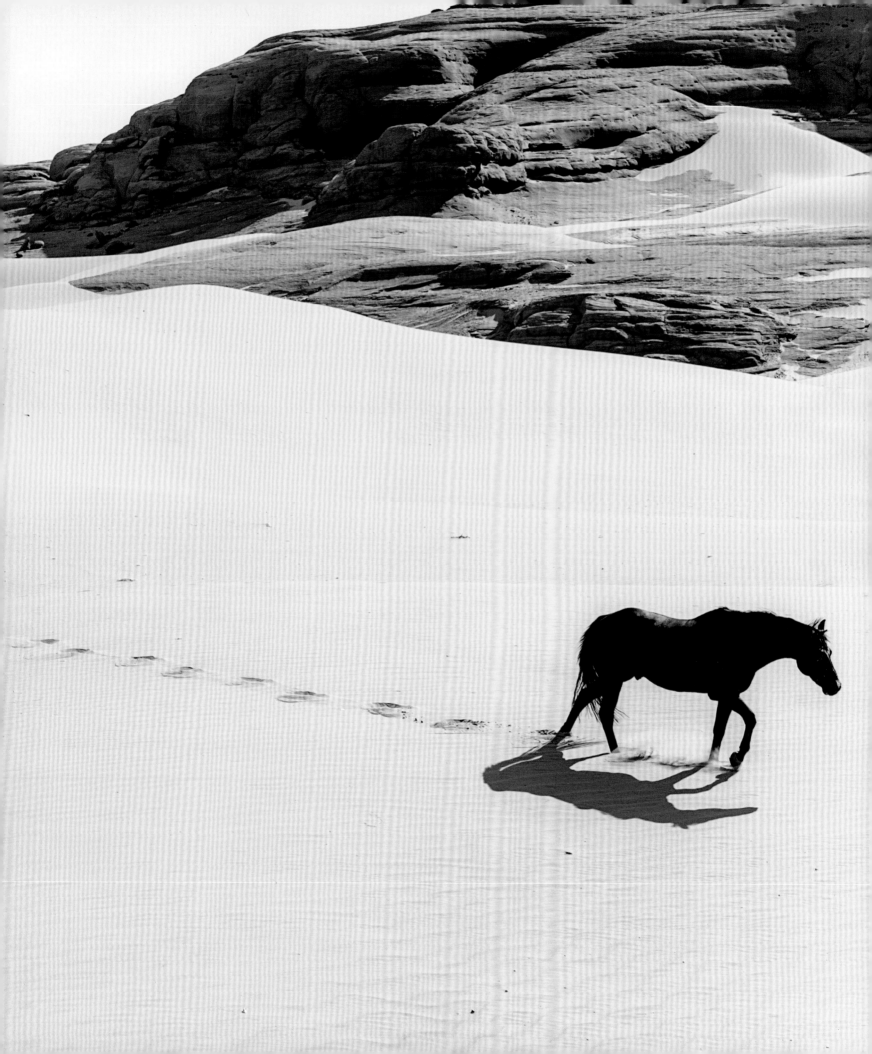

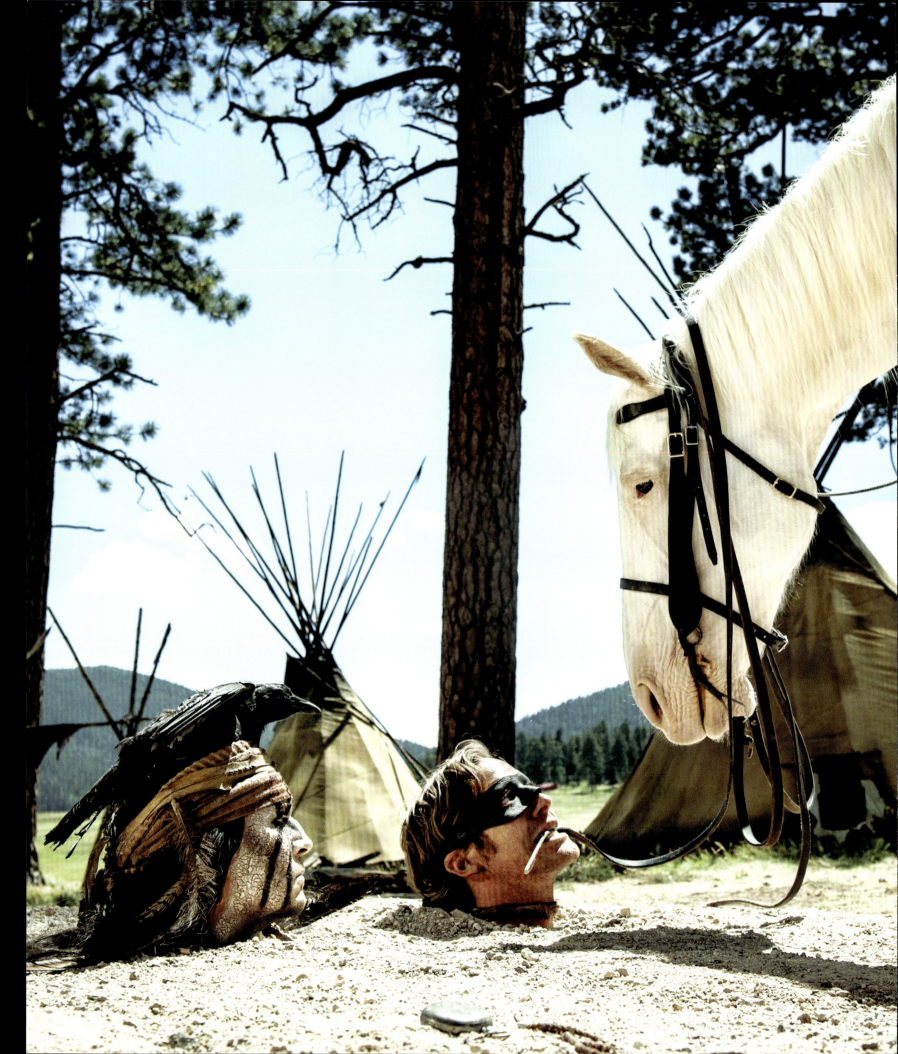

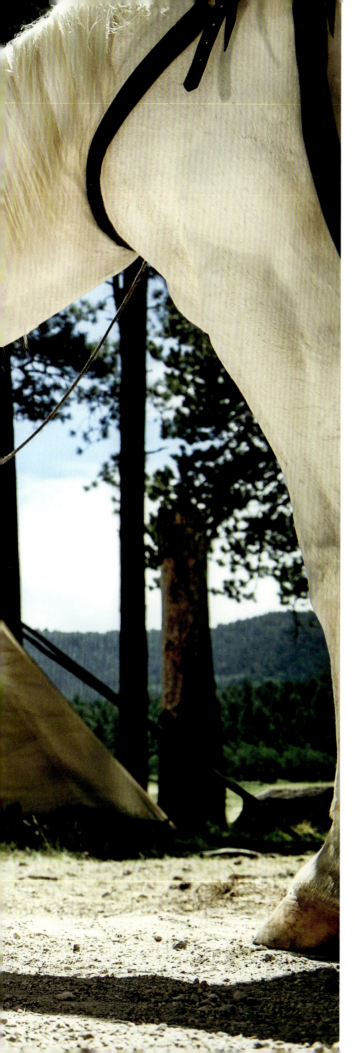

and enjoying it. We always try to make it easy for them, and that's why I do short lessons. I'll do a lot of them in the day, but never so that it's strenuous for them. That way they pay more attention, just like a little kid."

Lovgren notes that, when seeking the perfect horse to portray Silver, "you have to find ones that play and look the part. You have to find out what their personalities are, what they can and can't do, whether they jump well, or can stand quietly for a long time. All these things are very important." Luckily, the "hero" horse Lovgren chose to play Silver is also, incredibly enough, actually named Silver. Lovgren had already worked with the ten-year-old Thoroughbred–quarter horse mix a few years back. "It was nice going in with a horse that I knew and could rely on," he says.

EQUINE CASTING

ALTHOUGH SILVER PERFORMED most of the actions the role required, Lovgren also cast several other white horses, among them Leroy, Parrot, and Cloud, for specific actions. It's Cloud who races across the rooftops of Promontory Summit, a sequence that took weeks of preparation with Lovgren, the horse wranglers, and stunt rider Lyn Clarke. "That whole sequence was an unknown," admits Lovgren, "because that had never been done before, to my knowledge. Our biggest concern, as it is every day, is the animal's safety, making sure there was no room for error. We had a lot of rehearsals on lower containers, and for that sequence, we patterned the horses so that whenever they went up there they did exactly the same thing over and over again, which normally on a film set never happens because things change from scene to scene."

Tonto's mount, known as Scout in the classic television series, was played by two American paint horses, one called Sergeant and the other—believe it or not—called Scout! Lovgren began training Silver, Scout, and the other horses four months before filming began, at a facility called Horses Unlimited, a few miles from Albuquerque Studios. "It's always the slower things that are much more difficult," notes Lovgren. "Running, jumping, those are relatively easy. But standing there doing a certain behavior, like picking up a hat, or a bottle, many times in a row, you find out how patient a horse is. The question is how many times the horse can do it before I have to switch to the double, because everything we do is backed up by another horse."

Sometimes Lovgren was challenged by not only the horses' limitations, but his own as well, particularly for a shot of the Lone Ranger and Tonto sitting on their horses on the edge of a cliff at John Ford Point in Monument Valley. "I'm not fond of heights, so that was scarier for me than it was for the horses," he confesses.

OPPOSITE: The Lone Ranger entices Silver to rescue him and Tonto from an unhappy fate in a Comanche warrior encampment.

PAGES 130–131: Tonto believes that he can communicate with the "spirit horse"... and who's to say that he can't?

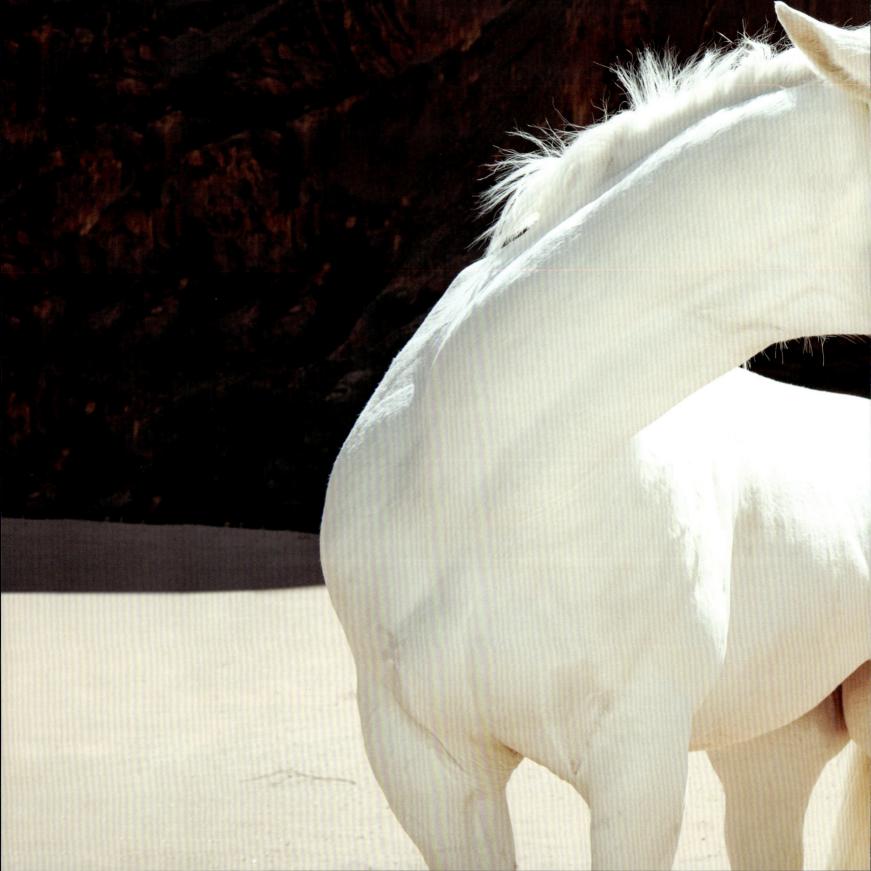

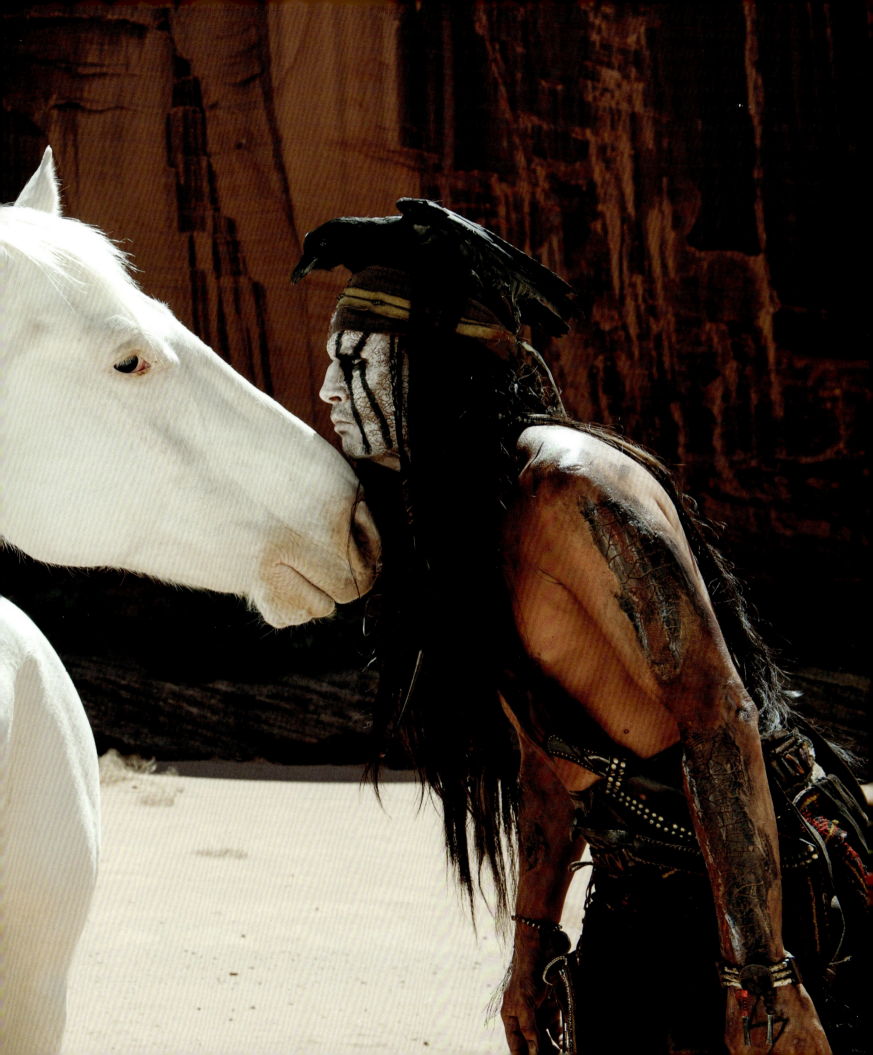

THE COMANCHE WAY

UNLIKE PREVIOUS INCARNATIONS OF THE LEGEND, IN THIS NEW VERSION OF THE LONE RANGER, THERE'S NO MYSTERY REGARDING WHICH NATIVE AMERICAN NATION TONTO BELONGS TO. AS JERRY BRUCKHEIMER NOTES, "IT MADE COMPLETE SENSE TO US GEOGRAPHICALLY, HISTORICALLY, AND CULTURALLY THAT, SINCE THE LONE RANGER IS FROM TEXAS, TONTO SHOULD HAVE BEEN BORN INTO THE GREAT NATION THAT HAD LIVED ON THOSE LANDS FOR GENERATIONS: THE COMANCHE."

At the height of its power, the Comanche Empire ranged from present-day eastern New Mexico to southern Kansas, all of Oklahoma, and most of northwest Texas. Known historically as being among the fiercest warriors in protecting their lands from the waves of outsiders who encroached upon them, and some of the greatest horsemen to traverse North America, the Comanche—who call themselves the Numunu—have survived culturally and linguistically against unbelievable odds. Although reduced in number from their population of some thirty thousand in the late eighteenth century, the Comanche today, based in Lawton, Oklahoma, remain strong and committed to their powerful history and promising future. Wahathuweeka-William Voelker, one of the greatest living repositories of his people's traditional knowledge, interpreted the Comanche's extraordinary way of life for the film. As the founder of Sia (the Comanche word for feather), the Comanche Nation Ethno-Ornithological Initiative conservation program, Voelker has bred more than four hundred eagles in captivity (many of them through revolutionary methods of artificial insemination) and restored their place in the natural order of Numunu spirituality.

OPPOSITE: Comanche warriors prepare to defend their village against the U.S. Cavalry.

BELOW: An authentic Comanche village constructed in Valles Caldera, New Mexico, including the *Numu kahni* (teepees) overseen by technical adviser Wahathuweeka-William Voelker.

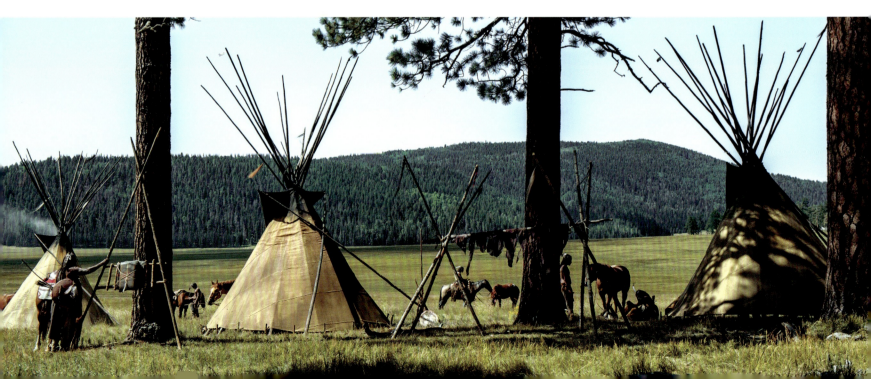

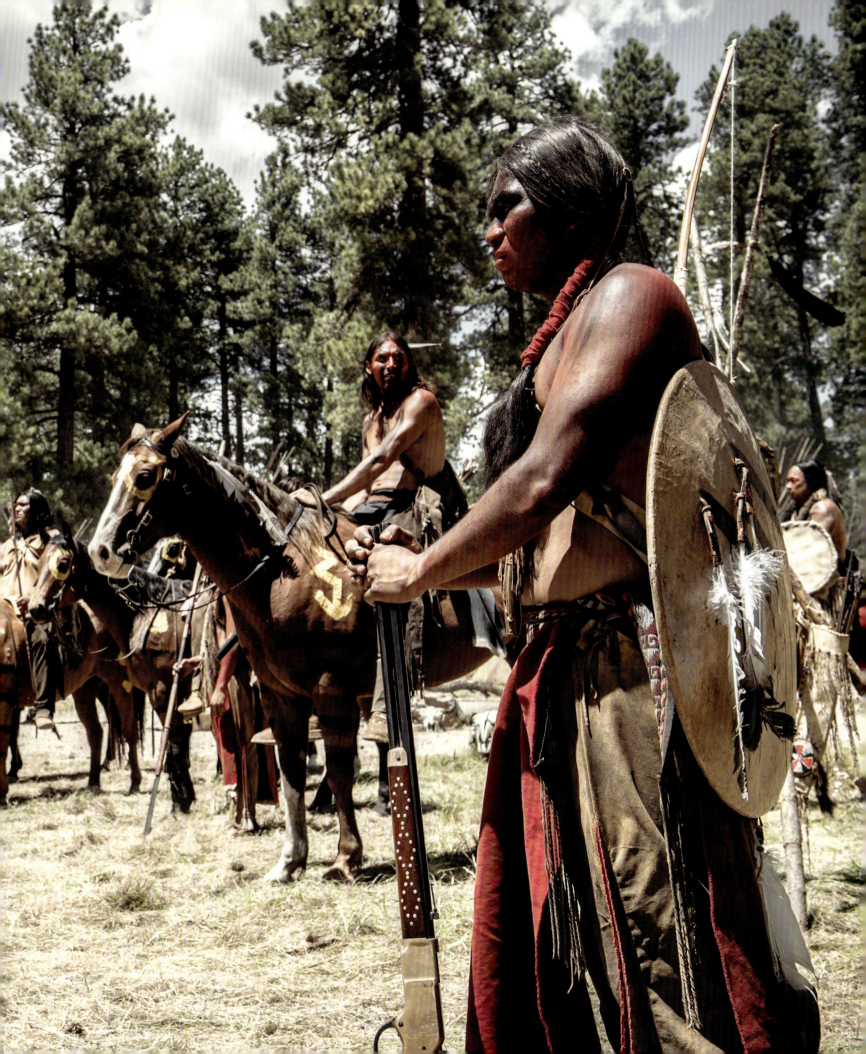

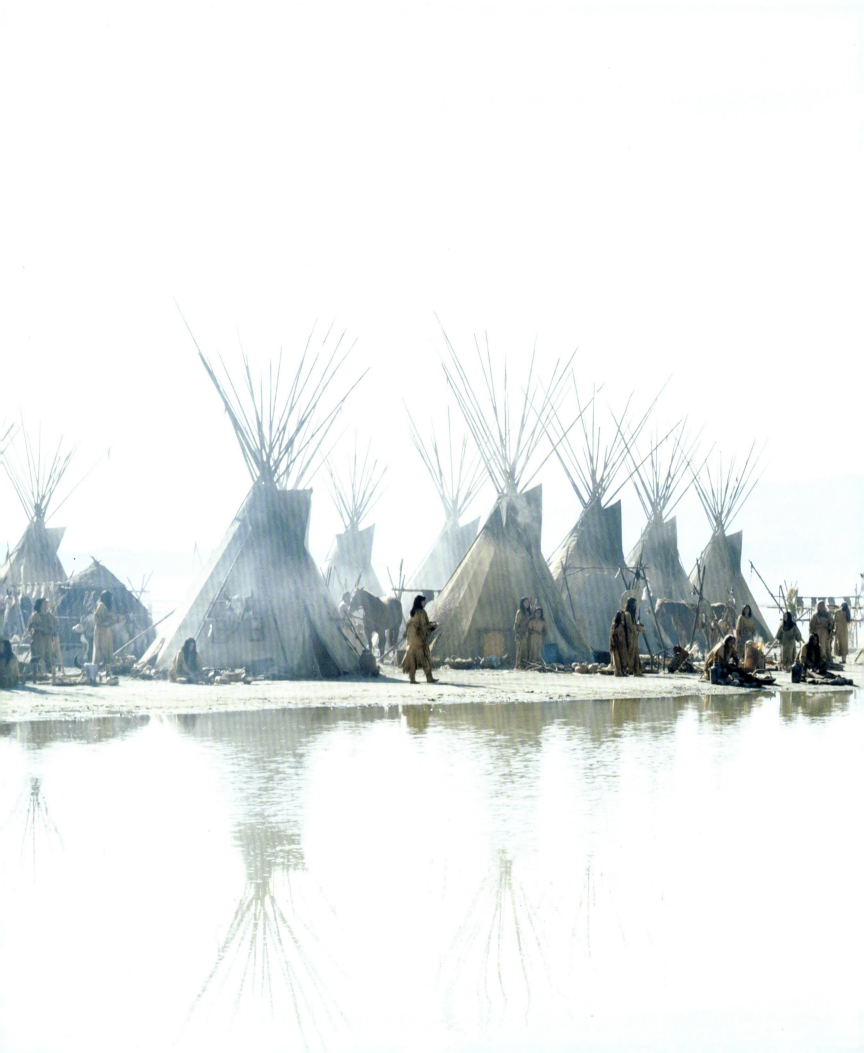

THESE PAGES: Young Tonto (Joseph Foy), holding his pet crow, brings two exhausted strangers into his village. This sequence, shot in Lone Pine, California, was the final scene to be filmed for *The Lone Ranger*.

PASSING ON THE PAST

Working on *The Lone Ranger* as a technical adviser along with Troy "The Last Captive," his longtime associate at Sia, Voelker served as a close consultant on the film to ensure historical and cultural accuracy on many levels. Voelker's wide range of responsibilities included coaching Depp on the Comanche language and assisting the production with accurate representations of Comanche *Numu kahni* (teepees), clothing, and weaponry. At the same time, however, he was also mindful that the film is a work of entertainment that occasionally takes dramatic license with the past. "Because of our life's work in cultural preservation, the movie industry at times will come knocking when there's an effort to involve historical accuracy," says Voelker. "Our primary work is preservation of culture and the eagle as a historical, spiritual, and ceremonial entity. But when it seems appropriate, we look at the project and agree to come on board, as we did with *The Lone Ranger*.

"We're not making a historical document with the film," continues Voelker, "but the production is committed to historical accuracy, to the extent to which it works for the film. We know we have to try to take a cooperative point of view on this. Not that we will compromise our culture, but we are focused on entertainment of the masses, done with sensitivity to our way of life. Unfortunately, we're living in a time where the Comanche people have fewer traditionally knowledgeable people, so anything of historical accuracy we can get before our young people is the primary reason we are involved."

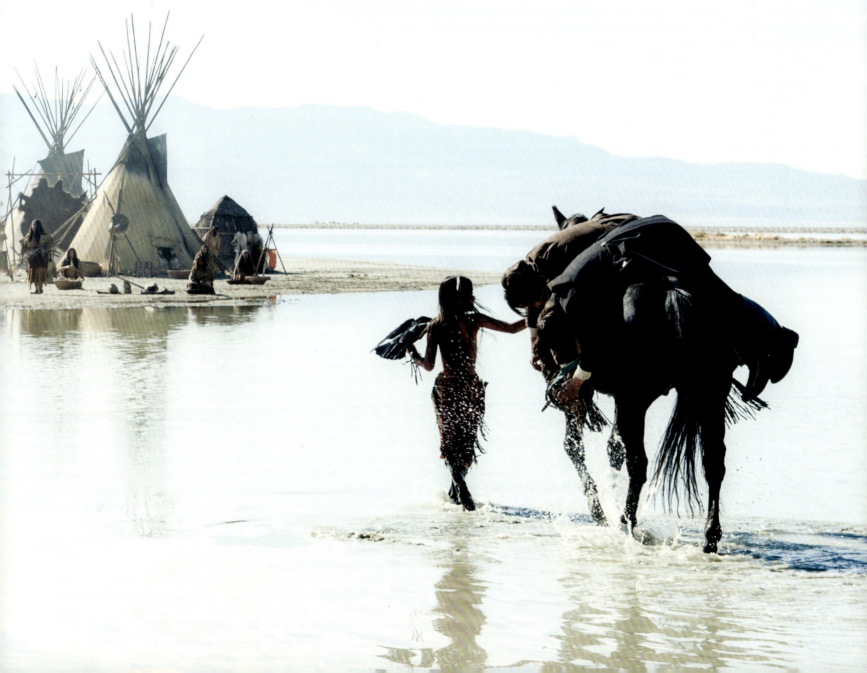

"We brought all the different departments together so that they could understand a little better about what we do and the living culture that we bring," Voelker continues, "and in dealing with them I can say with absolute certainty that they were all committed to working within an authentic historical framework." As a perfect example, Voelker and Troy worked in close collaboration with set decorator Cheryl Carasik, leadman David Manhan, and their team to develop and create accurate teepees for the Comanche camps in the film. Voelker proudly notes this is the first time such dwellings will be seen in a film. "We Numunu always get stuck with Northern Plains teepees, but this is one of the things that we got accurate in *The Lone Ranger*," he says. "Our *Numu kahni* had a four-pole foundation put together in a very specific way, and everything was built up from that. When you take into consideration that our villages were situated on the Southern Plains where there is nothing to break the wind, it was essential that our *Numu kahni* were set up in a way that fought back against the elements."

A NEW COMANCHE

THROUGHOUT PRODUCTION, Voelker and Troy were also pleased to develop a close relationship with Johnny Depp, advising him throughout the shoot on all manner of issues. "Johnny quickly revealed what a sensitive person he is, and a quick bond developed between us," says Voelker. "As a result of Johnny's great interest in who we are culturally, he has added words in Numunu that were not part of the original script where it seemed appropriate to call on our language. It's gratifying that he's so committed."

As one who has devoted years to the propagation of sacred birds, Voelker is uniquely qualified to address the most talked-about aspect of Johnny Depp's Tonto costume—the inanimate crow that adorns his head. "The crow is probably second only to the eagle in the level of medicine or power that the warrior would aspire to," explains Voelker. "We had an elite group of Comanche warriors, and the English translation of their name is the 'Crow Tassel Wearers,' of which I'm a direct descendant.

BELOW: The Lone Ranger tries to communicate with Comanche war chief Red Knee (Gil Birmingham, right).

A HAPPY MEDIUM

On *The Lone Ranger*, Bill Voelker and Troy worked closely with numerous departments, particularly production design, set decoration, and props, to find the middle ground between historical accuracy and the needs of the fictional film. "Gore has a very specific vision," confirms Voelker. "He's played these scenes over and over in his head many times. What we've been able to arrive at is a happy medium between what's absolutely historically accurate to us and what works within the palette that he has in mind. There's been a little bit of compromise, but not to the point where it's something we can't live with. We're making it work."

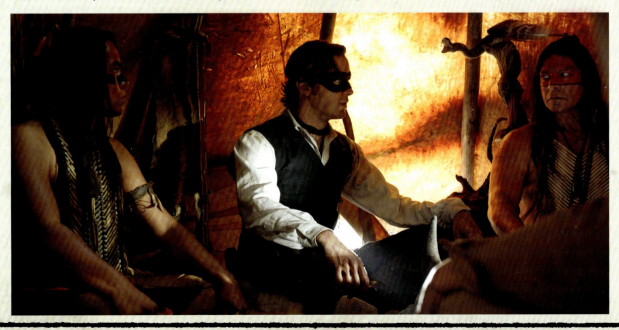

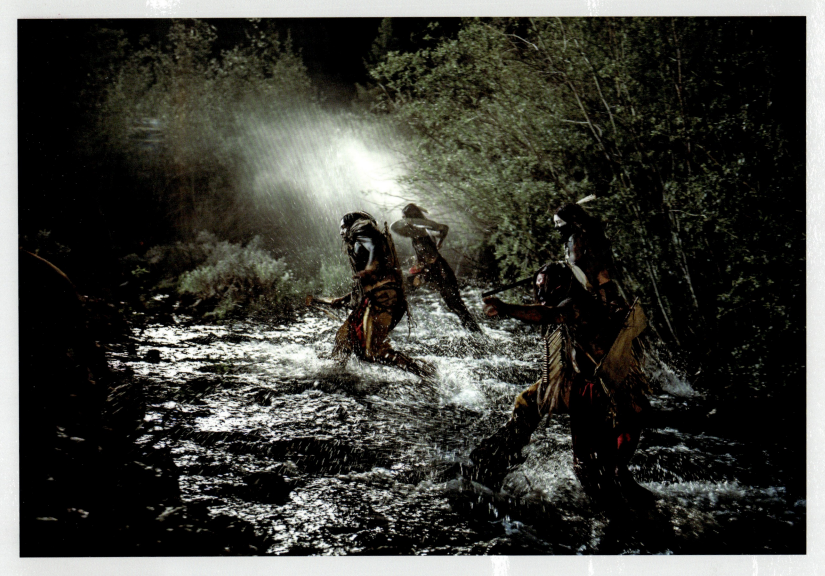

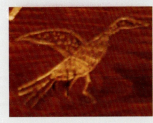

TOP: Comanche warriors make a desperate attack on the U.S. Cavalry at Silver Man Mine.

ABOVE: This petroglyph, based on ancient designs prevalent in the American Southwest, was hand-carved by visual consultant Crash McCreery inside of Tonto's diorama in the Wild West Exhibition tent set.

PAGES 138–139: Butch Cavendish's gang dressed as Comanche to give the false impression that homesteads are being attacked by the warriors.

The large cluster of crow and raven feathers on the head symbolize the fact that the individual was a member of this elite warrior society. The use of a whole bird or major parts of a bird on the head is something that transects many different tribal boundaries. It just so happens that with the Comanche, it is even more pronounced. So it's fitting that the Tonto character is one of us. A crow or feathers on the head is heavy-duty medicine, or spiritual energy, for our people."

The relationship between Wahathuweeka-William Voelker, Troy "The Last Captive," the Comanche Nation, and Johnny Depp continued beyond wrap. On September 29, 2012, just two days after completing seven grueling months of filming, Depp flew to Lawton, Oklahoma, to participate in the Comanche Nation Fair, fulfilling a promise he had made months earlier to the late tribal chairman Johnny Wauqua. In one very rainy and busy day, often in the company of Comanche tribal chairman Wallace Coffey, Depp rode side by side with his adoptive Comanche mother, LaDonna Harris, waving to cheering crowds in a soggy but joyous parade. He spoke eloquently in a gymnasium filled with Comanche children and teens along with Harris and Gil Birmingham, who portrays Red Knee in *The Lone Ranger* and is himself a Comanche. He also visited the beautiful Sia facility in nearby Cyril, Oklahoma, and paid his respects to the grave of the great Comanche chief Quanah Parker in a cemetery at Fort Sill, just across the road from the fairgrounds.

The love and warmth with which Depp was greeted by the Comanche people was returned to them in kind by the humbled and grateful actor. During his talk to those assembled in the gymnasium, Depp reminded the young people of their incredible heritage, saying that they could accomplish anything they wanted because they have the "warrior spirit" within them. As Depp discovered throughout the shoot, the survival of the Comanche is testament to a people of enormous inner strength and dignity who, unbowed, find their hopeful future in their proud past.

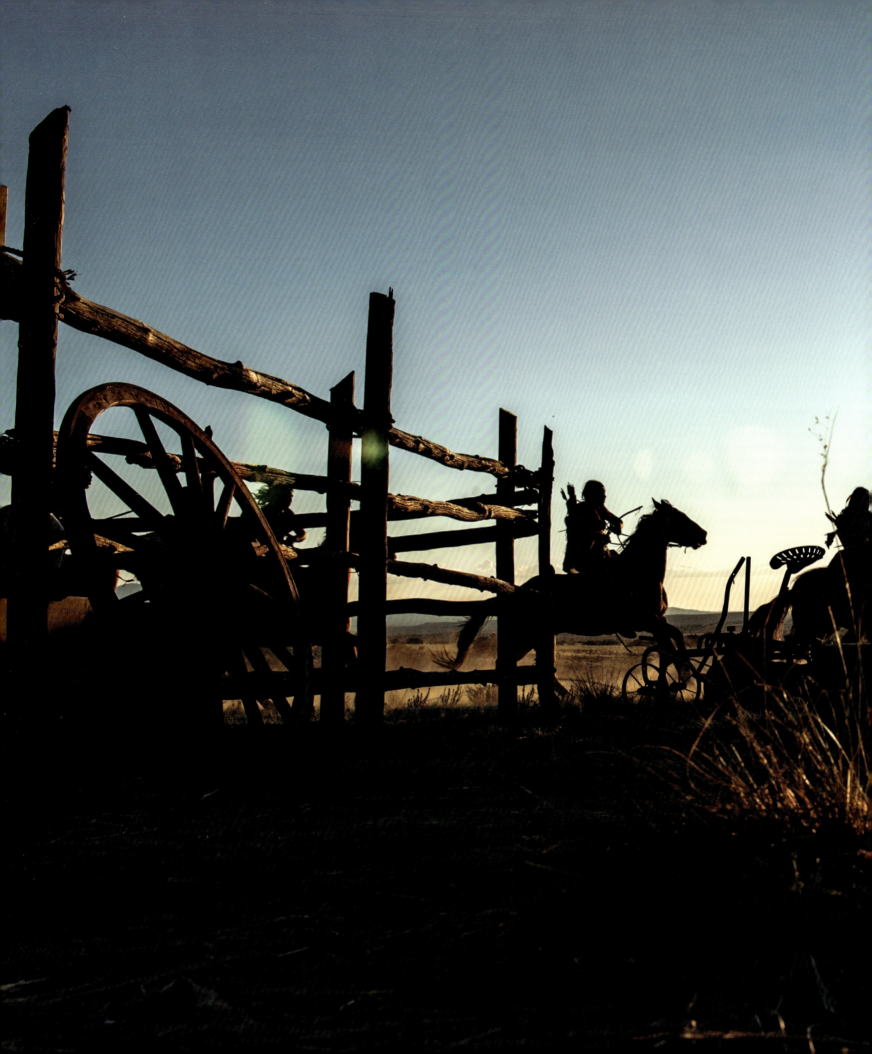

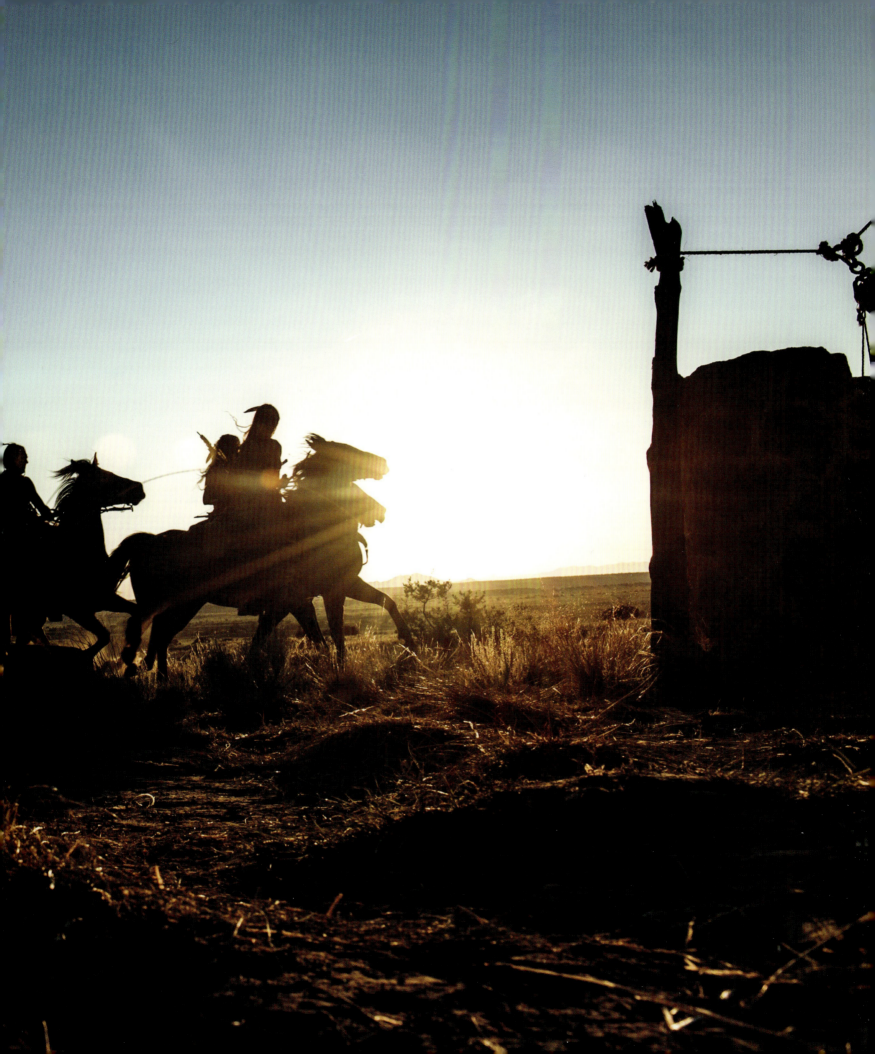

12

BOOT CAMP FOR COWBOYS & RAILROAD BUILDERS

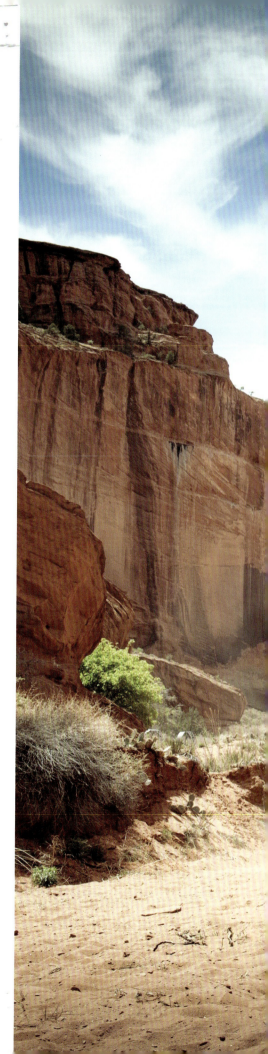

THE CAST AND BACKGROUND PLAYERS OF THE LONE RANGER DISCOVERED THAT IF YOU WANT TO BE A COWBOY, GUNSLINGER, OR RAILROAD BUILDER ON SCREEN, YOU'VE GOT TO GO BACK TO SCHOOL AND BE PROPERLY TAUGHT. "COWBOY BOOT CAMP" BEGAN THREE WEEKS BEFORE GORE VERBINSKI CALLED "ACTION" FOR THE FIRST TIME AND WAS ATTENDED BY THE VAST MAJORITY OF THE PRIMARY CAST AT THE HORSES UNLIMITED RANCH IN ALBUQUERQUE. THEIR TEACHERS INCLUDED STUNT MEN, HORSE WRANGLERS, PROP MASTERS, AND ARMORERS, AND NOBODY WAS CUT AN EASY BREAK—NOT EVEN THE GUY PLAYING THE FILM'S EPONYMOUS CHARACTER.

"Cowboy Boot Camp is basically all the actors running around like six-year-old boys," says Armie Hammer. "Horses for two hours a day, throwing lassos for an hour, shooting guns, riding in a wagon, putting on a saddle and taking it off, doing the tacking. It was like an immersion project. After just a few days of boot camp, I did more riding than I cumulatively had in my entire life."

"What Gore wanted," explains stunt coordinator Tommy Harper, "was to have a Cowboy Boot Camp where we basically teach each actor how to shoot a gun, how to saddle and ride a horse, along with other training. This way we get to know the actors, what their abilities are, and how to keep them safe. The main thing for me is to make sure that at the end of the movie they've done as much as they can do safely, and finish the movie being completely healthy." Although boot camp started before filming actually began, Harper points out that the actors' training went "all the way to the end. Just when you think you know everything, something backfires on you, so we never let them get too comfortable."

OPPOSITE: Butch Cavendish leads his gang in a scene shot in Canyon de Chelly.

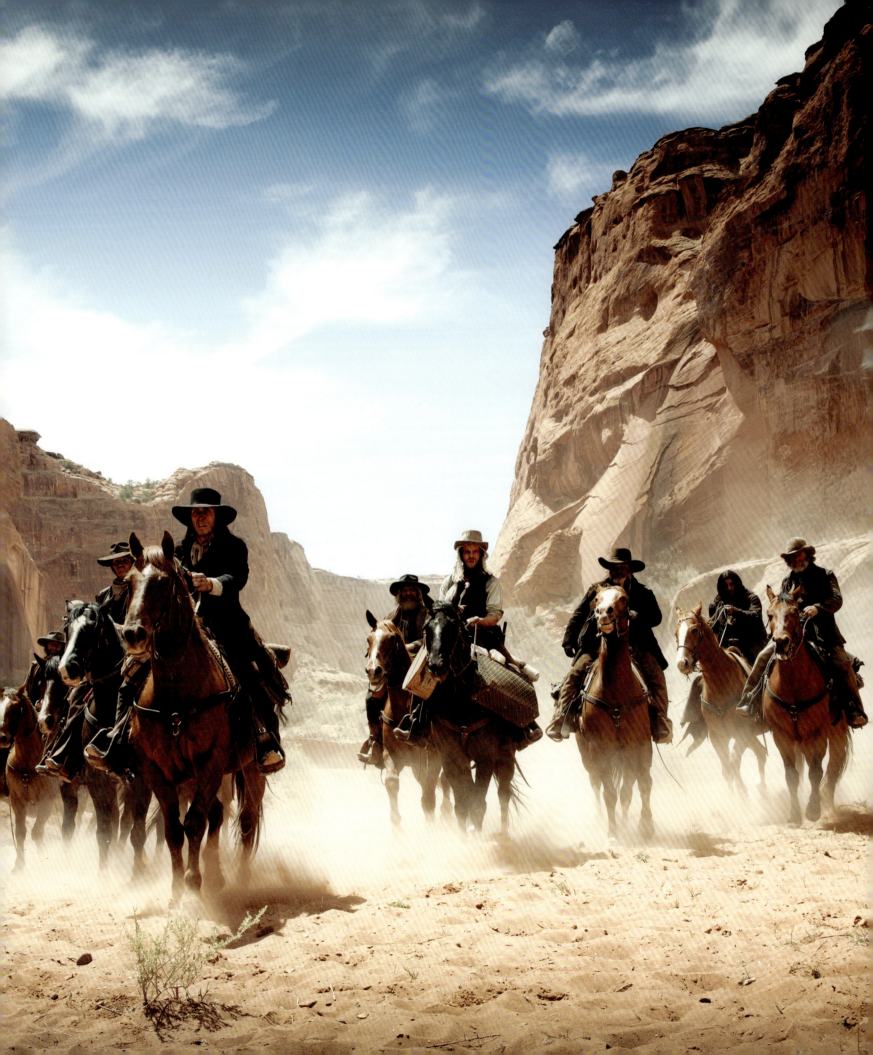

BUDDING GUNSLINGERS

CLEARLY, it was crucial for the actors to learn the correct handling of firearms, and for that they were under the expert tutelage of armorer Harry Lu. "Even though they're shooting blanks," notes Harper, "it's still a dangerous piece of equipment that they're working with, and we have to make sure that they know every bit of handling and how to look correct doing it." William Fichtner, who as ultimate badass outlaw Butch Cavendish had to feel absolutely secure with his weaponry, was glad to put himself in the safe hands of the experts. "With Mr. Harry Lu around, I'm comfortable with anything when it comes to firearms," says the actor. "It's hard . . . the first time you hold that heavy gun in your hand. But every time I would arrive on set and see Harry, I would ask him if I could handle the gun for a little bit, and he would always show me something new to practice, then show me a little more." After a time, Fichtner was doing dangerously cool flips and twirls with the gun, which were captured on film during shooting in Creede, Colorado. "You know why you try so hard with things like that?" asks Fichtner. "Because as an actor, you want little moments to equal everything else that's happening on this film. I wanted that gun move to be as good as the amazing backdrop and set we were shooting on in Creede."

While Lu was diligently working with the actors on the mechanics of firing six-shooters, shotguns, and Gatling guns, technical adviser and expert gunslinger Keith Meriweather demonstrated the finer points of gun handling, including quick draws and twirling. "I'm teaching them a little bit of fancy flourish," says Meriweather, who has been a stunt man for thirty years and performed in a Wild West show for three. "We want the actors to have a fluid, steady, smooth motion, so as they get comfortable doing things slowly, and all the body mechanics start to work together, the muscle memory starts taking over to the point where it becomes a natural thing."

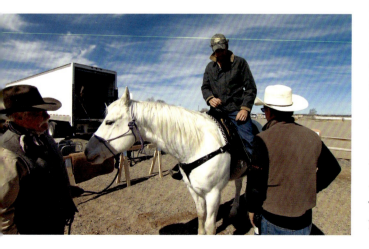

RIDING SHOTGUN

SCHOOLING THE TALENT on horsemanship were the film's crack wrangling team under the supervision of head horse wrangler Clay Lilley and wrangler gang boss Norman Mull. "A horseman can look at an actor and know that person can't ride a horse," says Harper. "You can just tell by how they walk up to it, or how they mount and dismount. So teaching them how to look correct was really important." Says Norman Mull, "What we're trying to do in boot camp is to get the actors comfortable with horses, pick horses for them, and teach them whatever we need to make sure they can ride. Some of the actors had some previous experience, including Armie Hammer and Ruth Wilson. "I've fallen off a few horses before," says Wilson with a laugh, "so I thought this was a good place to start learning properly." Wilson enjoyed being the only woman at boot camp. "Yeah, I loved it, surrounded by cowboys, it was quite fun. It was a really nice way of understanding the world of the movie."

The normally fearless Hammer, however, was actually a little nervous. "I'd been on horses before, but I thought, 'This animal thinks for itself, and that makes me a little nervous. What is it going to do if it sees a bunny?' But they don't give you a choice; they just stick you on a horse and say, 'Go ride.' It was nonstop fun for three weeks."

The other principal actors also had a blast at boot camp, although they acknowledged the rigors involved. "My experiences were very specific to my character, Captain Fuller," notes Barry Pepper. "He's a very rigid and proper officer who rides in an upright position, so the main focus was how to stay rigid in the saddle during a full gallop. The wranglers were just the best of the best and taught you how to properly position yourself, get your heels down, and just look like you know what you're doing."

James Badge Dale, the New Yorker who plays tough Texas Ranger Dan Reid in the film, had to come clean about his riding skills when he first met with Jerry Bruckheimer and Gore Verbinski. "I didn't have the job yet, and I met with the two of them," he recalls. "Jerry was just sitting quietly, as he often does, observing and listening carefully. Gore asked me if I knew how to ride a horse. I went back and forth with some story, and finally said, 'Gore, I'm sorry, I have no idea how to ride a horse. I'm from New York City!' Then Jerry suddenly starts laughing, and said, 'You're the first person who's come in here and told us the truth!' Then Gore added, 'Well, you're gonna learn.' And I did. I learned things about horses that I never thought I would. These wranglers are very good at what they do. They love their horses, and they teach you to respect them."

LEFT: Armie Hammer gets comfortable on Silver with the assistance of horse trainer Jess Brackenbury (left) and assistant prop master Curtis Akin (right).

OPPOSITE, TOP LEFT AND RIGHT: Armie Hammer and Ruth Wilson literally learn the ropes in Cowboy Boot Camp.

OPPOSITE, CENTER: Assistant prop master Curtis Akin inspects the saddles used for horse training.

OPPOSITE, BOTTOM LEFT: Armie Hammer and Silver get to know each other before filming begins.

OPPOSITE, BOTTOM RIGHT: Armorer Harry Lu teaches Ruth Wilson the fine points of firing a period pistol.

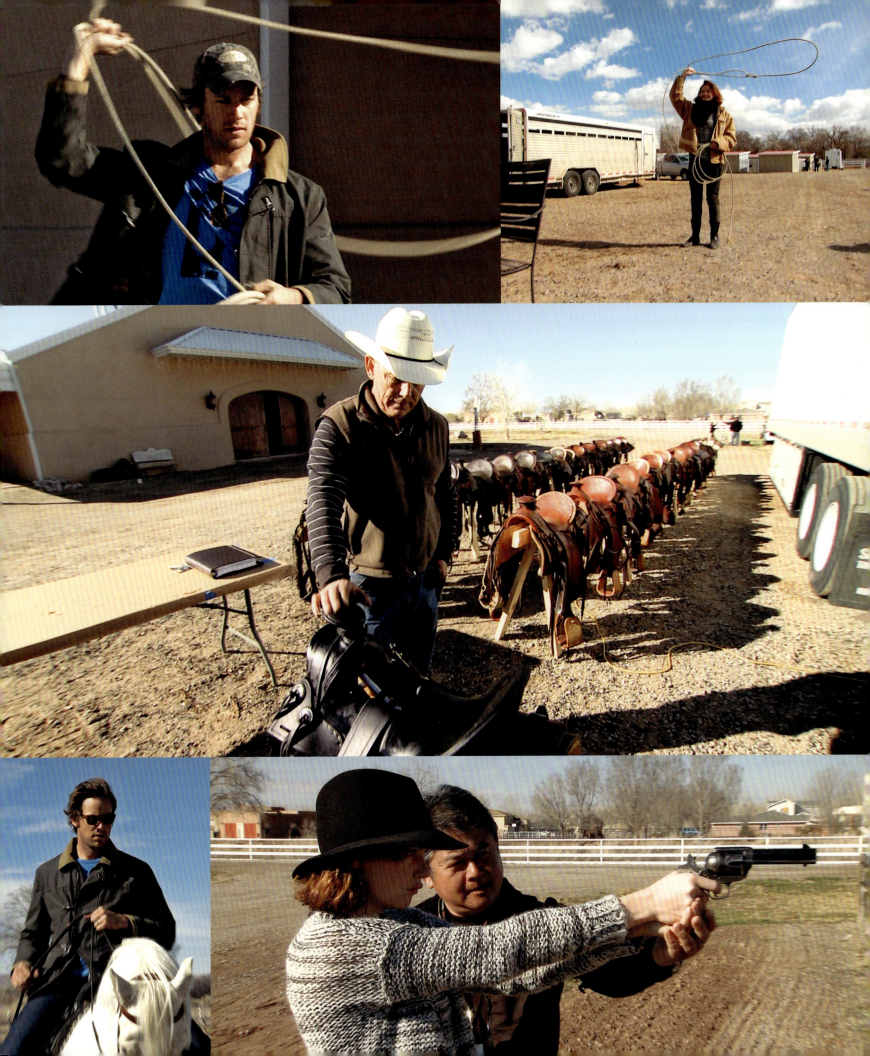

Like Ruth Wilson, actor Harry Treadaway, who portrays Cavendish Gang member Frank, is British and unaccustomed to American riding. "The wranglers are used to actors and horses, which is maybe a bit of a lethal combination," jokes Treadaway. "But they just chucked us out, there was no messing around. We rode five days a week for four hours in the morning. Little did we know that our first scene on horseback would be riding abreast to the top of a cliff in Monument Valley with a thousand-foot drop! I remember thinking, 'We didn't practice this in cowboy camp.'"

Fellow Englishman James Frain, who portrays the Cavendish Gang's Barret, recalls a similar feeling during that moment in Monument Valley: "It suddenly seemed like a month at Cowboy Boot Camp wasn't enough, but fortunately, horses don't want to plunge into an abyss. They were quite content to stop at the edge, but it was a thought-provoking moment."

Frain also enjoyed the learning curve of handling period authentic American firearms. "I've never fired these old-fashioned guns, and they're so different," he says. "The weight of them, the way you have to cock the hammer, trying to do tricks with them, and all the different things that can go wrong, it's really hard." Joaquin Cosio, who portrays the bandit Jesus, was enthusiastic by the end of cowboy camp: "I'm a cowboy now! The instructors were very patient with each of us, and helped me not be afraid of the horses." Adds Damon Herriman, the Australian native who portrays Ray, "I thought I could ride a horse until I got this role, but I could see how appalled the wranglers were following my very first session. But by the end of three weeks, I wasn't too bad. The gunslinging was also really fun, but it was a lot harder than I thought. I dropped my gun on my very first lesson, and it smashed to bits!" So what was the most valuable lesson that Herriman learned from boot camp? "Don't do gun twirling on a concrete floor. And don't claim you can ride horses unless you really can ride horses!"

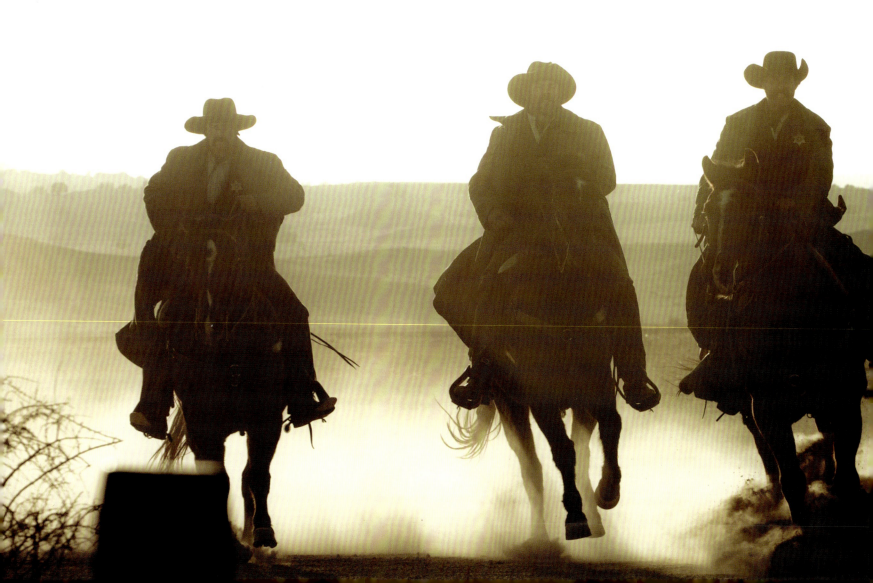

GETTING PROPPED UP

ALSO MAKING AN IMPORTANT contribution to boot camp was Kris Peck's prop department, it being responsible for providing the period-correct tack for the actors' horses. They custom made upwards of eighty Western saddles, twenty-five U.S. Cavalry saddles, and thirty Native American saddles. "We have to teach the actors how to take off all their props and look as if they know what they're doing," explains assistant prop master Curtis Akin. "They have all kinds of stuff that they're going to use for the camp scenes, so when they ride up they're going to get off their horses, pull all this stuff out, lay their saddles around the campfire, and lay their bedrolls out to make camp for the night."

There aren't too many films that require a pocket watch technical adviser, but the importance of that particular item for the story—and the distinctive way Latham Cole twirls, catches, and releases it—necessitated the talents of Steve Brown, one of the world's eight acknowledged yo-yo masters, an award-winning competitive yo-yo player, competition judge, and designer. Among Brown's amazing accomplishments was winning first place in the 2001 Bay Area Classic Invitational–Freestyle yo-yo competition, which he did while blindfolded. On The *Lone Ranger*, Brown worked closely with both Johnny Depp and Tom Wilkinson on mastering the pocket watch twirling technique, but he also spent some time showing his yo-yo wizardry to Armie Hammer, who eagerly picked up enough knowledge from the master to impress everyone with his own skill for the duration of the shoot.

THESE PAGES: The Texas Rangers: tough men with the hard job of enforcing the law in an often lawless West.

PAGES 146–147: The Texas Rangers make hard tracks through the desert landscape.

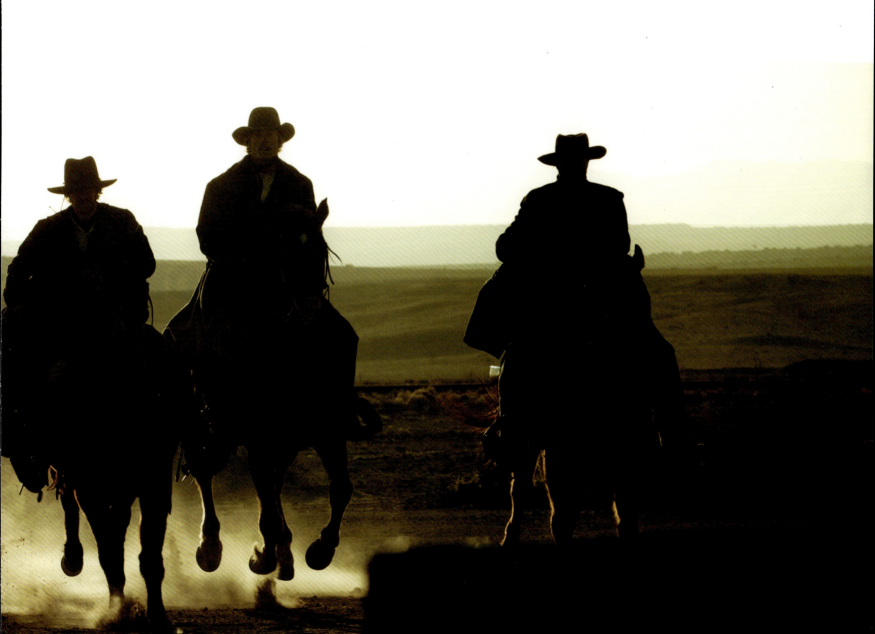

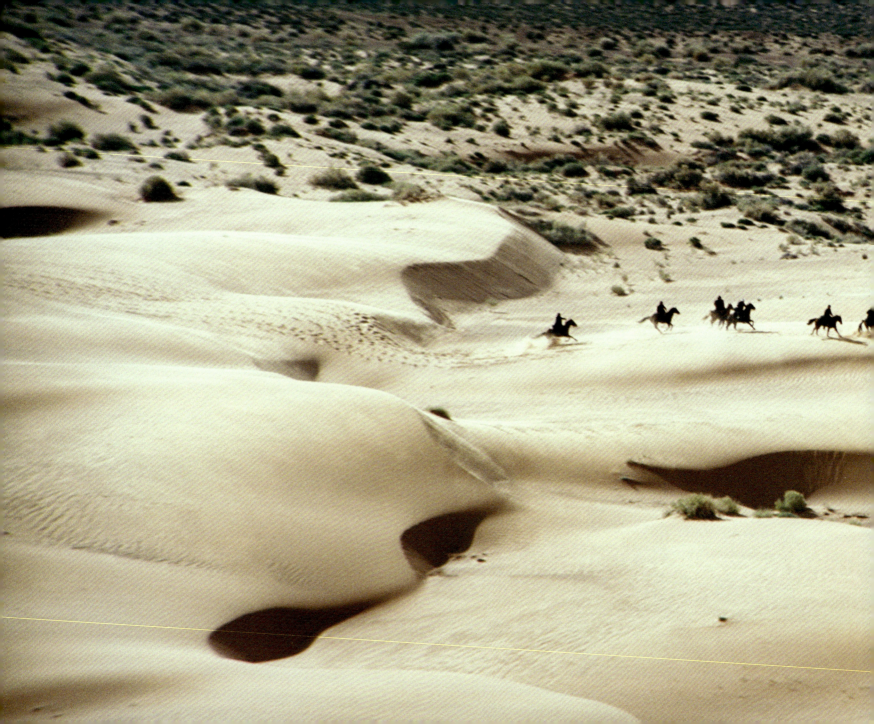

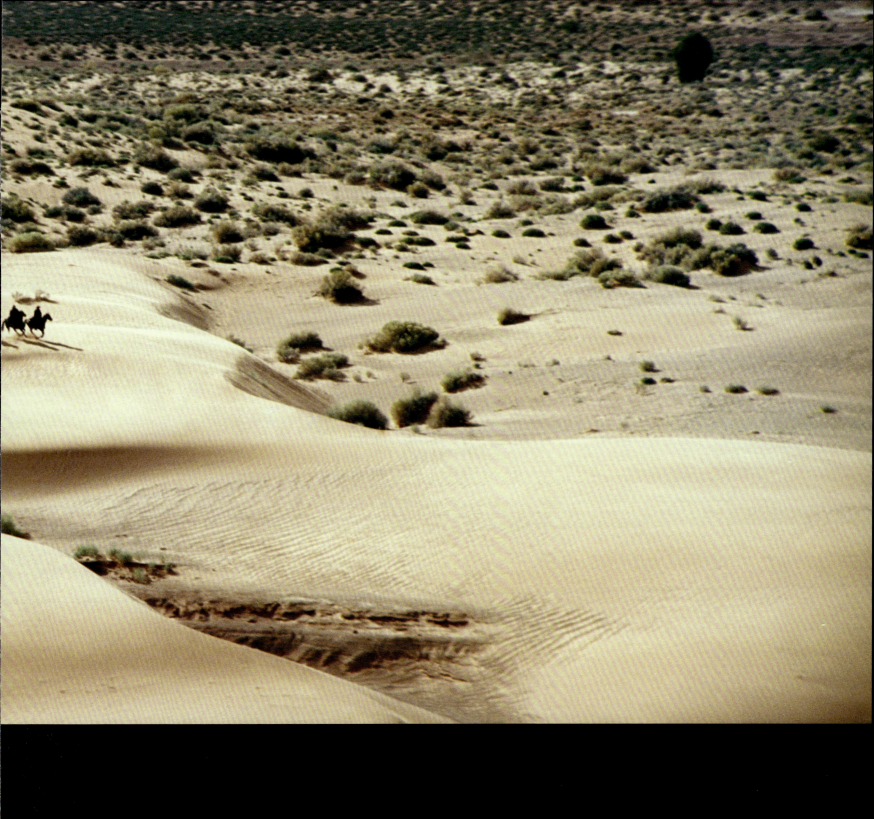

13

SPECIAL VISUAL PERFECTS

THE LONE RANGER'S SPECTACULAR SPECIAL EFFECTS WERE THE RESULT OF SEPARATE BUT OFTEN COLLABORATIVE EFFORTS BETWEEN VISUAL EFFECTS SUPERVISOR TIM ALEXANDER AND SPECIAL PHYSICAL EFFECTS SUPERVISOR JOHN FRAZIER. THE LATTER HANDLED THE STUNNING "IN CAMERA" MECHANICAL EFFECTS, WHILE THE FORMER WAS THE MAGICIAN TASKED WITH THE CREATION OF DIGITAL EFFECTS. THESE SUBTLE CGI WONDERS INCLUDED TRANSFERRING LANDSCAPES SHOT IN MONUMENT VALLEY TO THE BACKGROUND OF SCENES FILMED IN RIO PUERCO, AND NUMEROUS DIGITAL EXTENSIONS.

Tim Alexander, one of Industrial Light & Magic's young geniuses, had already worked with Gore Verbinski on a film that was all virtual reality—the rule-breaking *Rango*. In doing so, Alexander helped create a degree of realism theretofore unseen by audiences, raising ever higher the bar that had been set by Verbinski's previous films, from his more modestly scaled breakthrough movie *Mousehunt* to his three *Pirates of the Caribbean* films, where digitally animated characters like Davy Jones blend in seamlessly with the live action. Verbinski's overriding philosophy for visual effects is that they should never be used for the sake of it. "That's something that was drilled into my head during *Rango*," confirms Alexander, "that it had to be about the point of the shot, that CGI needs to be part of the story." On *The Lone Ranger*, Alexander would oversee a department of approximately thirty members during filming, which would grow in the all-important post-production phase to more than one hundred, with his work ending only a short time before the movie's July 2013 release date.

RIGHT: Although Johnny Depp and Armie Hammer were indeed running on top of a moving train, the visual effects department not only digitally erased their safety cables, but added an imposing butte in the background.

OPPOSITE: John Frazier's special effects department created the high-reaching fires in the military camp where the Lone Ranger delivers Butch Cavendish to justice.

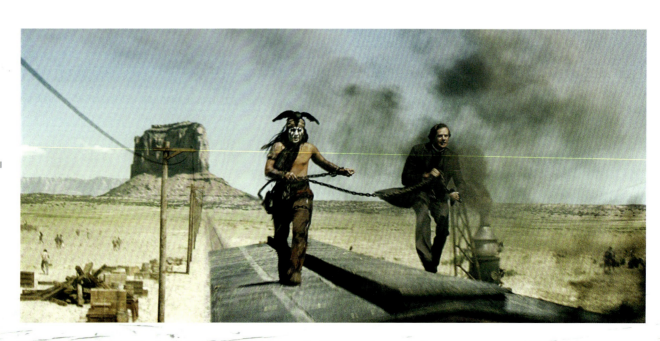

148

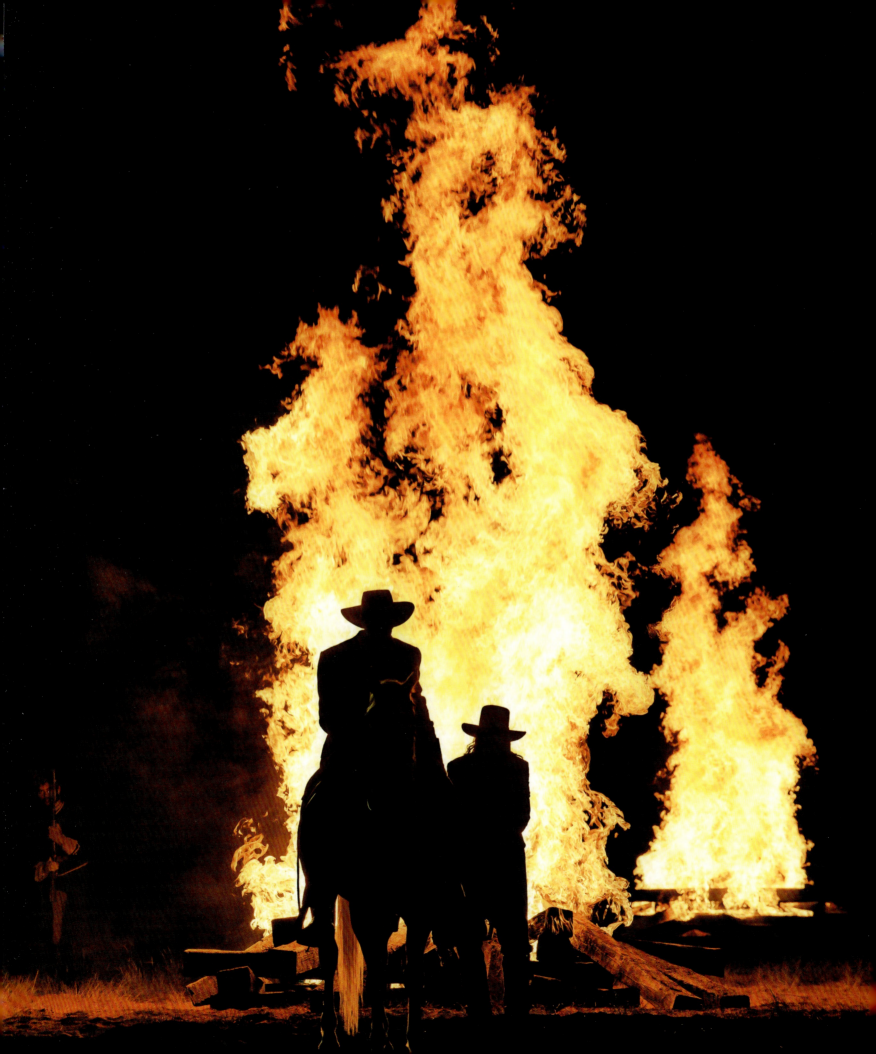

INVISIBLE EFFECTS

Tim Alexander's marching orders from Gore Verbinski were to make the visual effects *not* look like visual effects. "The effects are actually very big and extremely complicated in this film," notes Alexander, "and I think the trick for us will be in not allowing audiences to think of *The Lone Ranger* as a visual effects movie. It's about the story, not a big summer visual effects blockbuster." Not an easy task when one considers that the climactic train action sequence is one of the more complicated in recent film history. "It's huge," admits Alexander. "It requires about 350 visual effects shots, including rendering full or close-up trains. Gore wants the sequence to be a wild ride with two trains that are almost dueling each other, twisting, turning, crashing, and it just keeps going and going. And we've got to make it look real. So, all the real live-action footage that Gore pulled off gives us a basis for that, and we need to make sure that our CG stuff looks just as good."

THE 50% RULE

For *The Lone Ranger*, Tim Alexander explains that "Gore, myself, and the others came up with a philosophy that we called 'the fifty-percent rule,' where we wanted to always try to get at least half of something real into the camera frame to maintain as much realism as possible. Sometimes you can get stuck in a mode of just shooting blue screen on a soundstage, and you think everything is going great, but in the end all you have are a bunch of blue screens without anything real to grab on to.

"The other thing we did, along the same philosophy," continues Alexander, "was not to shoot blue screen on a soundstage. All our blue screens were shot outdoors in real sunlight so that they would match the rest of the film. Once you get on stage, it's often easier because it's more contained, but you're lighting for the sun instead of in the sun, and often it looks fake."

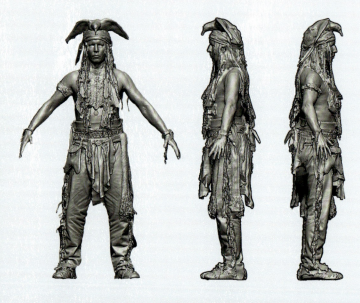

ABOVE AND RIGHT: This digital scan of Johnny Depp as Tonto, accurate to the most minute details, served as a model for required computer generated imagery of the character.

The requirement for approximately 1,300 visual effects shots in *The Lone Ranger* meant that in addition to ILM's work, Tim Alexander would also be supervising other contributing vendors as well, including the effects houses Moving Picture Company (MPC), based in London, and Lola, based in Santa Monica. As MPC's visual effects supervisor, Gary Brozenich, explains, his company is responsible for the Comanche attack at the Sleeping Man Mine sequence. "From the beginning to the end of that sequence," says Brozenich, "we're doing any number of things from set extensions, to adding a million Comanche arrows, to creating CG doubles getting hit by arrows, to face replacements and explosions. We're also doing CG scorpions and some backgrounds and landscapes that will be peppered throughout the film."

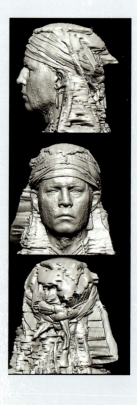

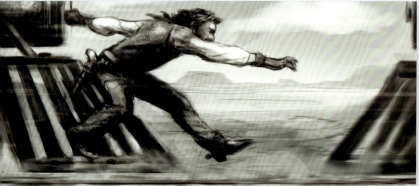
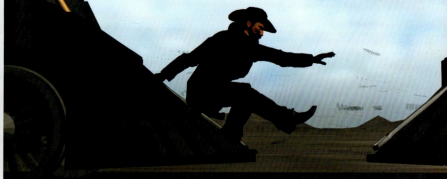

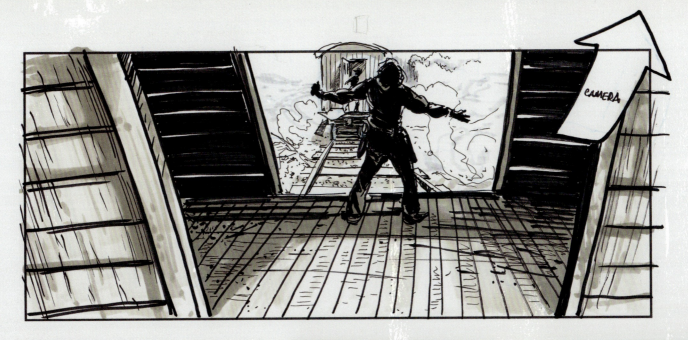

GETTING REAL

Brozenich says that working with Gore Verbinski and visual consultant Crash McCreery "gave us a strong vision from the start. Gore will do anything he can to get it real. There's a holistic vision for *The Lone Ranger*, which guides us into working within the structure of the vision of the film. It's very clearly laid out, although there's also room for creative breathing." One of the methods Verbinski and his team used were detailed pre-visualization (pre-vis) animatics to map out the more complex sequences. These essentially function as moving storyboards (another technique the meticulously prepared Verbinski relied on heavily), although Brozenich points out that "it technically guided the work rather than dictated it."

At the end of the long shoot, both Alexander and Brozenich knew that some of their most consuming work still lay ahead of them, but they were ready to take the bull by the horns. "I'm definitely really tired," said Alexander two days before wrap, "but I'm excited to get into the next phase now, because I can get back to ILM and start looking at the work everyone has been doing there for almost two months. I know it's going to be hard, with long days and nights, but with so much material to work with, it's time to start implementing." Added Gary Brozenich, "You can already tell that we're working on a great film, which is why motivating everybody to put in those late hours is not going to be a problem for me."

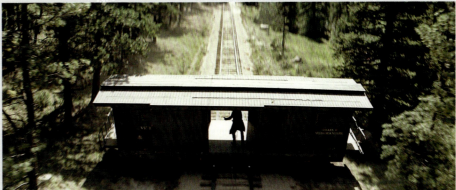
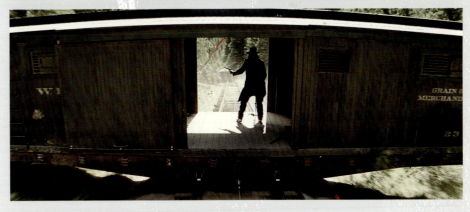

ABOVE AND BELOW: Two key action sequences involving William Fichtner as Butch Cavendish, from storyboard, to concept artist Joshua Hayes's illustrations, to live-action "reality".

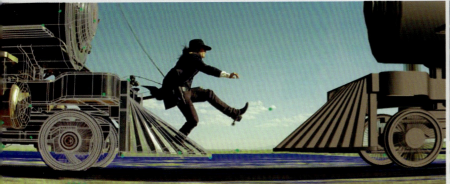
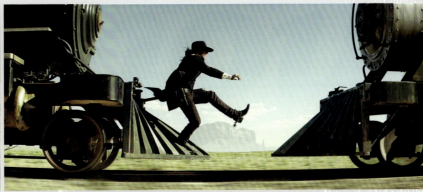

14

TRANSFORMATIONS: MAKEUP & HAIR

A CADEMY AWARD–WINNING MAKEUP ARTIST JOEL HARLOW CAN TAKE ANY PERSON AND TRANSFORM THEM INTO WHATEVER HE WANTS. HIS TASK IS MADE MUCH LESS CHALLENGING, THOUGH, IF THAT PERSON HAPPENS TO BE JOHNNY DEPP, WHOM HE HAS MAGICALLY TRANSFORMED INTO THE ICONIC CAPTAIN JACK SPARROW IN ALL FOUR PIRATES OF THE CARIBBEAN EPICS, THE MAD HATTER IN ALICE IN WONDERLAND, 1960S JOURNALIST PAUL KEMP IN THE RUM DIARY, AND THE VAMPIRIC BARNABAS COLLINS IN DARK SHADOWS. NOW IN THE LONE RANGER, HARLOW AND DEPP HAVE WORKED TOGETHER TO COMPLETELY REIMAGINE TONTO, AND THE RESULTS ARE UNFORGETTABLE. "JOHNNY AND JOEL ARE KINDRED SPIRITS," OBSERVES JERRY BRUCKHEIMER, "WITH A LOVE OF THE OFFBEAT AND UNUSUAL. THEY ALWAYS SEEM TO VISUALLY FIND A WAY INTO THE HEART OF THE CHARACTERS JOHNNY PLAYS."

Harlow, who took home an Oscar for his imaginative work on J. J. Abrams's *Star Trek*, was also *The Lone Ranger*'s makeup department head, leading a talented department of some twenty-five souls. And whether attending to the film's stars, or inventing fantastically bizarre creations ("goat skeleton marionette" or half-man, half-woman, anyone?) for the "Hell on Wheels" sequence, Harlow and company worked to the very limits of their capabilities—and beyond. He and his team were responsible not only for Depp but also for the entire cast, right down to the background players.

TONTO REBORN

THE LOOK FOR TONTO (as explained in Johnny Depp's afterword to this book) began during the filming of *The Rum Diary* in Puerto Rico during the hot summer of 2009. "I came across a really interesting painting by Kirby Sattler titled *I Am Crow*," recalls Harlow. "I showed it to Johnny, who thought it could be a great inspiration for the character and look of Tonto. Johnny then showed the image to Jerry and Gore, which really got the fire going."

Sattler's painting shows a Native American warrior with very strong features, face painted white with four vertical black stripes on either side of his nose, long hair adorned with eagle feathers, and most striking, a crow atop his head. On his website, Sattler explains, "The display of face paint design, crow feathers, and crow headdress in the painting *I Am Crow* is an illustrative interpretation of the inseparable relationship between the Native American and their spiritual and natural world."

"I wanted to incorporate a cracked-earth feel," notes Harlow, "the idea being that Tonto has smeared this earth on himself and it's dried over a period of time, and has cracked almost like a mud mask. I could have smeared a kind of mud mask material on Johnny's face and let it crack naturally, but there's no way that would have held up, and waiting for it to dry would be ridiculous. So what I did was to take a life cast of Johnny, and smear molten clay on it; in that state it has the same texture as mud. Then I took that off his life cast, molded, cast it in plaster and scribed crack marks into it, to turn it into a silicone prosthetic."

As Harlow notes, there were times when Depp would wear his prosthetic Tonto makeup over multiple days without removing it at wrap, not only because it would save time for the hour-and-a-half makeup process each day, but also because

OPPOSITE: The bold makeup design for Johnny Depp's Tonto emphasizes the character's warrior nature and connection with the Western landscape.

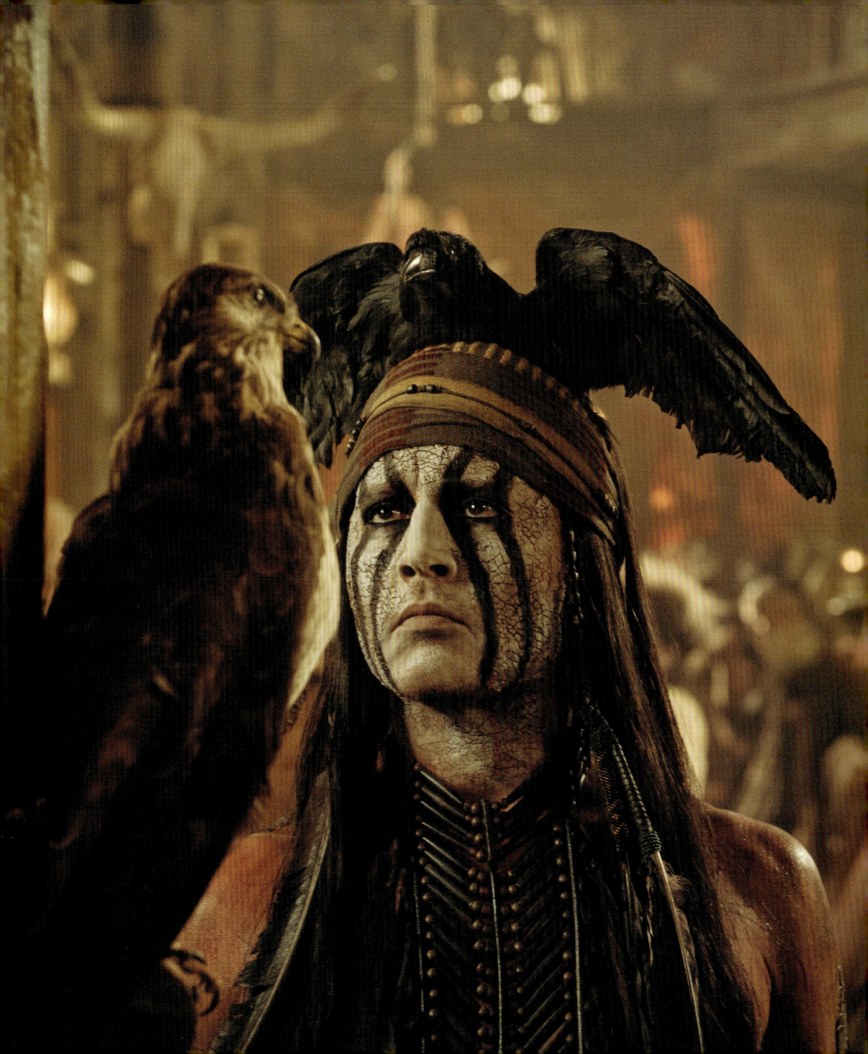

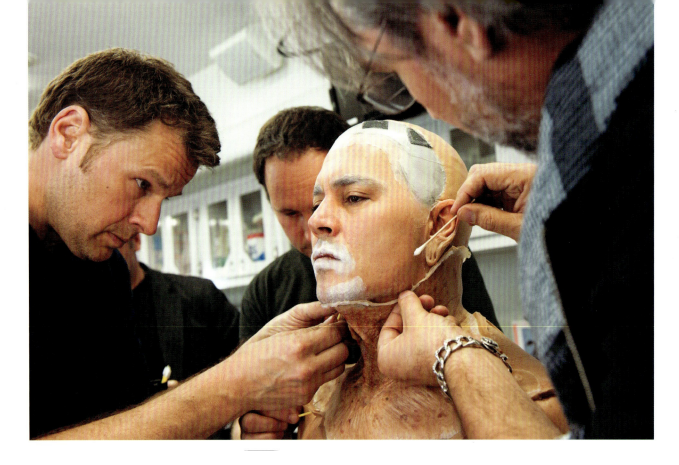

"this makeup specifically looks better the longer you sleep in it, as long as it's not more than three days." A prosthetic nose in conjunction with four body pieces and four facial pieces comprised the look of Tonto, painstakingly manufactured and applied in a process Harlow eventually managed to refine to just ninety minutes. Depp's numerous tattoos were also a challenge for the makeup artist. "Some were period-correct and we were able to leave them," says Harlow. "Tonto is a nomad, in exile from his Comanche tribe, so we could take some liberties with his look based on the journey he had undergone since he was a boy. The tattoos that didn't work were covered with the same sort of mud that covers Johnny's face, which keeps his look consistent." In one case, a tattoo that began as a temporary makeup—the jagged lightning bolt on Tonto's hand—became real when Depp had the design permanently tattooed on his skin partway through production!

The ever-present crow that straddles Tonto's head was also a responsibility of Harlow's department. Some fifteen different versions of Tonto's crow were created from a combination of taxidermic, imitation, and sculpted birds in a subsection of the department known as "the Lab," run by shop supervisor Steve Buscaino and his team of delightfully mad scientists. As for Tonto's long mane, hair department head Gloria Pasqua Casny fabricated the elaborate wig, mysteriously streaked in the back with what looks suspiciously like bird droppings. Finally, Comanche technical adviser William Voelker provided the beaded feathers that are knotted into Tonto's hair.

Harlow's greatest challenge for *The Lone Ranger* was creating the elaborate prosthetic full-body makeup for Depp's appearances as a century old Tonto, who in the film's framing device is the "unreliable narrator" telling his story to a young boy in a Wild West exhibition tent in the easly 1930s. The extensive makeup consisted of twenty-two separate silicone prosthetic pieces that took as long as six and a half hours a day to apply to Depp, and two hours to remove. "The pieces include a full chest piece," explains Harlow, "full arms, hand pieces, chin, neck, cheeks, nose, upper and lower lip, and a different bird than the one we usually see in the film, because it's at least seventy years older." Harlow's big concern was making an actor, albeit a man of such infinite patience as Depp, sit still for a six-and-a-half-hour makeup process. "I would never willingly want to do that to him, but we all knew that this was what it needed to be. In order for it to work correctly, the makeup needed to be something that Johnny was completely glued into rather than a suit. It needed to be able to move with him, breathe with him, basically *be* him. And once it was done, Johnny loved it. He is very involved in the process and he'll see things in the mirror that I don't. It's very collaborative. He's as much of a makeup artist as I am when it comes to creating these characters."

TOP AND RIGHT: A before and after look at the long process of Johnny Depp's conversion into Old Tonto.

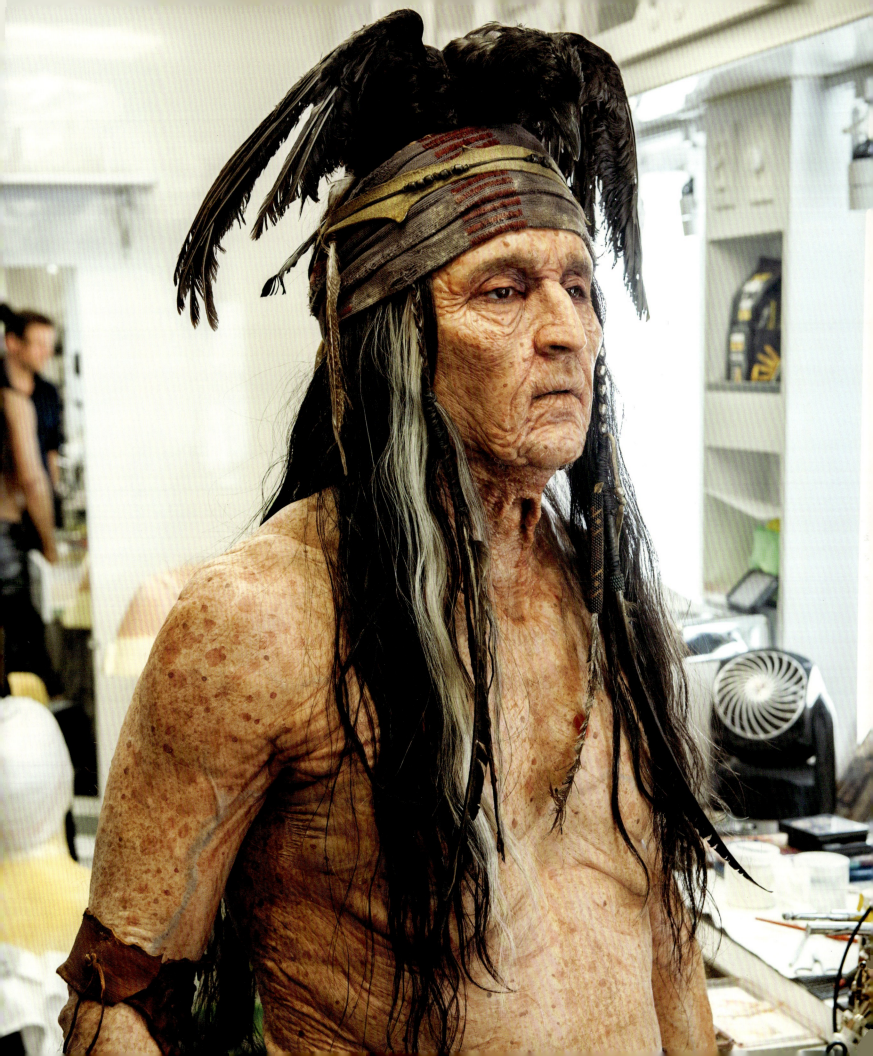

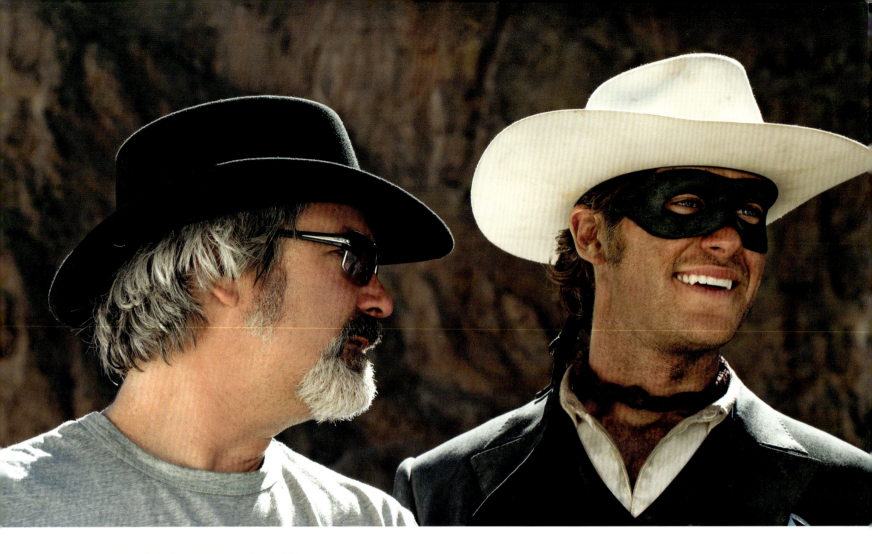

BEHIND THE MASK

ARMIE HAMMER DIDN'T REQUIRE quite so much attention in his role as the Lone Ranger, but the hero's all-important mask was also under the supervision of Harlow's department. Despite the seeming simplicity of the item, it required a huge amount of work to get it to where everyone needed it to be. "The shape was very important," says Harlow. "I worked very closely with Gore and Crash McCreery on that because just a little bit of difference in the contours of the mask and you go from the Lone Ranger to a superhero. Once we got the shape, it became a question of material, because Tonto uses the murdered Dan Reid's vest to make the mask for his younger brother, John. The material of the mask needed to match the material of the vest but also needed to look like its own element. The eye holes are cut from bullet holes in the vest, which I think is genius."

In all, getting the mask right required ten different designs and seven fittings with Armie Hammer. "It's not as easy as just tying a piece of leather to a guy's face," continues Harlow. "That's an iconic image, and you want to make sure that it's correct through the whole film." As a result, the actual fabrication of the Lone Ranger's mask had to be every bit as painstaking as its design. "The mask is made out of very soft goat skin leather," explains Lenny MacDonald, who fabricated the masks in the Lab. "It was vacuum-formed right over Armie's face so that it fits nice and skintight. The leather is heated with warm water, which makes it pliable, and wrinkles are forced into it so it hopefully looks natural." As always with such designs, there was a period of trial and error. "It's very similar to the iconic look," MacDonald continues, "but we wanted to make it more realistic than the original, which was pretty much what you can buy in a costume store."

"The first time I put on the mask," recalls Armie Hammer, "I was in a tailor's back office in Burbank. It was the first version they made, which didn't fit right. Two or three days later, they came back and said, 'We finished the mask, come on in.' So I showed up, and it was vacuum-formed and fit my face perfectly. I remember putting it on and just thinking, 'Damn, this is badass. This is actually going to be very cool.'"

TOP: Gore Verbinski and Armie Hammer between scenes, keeping a difficult production as lighthearted as possible.

OPPOSITE TOP AND BOTTOM: Makeup department head Joel Harlow (right) and key makeup artist Michael Smithson (left) transform William Fichtner into the terrifying Butch Cavendish.

PAGES 158–159: The Lone Ranger's long trek with his prisoner, Butch Cavendish, takes them through a wide spectrum of stunning Western landscapes.

THE FACE OF EVIL

ANOTHER ACTOR THAT HARLOW and the makeup department unrecognizably and unforgettably transformed was William Fichtner as Butch Cavendish, his terrifying visage a true reflection of the evil inside of his soul. "Bill is a great actor who's very recognizable," says Harlow, "and Gore wanted to change his look for the role. At first, I messed with the design of Butch's nose tip, and just kept going and sculpted a piece that had a cleft lip. Then, in conjunction with that, we created an effect where we grafted a piece of wire onto a denture with a silver tooth, then forced up the lip, which reveals the tooth.

"Then, since Gore talked about how he wanted Butch to be reptilian, on the morning of the first day that Bill started, we got a rattlesnake tail and stuck it in Butch's hair," Harlow continues. "Gore and Bill both loved Butch's look, and based on that, we decided that each member of the Cavendish Gang would have their own distinctive physical signatures. For example, Ray, who is played by Damon Herriman, probably has the most extreme signature of the gang, because he was a victim of a failed hanging. So we sculpted a prosthetic that cuts across his neck and up the side of his face rather than the back of his head."

Fichtner himself was deeply impressed by his makeup, along with everything else he encountered during his time on the film. "I've never been more inspired by a first day on a project," he says. "Two days after I talked to Gore about playing Cavendish, I got off the plane in Albuquerque, went right to Horses Unlimited to get on a horse—which I hadn't done in thirty-eight years—only to be told that the first thing they were going to ask me to do was to jump out of a train onto a galloping horse. Then I went to see the incomparable Joel Harlow, who created a look within a matter of two hours to which I could only respond, 'Wow!' It's what happens when you have a group of people who are at the absolute top of their game."

Throughout the production Joel Harlow was impressed by how much creative leeway he and the other department heads were given. "I can't express how much I appreciate both Gore and Jerry Bruckheimer," adds Harlow, "because when you have a free flow of ideas, their ideas feed my ideas, it's a back-and-forth creative process. You're not stifled, and you can push the envelope. We were allowed to go crazy."

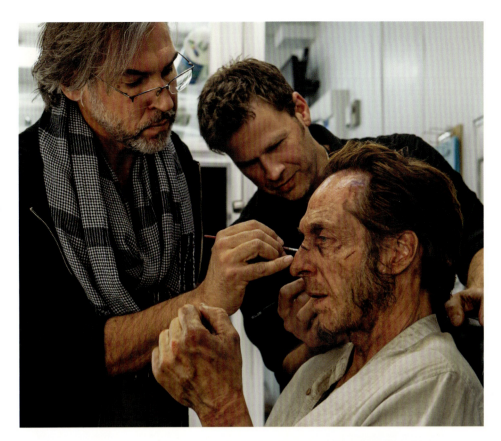

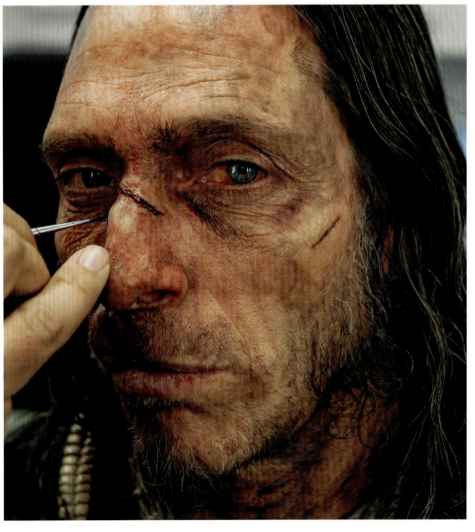

TRANSFORMATIONS: MAKEUP & HAIR 157

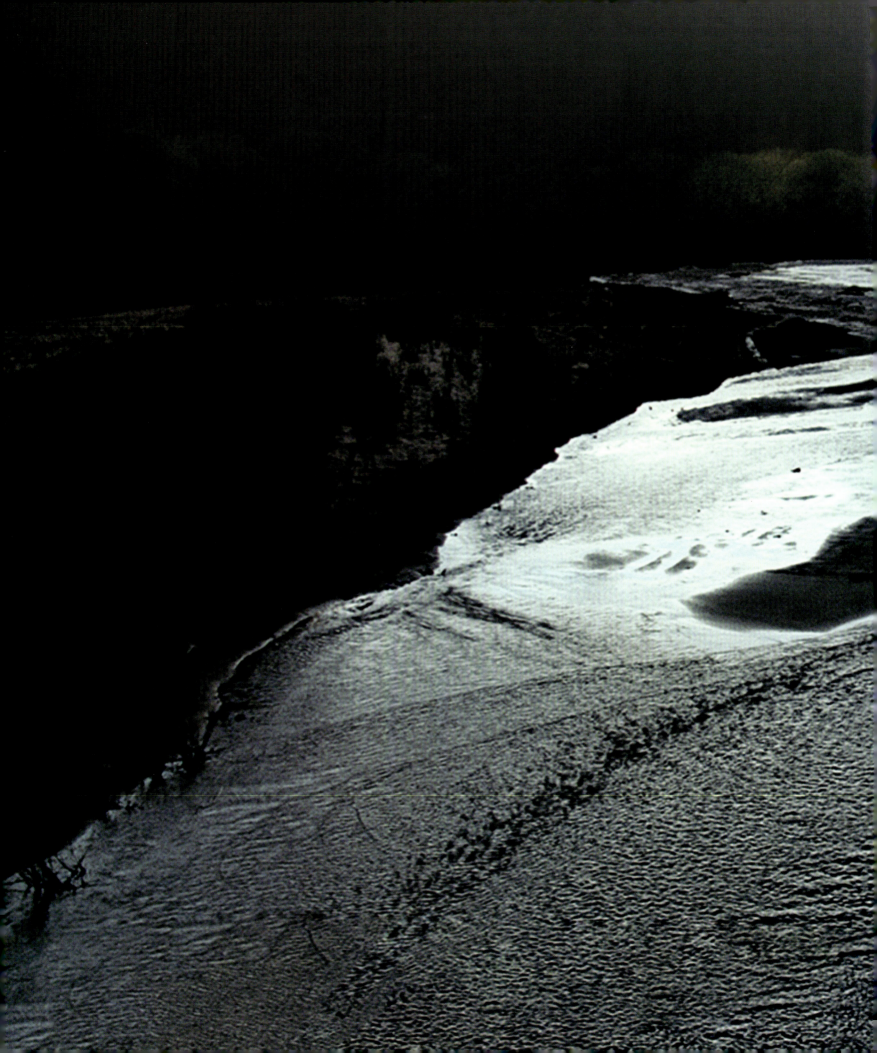

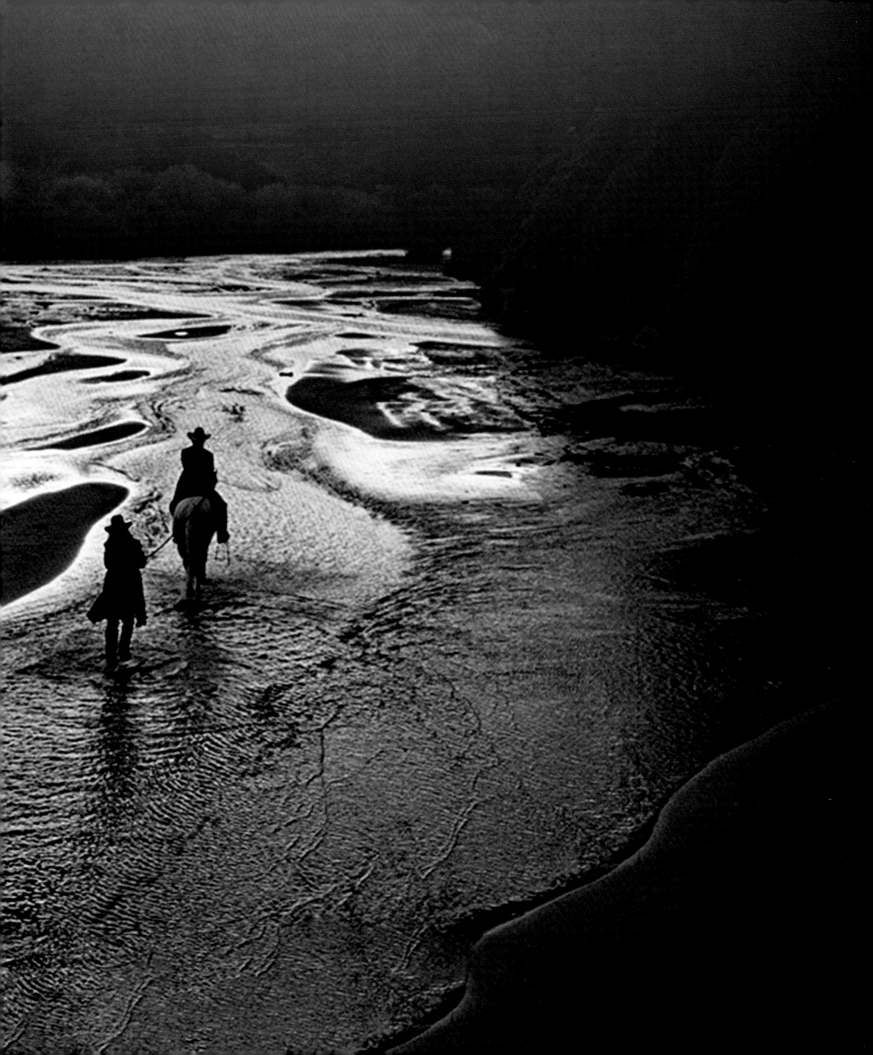

GORE'S SCRIBBLES

While thriving on the spontaneous spark of the moment, director Gore Verbinski is also a filmmaker of meticulous preparedness. One of the techniques he uses has come to be known as "Gore's Scribbles." These "scribbles" are very personalized storyboards hand-drawn by the director either in the margins of his scripts or on large white boards, which are displayed right next to his director's chair and video monitors. They can also be found on nearly every other space Verbinski inhabits in the course of making a film!

Deceptively simple in style, these drawings are essential tools in helping Verbinski and his team keep track of exactly which setups are required for each scene. When completed, the filmmaker then crosses off the scene like a date on a calendar. "I try to scribble the shots down loosely and quickly in order to keep ideas fluid and malleable," Verbinski explains. "This becomes the vocabulary of the film for me, and my office, trailer, and script are swimming in them."

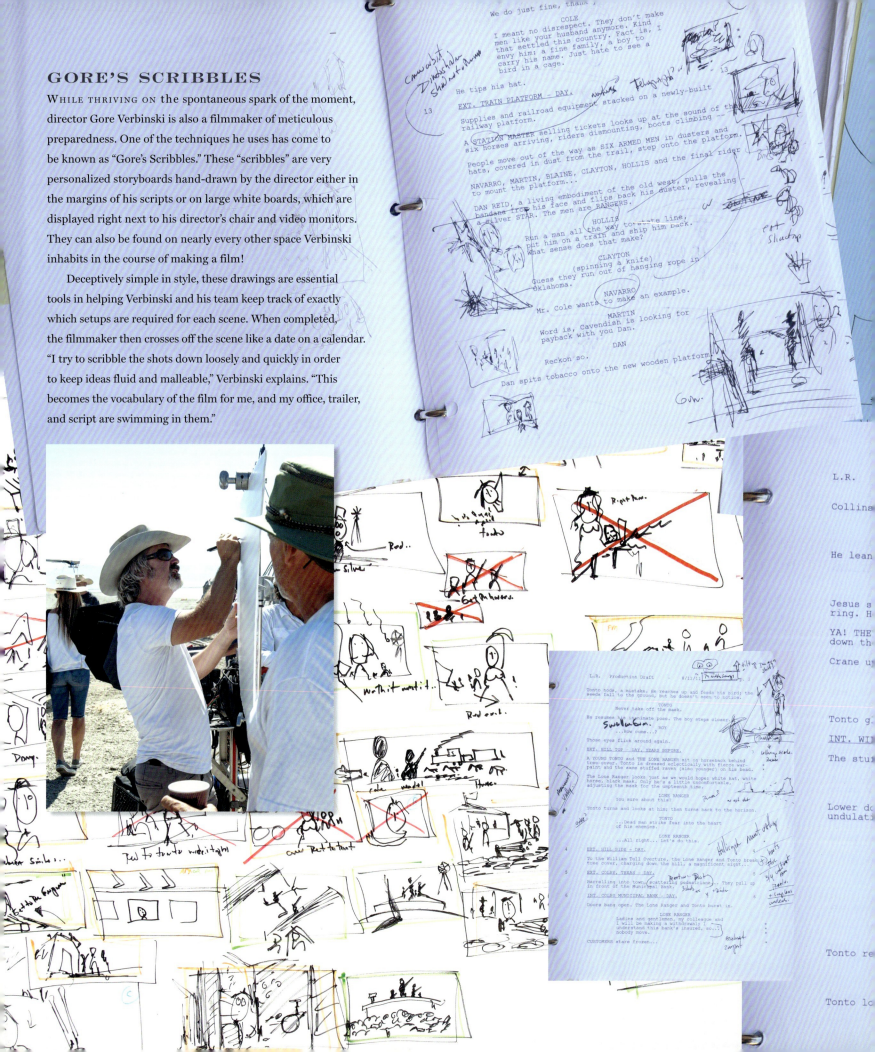

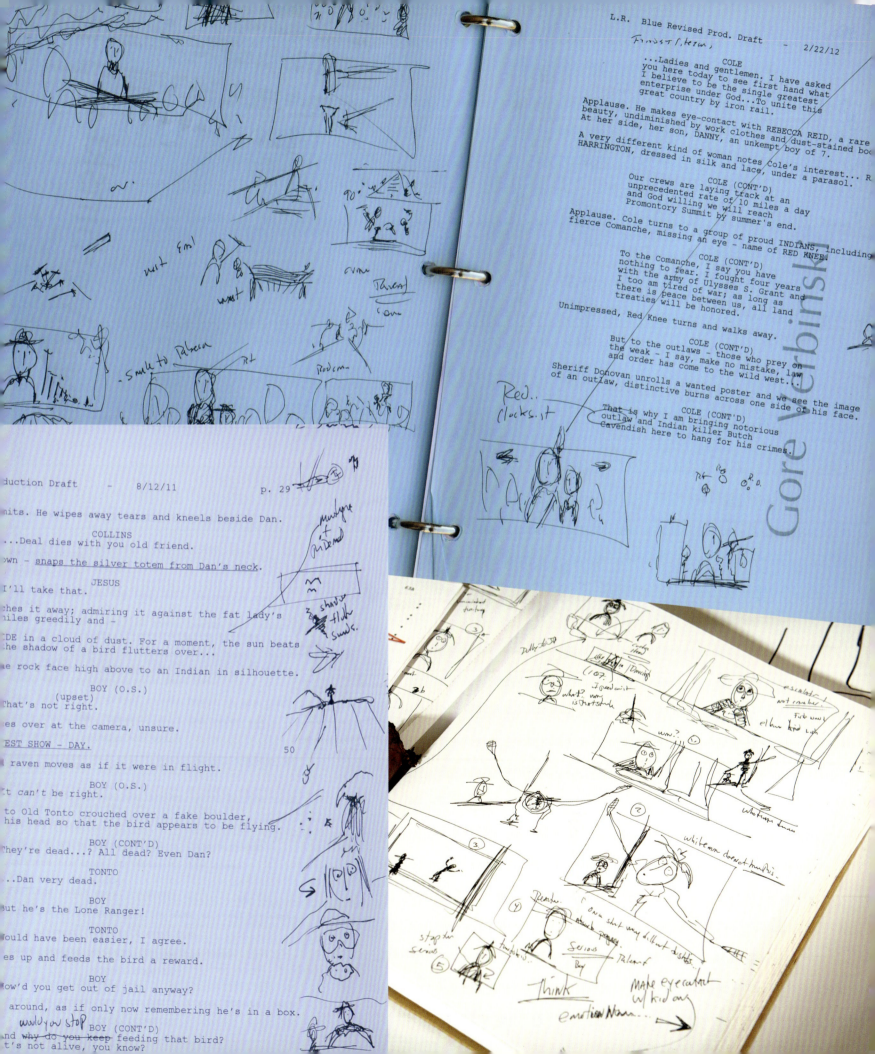

POSTSCRIPT

THE END OF PRINCIPAL PHOTOGRAPHY, on September 29, 2012, hardly marked the final lap of *The Lone Ranger* marathon. Rather, it was the beginning of a new, and perhaps just as challenging, race to a finish line that wouldn't come into view until July 3, 2013, when the film would finally open in theaters around the world. The punishing post-production schedule was about to ensue, with the millions of puzzle pieces created during the shoot needing to fall into just the right place, all under the supervision of Gore Verbinski, Jerry Bruckheimer, and associate producer and post-production maestro Pat Sandston.

Editing bays were prepared in Pasadena, California, where film editors Craig Wood (a Verbinski collaborator from *Mousehunt* to *Rango* and almost everything in between) and James Haygood set to work on assembling the vast amount of footage shot over the previous seven months. There would be sound mixing, looping, and dubbing to be accomplished. Up in the Bay Area, visual effects master Tim Alexander would oversee an ever-growing team of artists to create the necessary magic, while across the Atlantic in London, the Moving Picture Company's Gary Brozenich would be doing the same. Longtime Verbinski and Bruckheimer musical collaborator Hans Zimmer, who gave Captain Jack Sparrow his unforgettable theme, would now be doing the same for Tonto and the Lone Ranger. And of course, there was the ubiquitous "William Tell Overture" to deal with. "We're going to hold back on it, and perhaps deconstruct and dissect it for a

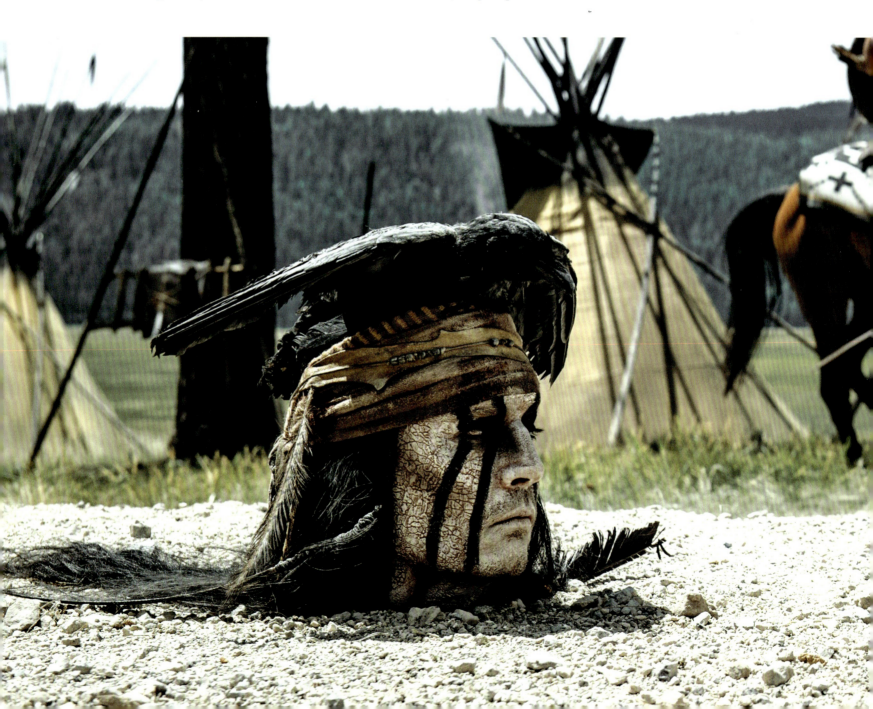

while," says Verbinski. "It's like foreplay for most of the movie, because John Reid hasn't quite yet become that guy. Then, at a certain point, he wears the mask in a slightly different way. It fits better, the white hat fits better, the attitude's better, and then we boldly break out the "William Tell Overture" in our last reel. Ultimately, we're going to deliver *The Lone Ranger* in the classic sense—we're just going to get there in a completely different way." Also contributing his prodigious musical talents to the film would be Jack White, as uncompromising an artist in his field as Verbinski is in his.

What would remain for *The Lone Ranger* cast, department heads, and crew members were the thousands of cherished memories left by an incredible, if often challenging, shared experience. Together they had brought back to life characters deserving a rebirth as imaginative, vibrant, ambitious, and fearless as the one that *The Lone Ranger* delivers. Says Jerry Bruckheimer, "We may not have seen the Lone Ranger and Tonto on screen for quite some time, but they've always been with us. The odd friendship between these two very different men, and their fight for justice, touched something in audiences around the world, and that spark has always been there."

Reflecting on all of the challenges he had faced before, during and after filming of *The Lone Ranger*, Gore Verbinski says, "The only way out is to make a great movie, because compromising just doesn't work. In the end, the question is whether you made the best movie you could. And you have to make every movie like it's your last."

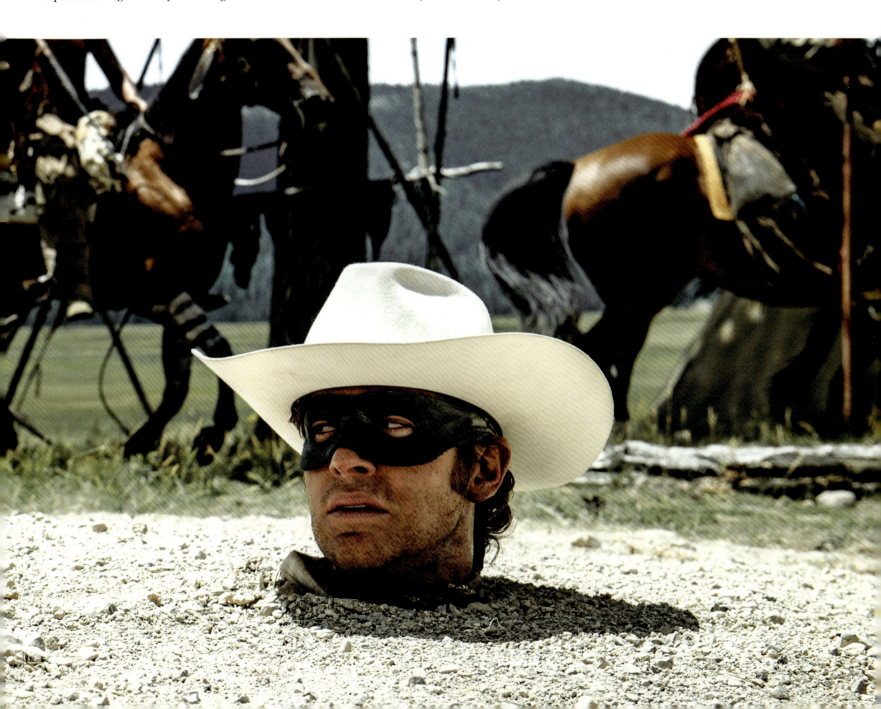

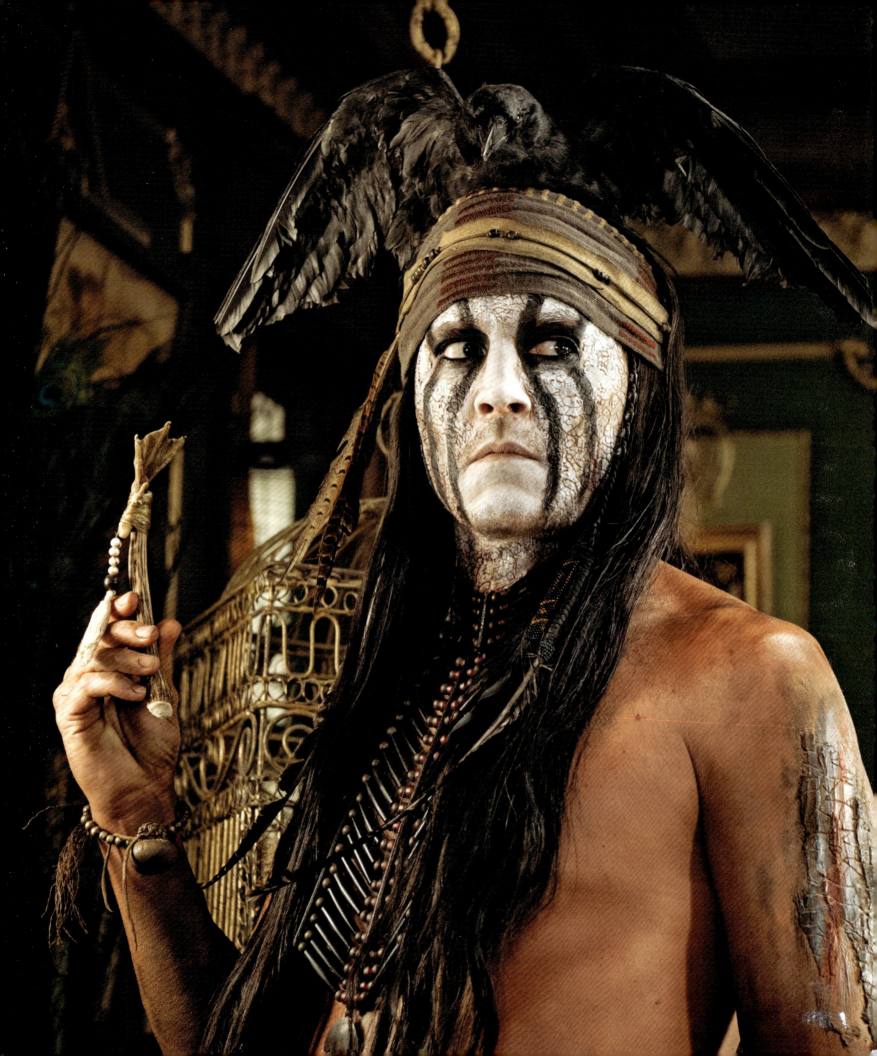

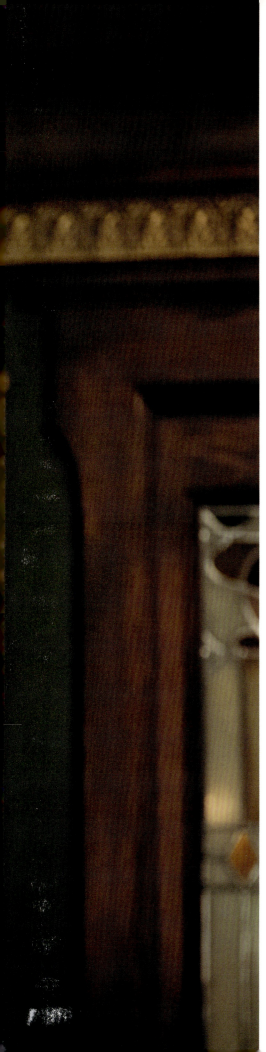

AFTERWORD
JOHNNY DEPP

WELL, SOME JOURNEY. From a crazed impulse some years ago, to the here and now, approaching camera wrap on *The Lone Ranger* in Los Angeles, late September 2012. But, as well we know, it's not about the destination so much as it is about that journey . . .

Starting with a highly productive character test one Sunday afternoon between myself, makeup artist Joel Harlow, and photographer Peter Mountain in Puerto Rico, summer of 2009, to discussing the concept with Jerry Bruckheimer and Dick Cook back in Los Angeles. *The Lone Ranger* would not have been made without these two great men. Then to the working and reworking of the script, ultimately delivered by Justin Haythe, the stage was finally set. My dear friend, Gore Verbinski, was the first and only choice to direct. He's the one man I knew to be insane enough to say yes. His wild animal stamina and mad vision was, as always, a joy to experience, while I'd also like to tip my crow to Armie Hammer for coming into this maelstrom and making the Lone Ranger his bitch.

To the people of Albuquerque, where we began shooting in February 2012, I would like to thank you for your warm welcome and kind hospitality. I would like to extend the precisely same praise to the wonderful people of Creede, Colorado. To the wonderful people of Canyon de Chelly and Monument Valley in the Navajo Nation. To the wonderful people of Moab, Utah. To the wonderful people of Santa Fe, Laguna and Jemez Pueblos, Angel Fire, and other communities in New Mexico. To the wonderful people of Lancaster, Acton, Arcadia and Lone Pine, California. You took us in. You looked after us. And we cannot thank you enough for your love and kindness. It will never be forgotten.

To the cast and crew of the film. Too many names to mention. But you know who you are. We've been on this journey before. We'll go on this journey again. I know you've got my back, and I've sure as hell got yours.

To the Lords of the Southern Plains, the Comanche Nation. To LaDonna Harris and the Tabbytite family, to Chairman Coffey, to William Voelker, to Troy, to Celli Crawford, to the late Chairman Wauqua and to all those in the Nation who I had the pleasure of meeting. You brought me in as one of your own, and for that I am eternally blessed. I hope that I can serve you proudly, in inhabiting the warrior skin of your magnificent people. I am honored and privileged. Your brotherhood is a gift unlike any other I have ever, or will ever, receive. I remain humbly yours until I become smoke.

And finally to you, dear reader. As you can see, the journey has been long for us, but it has only just started for you. Or perhaps not. Perhaps you have long followed the stories of the Lone Ranger and Tonto, from their earliest incarnation on the wireless, over to their transition on the small screen. If so, to you I say watch closely, since the tale is about to take a turn. A turn for the better, and perhaps one that it should have made a long time ago, since I believe much of what drove me to take the role was to be able to serve not just one Indian nation, but to serve all Indian nations, all Native peoples. To do what little I could, in exploiting the spotlight that my curious profession affords, by bringing a positive message to a long problematic situation, to incite global attention to a cause, still much in need. Here is not the place, but it is my wish that you will educate yourself in this regard, by voices far more knowledgeable than my own. You will quickly see that there is much to learn, much to celebrate, and much to be done.

Now, enough from me. On behalf of all the grand personages that you have met in these here pages, written by my noble friend of many years, Michael Singer, we thank you for visiting our new world and hope that you will continue to enjoy your journey, wherever it might take you, up on that silver screen.

Udah,

Johnny Depp

Los Angeles

September, 2012

ACKNOWLEDGMENTS

The Lone Ranger was more than a movie to those of us who spent the better part of a year on location (some considerably more than that) . . . it was our life. And subsequently, cast and crew members were more than just colleagues . . . they were family. There are way too many members of that extended clan to mention (it would require a separate book), so I'll just thank each and every one of them, as well as the wonderful new friends I made along the way in New Mexico, Colorado, Utah, Arizona, the Comanche Nation, the Navajo Nation, and several of the nineteen Pueblos of New Mexico. But to some, special attention must be paid. To Jerry Bruckheimer for gracing me with yet another amazing cinematic and real-life adventure, and his inspiring leadership. To Gore Verbinski for raising the bar high and never letting it fall under any circumstances. To Johnny Depp and Armie Hammer for providing such marvelous afterwords and thereby sanctifying the entire project with their personal thoughts and recollections, not to mention their beautiful spirits.

Thanks to everyone at Jerry Bruckheimer Films, including Mike Stenson, Chad Oman, Melissa Reid, Jill Weiss, Pat Sandston, Charlie Vignola, and John Campbell; to Christi Dembrowski, Stephen Deuters, Nathan Holmes, and everyone at Infinitum Nihil; to Morgan Des Groseillers at Blind Wink for her tremendous efforts in making this book a worthy companion to the film. Thanks to Jessica Bardwil, Dale Kennedy, Christopher O'Connell, Jeffrey Sotomayor, and Leslie Stern at Disney Franchise Management, and to Fredi Edwards and Laurence Schroeder in Disney Global Materials. Also, I am grateful to Jon Rogers for his help in getting this project off the ground and shepherding it at least halfway to its conclusion. At Insight Editions, I am indebted to editor Chris Prince for his patience, great good humor and surgical skills in eliminating what was unnecessary, as well as to Raoul Goff, Robbie Schmidt, and Chrissy Kwasnik. At Herzog Productions, thanks to the amazing Jack Kney, as well as to Mark Herzog, Joy Lissandrello, Anna Yeager, Ajay Clark, Joshua Rosenfield, and Ryan Schiavo. A deep bow of gratitude to unit photographer Peter Mountain, my friend and colleague, whose magnificent images grace this book. And to my wife, Yuko Kikuchi Singer, and our daughters Miya and Kimi, who somehow, after my absence of eight months' duration while on location with *The Lone Ranger*, were miraculously still at home waiting for me when I returned . . . *domo arigato gozaimasu.*

MICHAEL SINGER
Los Angeles, California
March 2013

COLOPHON

PUBLISHER Raoul Goff
EDITOR Chris Prince
ART DIRECTOR Chrissy Kwasnik
PRODUCTION MANAGER Anna Wan
ACQUIRING EDITOR Robbie Schmidt
PRODUCTION EDITOR Rachel Anderson

Additional editorial support by Elaine Ou and Emily Crehan. Additional design support by Jon Glick.

INSIGHT EDITIONS would like to thank Chris O'Connell, Jessica Bardwil, Dale Kennedy, Morgan Des Groseillers, Michael Singer, Gore Verbinski, Jerry Bruckheimer, Jon Rogers, Jason McNaughton, Armie Hammer, and Johnny Depp.

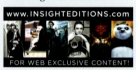

PO Box 3088
San Rafael, CA 94912
www.insighteditions.com

 Find us on Facebook: www.facebook.com/InsightEditions
 Follow us on Twitter: @insighteditions

Copyright © 2013 Disney Enterprises, Inc., and Jerry Bruckheimer, Inc. THE LONE RANGER property is owned by and ™ & © Classic Media, Inc. an Entertainment Rights group company. Used by permission

THE LONE RANGER ™ & © Classic Media, LLC. Used by permission. THE LONE RANGER theme music is a registered sound mark of Classic Media, LLC.
All rights reserved. No part of this book may be reproduced in any form without written permission from the publisher.
Library of Congress Cataloging-in-Publication Data available.
ISBN: 978-1-60887-210-7

Insight Editions, in association with Roots of Peace, will plant two trees for each tree used in the manufacturing of this book. Roots of Peace is an internationally renowned humanitarian organization dedicated to eradicating land mines worldwide and converting war-torn lands into productive farms and wildlife habitats. Roots of Peace will plant two million fruit and nut trees in Afghanistan and provide farmers there with the skills and support necessary for sustainable land use.

Manufactured in Hong Kong by Insight Editions

10 9 8 7 6 5 4 3 2 1

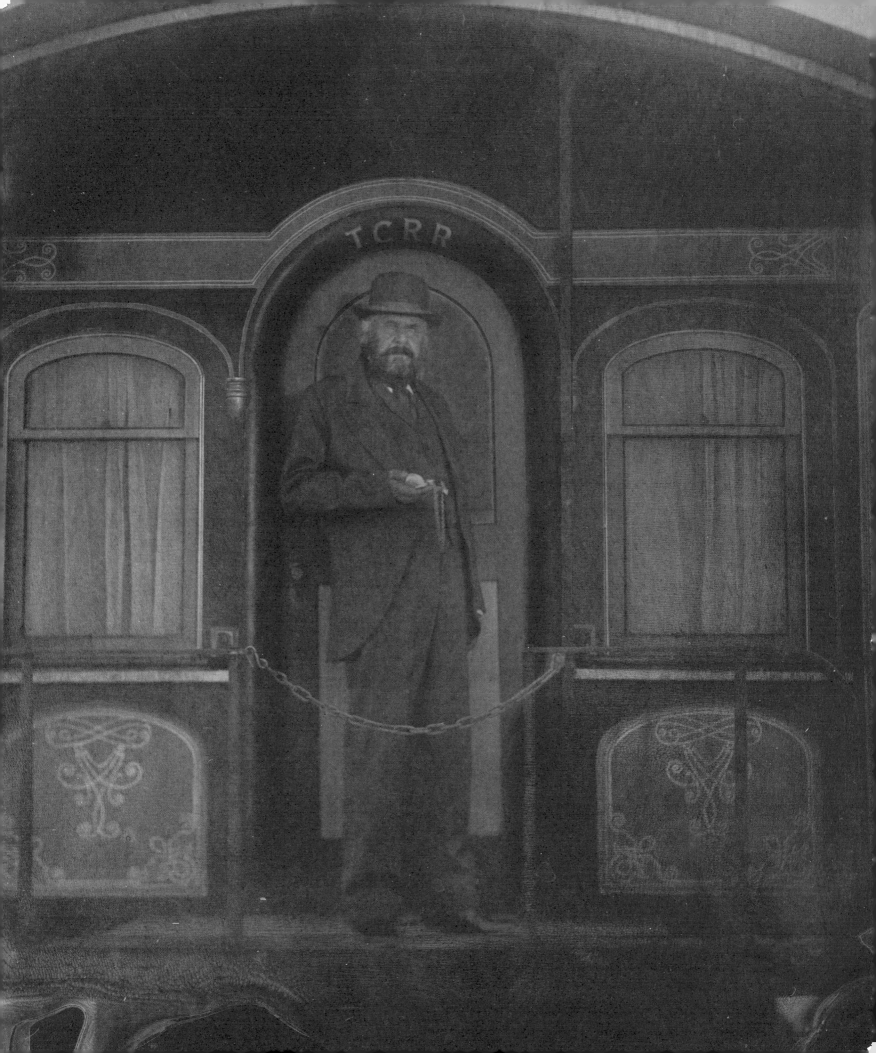